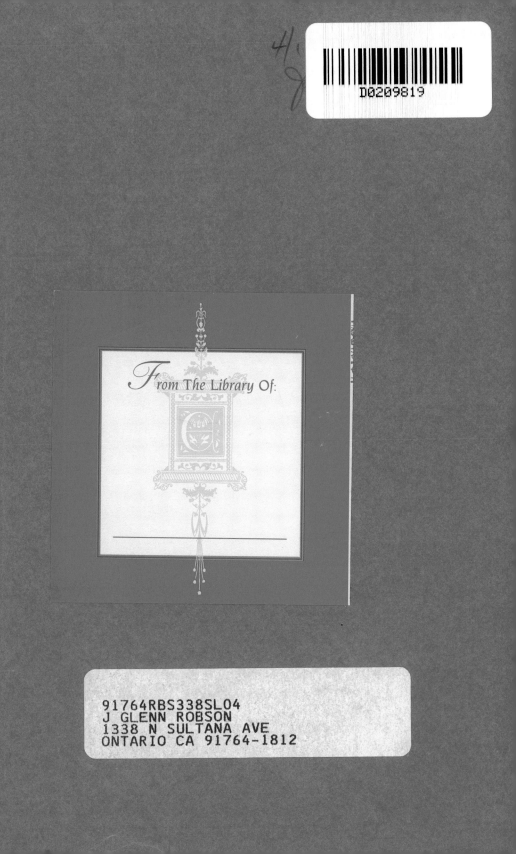

The
Stuff of
HEROES

The Eight
Universal Laws
of Leadership

WILLIAM A. COHEN, PH.D.,
MAJOR GENERAL, USAFR, RET.

LONGSTREET
Atlanta, Georgia

Published by
LONGSTREET
A subsidiary of Cox Newspapers,
A subsidiary of Cox Enterprises, Inc.
2140 Newmarket Parkway
Suite 122
Marietta, GA 30067

Printed in The United States of America
1st printing, 1998
Library of Congress Catalog Card Number: 98-066359
ISBN:1-56352-524-0

Book and jacket design by Jill Dible
Typesetting by Burtch Hunter

TABLE OF CONTENTS

THIS BOOK IS DEDICATED TO ALL THOSE WHO PRACTICE THE STUFF OF HEROES, WHETHER THEY PRACTICE IT IN UNIFORM OR IN CIVILIAN DRESS.

FOREWORD
GENERAL RONALD R. FOGLEMAN, USAF (Ret.)
Former Chief of Staff, U.S. Air Force

I am normally very suspicious of the whole genre of short special-topic books purporting to distill very complex subjects into a few basic laws or principles. So many of these books have been written on the subject of leadership that producing a first-rate, innovative, and substantive work would be a major challenge for anyone. With *The Stuff of Heroes*, Dr. Bill Cohen succeeds in not only producing a great primer on "the eight universal laws of leadership," but through his methodology and presentation the book becomes a well-told story of great adventure. From both successes and failures on the battlefield come revelations applicable to the modern corporate world.

Having been exposed to this work in draft form, I could not wait for it to be completed. I have been using material from the draft in speeches and presentations for the past six months. At the same time, I am not sure whether eight is the precise number of laws of leadership one needs to study and practice. Depending on how you might package the principles or laws, the number will vary. However, Dr. Cohen has done a meticulous job of researching the subject and certainly addresses the key elements in a comprehensive way. There is no doubt that his listing of integrity as the first principle is right on target. The demonstration of absolute integrity in professional relationships remains the singularly defining attribute of any leader. Leaders with integrity may come up short on one or another of the laws and still succeed, but nothing will undermine an organization more quickly than to have its leader be found wanting in the area of integrity. From the introduction through the epilogue the reader and/or student is exposed to each of the eight laws in a refreshing way that should have a lasting impact.

Moreover, Cohen does not stop at stating and explaining the laws he has uncovered or in dramatizing their application through real business and military examples. He takes that important extra step and tells the reader exactly how to follow each law. For the crucial law of maintaining absolute integrity, he explains four ways to do this: keep your word, chose the harder right over the easier wrong, guard your principles, and do the right thing. To know your stuff, he shows how this means knowing your people, learning from the bottom up, learning from every experience, learning from your subordinates, and never ceasing to learn. He shows us six ways to declare our expectations, five ways to show uncommon commitment, four ways to expect positive results, five ways to take care of our people, five ways to put duty before self, and five ways to get out in front. That's thirty-nine separate lessons on implementing the eight universal laws. The professor has served up a full course of instruction for the most demanding palate!

In earlier works, Dr. Cohen demonstrated how military leadership principles could be applied to all organizations. In this book he goes to the next level by examining not just what was successful for any given military leader, but what traits and actions provided the foundation for that success throughout the history of warfare. His use of the combination of survey and interviews resulted in the conclusions he presents in the book. Because of his background as a professional airman-scholar, Bill Cohen is uniquely qualified to interpret and present the findings. The richness of his research and details of his narrative will make this book a valuable addition to any aspiring leader's library and a superb tool in any case study presentation of the subject.

What the Stuff of Heroes Is All About

No man is a leader until his appointment is ratified in the minds and hearts of his men.

—Anonymous, *The Infantry Journal*

There are many books on leadership. And many books based on leadership in battle. But this one is different. Unlike others, this is not a "business is war" book. Like my earlier book, *The Art of the Leader* (Prentice Hall, 1990), it is a "swords into plowshares" book. In *The Art of the Leader*, I explain how to take various military leadership techniques and apply them to all organizations.

I wrote that book just before Operation Desert Storm. Even then, it was far from the first book on military leadership. Thirty years earlier, my professor, friend, and mentor Peter F. Drucker wrote that the first systematic book on leadership was written by Xenophon two thousand years earlier and was still the best on the subject.[1] Xenophon described leadership during a five-month campaign in which he and others led ten thousand men in a retreat from Babylon to the Black Sea, though surrounded by a hostile and numerically superior foe.

If a book describing military leadership written more than two thousand years ago is so powerful that it attracts the recommendation of probably the greatest management thinker of our time, the subject is worthy of deeper exploration. But why? Conventional wisdom is that military leadership is bad, not good. However, as Peter Drucker is so fond of saying, "What everybody knows is usually wrong."

The battlefield probably represents the greatest challenge for any leader. In combat, conditions are severe. There are terrible hazards. There are poor "working conditions." There is probably greater uncertainty than in any other type of human activity.

As Drucker pointed out to me at a recent meeting, "In no other type of leadership must the leader make decisions based on less, or less reliable, information."[2] "Workers" may need to perform their duties with little food and irregular sleep. All must take great risks. Most followers and leaders alike would prefer to be somewhere else and doing something else.

While there are true military geniuses in battle, the vast majority, as in most organizations, are ordinary men and women. Not all are suited to their jobs. Professional or amateur, all are stressed far more than in any civilian situation or occupation. Moreover, leaders must not only carry out the mission, but do their best to protect the lives of those they lead at the same time. So battle probably represents a "worst-case" condition. No wonder such traditional motivators as high pay, good benefits, and job security aren't much good. There is no "business as usual" on the battlefield.

To some, military leadership is not something to emulate. It means running around shouting orders as in a Hollywood movie. It means obeying stupid orders simply because someone else is in authority. But those who have been there know better. Sure, as in any organization, there are some combat leaders who do a poor job. They operate as martinets and provide the models for those who seek to ridicule anything military. However, the vast majority of combat leaders are not of that mold. Instead, these leader-heroes enable ordinary people to routinely accomplish the extraordinary. In battle situations, leaders help their followers reach difficult goals and complete arduous tasks. People in combat cannot be managed. They must be led. And in leading under terrible conditions, successful combat leaders have built amazing organizations that have gotten things done ethically, honestly, and for the most part humanely.

Although I appreciate the value of what I personally learned about leadership in battle, which formed the basis of most of my recommendations in my first book on leadership, I wondered whether there were underlying principles or lessons from warfare that were at the root of all leadership success.

Without question, such lessons are desperately needed now.

This is a time of great change that threatens the very fabric of society. In the wake of the breakup of the Soviet Empire, ethnic groups in the Balkans are at each other's throats — to the death. In America, for better or worse, leaders raised during the "me generation" are gaining positions of power. Women and minorities struggle for equality and increased power while organizational leaders weigh their responsibilities for social issues with their responsibilities for mission accomplishment. After years of relative calm, management and labor jockey anew for position and power, with management claiming the need for tight purse strings in order to be competitive and labor demanding better conditions and compensation for its members. It is a time when the industrial power of the United States has already been successfully challenged by other rising institutions throughout the world. Indeed, as America strives to remain internationally competitive, the rising colossus of China is on the horizon. This new, great power dwarfs the former commercial threats from the juggernauts of Japan and Korea. In business, leaders worldwide are about to enter a fight for our lives and futures.

If general principles of leadership from the worst-case scenario of warfare could be uncovered, they could have an extremely important impact. Leaders from all organizations could use these principles to dramatically increase productivity and the likelihood of success in any project in which they were engaged.

To discover such desperately needed principles, I sent a survey to more than two hundred former combat leaders and conducted conversations with many more. I especially sought out those who had become successful in the corporate world or in other nonmilitary organizations after leaving the armed forces. Among the responses I received in the initial phase, sixty-two were from generals and admirals. I asked these extraordinary leaders what they had learned from leadership in battle. I asked about the tactics they used, about the importance of their style, and about the most important actions a leader must take. I asked about the ways in which they adapted these lessons in their civilian careers.

I found that while successful leaders practiced many different styles, there were universal principles that such leaders followed to dramatically boost productivity and achieve extraordinary success in all types of organizations. I asked respondents to list three or more leadership principles, so I expected a huge list. The Emperor Napoleon, one of history's preeminent military leaders, developed and published 115 maxims on the conduct of war. How many hundreds of leadership principles would I uncover after analyzing and tabulating the input from such a large number of respondents?

Surprisingly I discovered that 95 percent of the responses I received boiled down to only eight principles. Each of these leaders had seen one or more of these eight principles help them achieve extraordinary results in their careers.

More than a few wrote special notes or letters to express their support for my project. They had seen payment in blood for what they had learned. They know its value, and they don't want to see it wasted.

In a latter phase of my research, I interviewed other success-ful senior business leaders. I also reviewed dozens of corporate situations and the actions taken by the corporations' senior leaders. Some had combat backgrounds. Some did not. Some allowed me to use their real names and companies. Some pre-ferred to remain anonymous. Some had developed their own lists of leadership principles over the years. While their lists dif-fered, they invariably included the eight responses I had previ-ously developed from my surveys. I also looked at seven thou-sand years of recorded history to confirm these concepts. An abundance of evidence supported these principles.

I decided that these eight points were far more than princi-ples — they were actually universal laws of leadership. People may follow hundreds of excellent techniques and rules in lead-ing others. But these eight universal laws are essential. I believe they are the very essence of all leadership. These eight laws are simple, but even one of them can make the difference between success or failure in any project in any organization. You can make a lot of mistakes and still succeed as a leader. But if you violate these universal laws, you will probably eventually fail. No one can guarantee success, because other factors can over-ride anything a leader may be able to do. But, there is no ques-tion that if you follow the universal laws, you increase your chances of success. I believe these laws are that powerful. The consequences of following them or not can be the determining factor for success for most leaders in most situations. These are the eight laws:

1. Maintain Absolute Integrity
2. Know Your Stuff
3. Declare Your Expectations
4. Show Uncommon Commitment
5. Expect Positive Results
6. Take Care of Your People
7. Put Duty Before Self
8. Get Out in Front

However, if that's all there was to it, we could end the book now. But, it isn't. Jodie Glore was once a combat infantry company commander in the 101st Airborne Division in Vietnam. His company was located at the very northern-most tip of our troops facing the North Vietnamese border. When he returned from Vietnam, he taught military psychology and leadership at West Point. Today, he is president and chief operating officer of Rockwell Automation, a $4.5 billion company. President Glore states, "There is no question of the importance and the universality of these eight laws." "But," he says, "there is more to it." What must a leader do to follow these laws? And when two or more conflict, in what situation is one of more importance than another?[3] In addition to explaining the eight laws and giving both military and civilian examples of their application, I have tried to explain what a leader must do to follow the laws and when each is of particular importance.

As I said earlier, I found that many successful leaders in businesses and organizations of all types used the universal laws even though they had never been in battle. For example, a girls' high school soccer team in New York had five straight undefeated seasons. That was more than forty victories without a loss. What made this possible? A leader by the name of Arthur Resnick.

When there was no money for uniforms and equipment, Resnick used his own or got out in front and helped his students raise money. That's universal law number eight: get out in front.

Many coaches think it's a good season if they win more than they lose. Resnick expected to win every time. That's universal law number five: expect positive results.

Other coaches believe that rank has its privileges. No matter the situation, Resnick saw to his players' welfare before his own.

That's universal law number seven: take care of your people.

Other coaches take the credit for their victories and imply that one or more of their players had a bad day when they are defeated. Resnick gave the credit for victory where it belonged — to his players. If things didn't go quite right on the soccer field, Resnick took the blame. That's universal law number one: maintain absolute integrity.

Is it any surprise that Resnick's players rewarded his efforts by winning year after year? That Resnick's players would do almost anything rather than lose? Coach Resnick practiced the stuff of heroes. As a result, Coach Resnick led his girls' soccer teams to victory after victory, no matter who their competitor or what odds they faced.

I believe if you put the eight universal laws in this book into practice, you have the basis of what you need to lead any organization under a wide variety of conditions. It doesn't make any difference whether you are a CEO of a major corporation or the coach of a girls' soccer team. You will find:

- Real-world examples from business as well as battle that will give you the know-how and confidence to lead in any situation.
- Proven strategies and results-oriented techniques to apply the universal laws and multiply the productivity of any group or organization.
- New ideas for motivating people and helping them achieve greater heights of personal and group performance.
- Little-known but highly effective methods for building team-work and esprit de corps.
- Methods with which to develop yourself as a leader and to reach your full potential.
- Strategies used by combat leaders to accomplish goals others thought impossible.

The fact that you have this book in your hands means that you are a leader who is in a lifetime learning experience. This is important because being a leader is different from all other human endeavors. Being a leader has to do with a trust, which you have accepted. It is a trust in which you have agreed to accept responsibility for a mission, whether this mission is great or small. It is a trust in which you have agreed to accept the responsibility for others, for their welfare, and for what they accomplish and fail to accomplish. And it is a trust in which you have agreed to put these first two responsibilities before your own personal interests. You have accepted the responsibility for getting things done. You and I share these trusts, and we share it with all others who have accepted the mantle of leadership since the tribe of man first banded together to accomplish what one alone could not accomplish by him- or herself.

The lessons from my research and the basic message of *The Stuff of Heroes* are contrary to conventional wisdom:

• You don't get ahead by fighting your way to the top. You get ahead by helping others to the top. When you help others, they elevate you to successively higher levels of leadership.
• You don't succeed by trying to get the most work out of your employees. You succeed by giving the most help to your employees. When you start focusing on helping your employees, their performance and output will amaze you.

The eight universal laws are simple but not always so easy to follow. One definition of the word "hero" is someone of distinguished valor and admirable exploits. Those who follow the eight universal laws have the stuff of heroes. I hope you are one of them.

William A. Cohen
February 1998

ENDNOTES

[1] Drucker, Peter F., *The Practice of Management* (New York: Harper and Row, 1955), 194.
[2] Drucker, Peter F., meeting with the author, November 7, 1997.
[3] Glore, Jodie K., telephone interview with the author, January 9, 1998.

MAINTAIN ABSOLUTE INTEGRITY

No matter how lacking a man may be in humanity, if he would be a warrior, he should first of all tell no lies.
— ASAKURA SOTEKI (1474-1555)

Integrity . . . is the willingness to do what is right even when no one is looking. It is the "moral compass" – the inner voice; the voice of self-control; the basis for the trust imperative in today's military.
— UNITED STATES AIR FORCE CORE VALUES, IDEALS DEVELOPED UNDER
THE LEADERSHIP OF GEN. RONALD R. FOGLEMAN, USAF (RET.),
FORMER CHIEF OF STAFF, UNITED STATES AIR FORCE

Back in 1989, then Major Clay McCutchan was an air commando and pilot of an AC-130 gunship in the U.S. Air Force Reserve. The AC-130 was a descendent of earlier prop-driven aircraft developed primarily to attack traffic on the Ho Chi Minh Trail during the Vietnam War. The C-130 was a transport aircraft. Extensively modified with side-firing guns and the latest acquisition electronics, it became the AC-130, a formidable flying gunship. The AC-130 could loiter for long periods of time until needed. Then it could provide unparalleled firepower, destroying most targets as long as the ground defenses were not too heavy.

In late December, Clay McCutchan and his crew were one of two air force reserve crews who volunteered to relieve an active duty AC-130 crew assigned to Panama during the Christmas holidays. This was nothing new. They had relieved active duty crews in Panama three times before. There had been an ongoing problem with Manuel Noriega, the Panamanian dictator. But few realized how rapidly the United States was approaching war at this time . . . certainly not Clay McCutchan and his crew.

What McCutchan and others didn't know is that the decision to invade Panama and capture Noriega had already been made a few days earlier by President Bush. The invasion, called Operation Just Cause, was set for the night of December 19, 1989 — as luck would have it, only two days after McCutchan's arrival.

The objectives of Operation Just Cause were to oust and capture Noriega, return him to the United States to stand trial on drug charges, and install a new, more democratic government in Panama. The Air Commandos, or Air Force Special Operations as it was now called, were to spearhead the invasion. Active duty gunship crews had practiced for months firing at and destroying mock-ups of certain predesignated targets. Since McCutchan's crew hadn't participated in this earlier training, they were given a different mission at first. His crew was put on standby alert to guard Howard Air Force Base, the American air base in the Panama Canal Zone, in case it came under attack. It didn't.

Says Clay McCutchan, "Before the war started, we got a twenty-minute briefing on the mission." Afterward they were ordered into the air to respond, if called upon, to help friendly troops fighting on the ground.

However, there was considerable confusion in communications with the ground. For some time they flew around over Howard without an assignment. Then they were sent to aid a group of civilians at another airfield immobilized by a sniper. A few rounds from their 40mm guns took care of that problem. Then they flew around again waiting for a new assignment. Hours went by. No one seemed to need them. Or at least, no one communicated with the crew.

With only about an hour's fuel remaining, they were sent to a fortified area known as Fort Amador where there was a large fight in progress on the ground. When McCutchan's crew arrived, they couldn't tell the good guys from the bad guys. They couldn't even establish radio contact. Without radio contact, they couldn't get instructions or permission to fire. Communications were made more difficult because they were given three different call signs to use depending on to whom they were talking. Even worse, McCutchan, flying at only 4,500 feet, was the lowest of a number of AC-130s orbiting at different altitudes and only under marginal control of someone on the ground. When an unseen AC-130 at a higher altitude opened fire through the crew's flight orbit and almost hit them, McCutchan decided it was time to depart. He altered course to take his AC-130 out of the area.

As they flew away from the ground fighting, McCutchan's crew was ordered to attack three armored cars on the Fort Amador Causeway. The vehicles were not a type used by our forces. The crew tried calling a controller on the ground, and, this time, made radio contact with the forward air controller (FAC) right away. The FAC's job is to control all friendly air strikes in his assigned area.

"They're not friendly; you can open fire on them," advised the voice of the FAC.

McCutchan planned to start with 40mm armor-piercing ammunition and then use high-explosive ammunition to finish the armored cars off. As he prepared to fire, his sensor operator and fire-control officer (FCO) spotted thirty to forty troops coming out of the jungle.

McCutchan's FCO called the controller on the ground and told him about the arrival of these new forces. "Take them out; they're not ours," said the controller. In the AC-130A, which McCutchan flew, the pilot fired the guns using a thumb trigger. As his thumb began to itch in readiness, his crew studied the situation closely using infrared and television sensors.[1] The more they looked, the more convinced they became that these troops were Americans. McCutchan had just rolled his airplane in to attack when one of his crew stopped him with a sudden warning: "Don't fire. We think they may be friendly!"

McCutchan took his thumb off the trigger. After talking it over with his crew, he spoke to the FAC on the ground again and told him that they had identified the troops with the vehicles as possibly American.

"Negative, negative, they are not friendlies. They are enemy, and you are cleared to fire," the controller responded, the frustration clear in his voice. By now the FAC was excited. "Shoot, shoot, shoot," he intoned.

McCutchan called his command post back at Howard Air Force Base and briefed the officers there on the situation. He asked for positive confirmation before firing. After several minutes the command post duty officer came back with a decision. "These are confirmed enemy. You are ordered to fire."

Now McCutchan's actions were no longer discretionary. He had been given a direct order. He had also been given the supreme test of integrity. He and his crew believed that these were friendly troops with the enemy vehicles. Usually the FAC on the ground had a much better picture of what was going on. But with the AC-130A's sophisticated equipment, they might be in a better position to judge whether the troops were friendly or enemy in this instance. "Our forces were not being fired on by these vehicles or these troops, and they were not an immediate threat to anyone," reasoned McCutchan. "If they were enemy and they lived, it would make little difference to the war. But if they were friendly and we killed them, we could never bring them back to life."

Clay McCutchan told the controller he was leaving the area to return to base. He was not going to fire. "I was convinced I was going to get court-martialed because three times I disobeyed a direct order to fire," he told me.

The commander met them as they landed at dawn. "You're either a hero or in a lot of trouble," he told McCutchan.

McCutchan spent a sleepless morning despite his fatigue. He had been up all night and in the air almost six hours. By noon the whole story came down from higher headquarters. Contact had been made with the troops surrounding the vehicles. McCutchan and his crew had been right. The group was American Special Operations troops who had captured the enemy armored vehicles. They had been unsuccessful in contacting anyone by radio to identify them. McCutchan and the others on his crew were awarded medals for having the moral courage — the integrity — not to fire, even when ordered to do so.

Typical of an outstanding leader of integrity, McCutchan gave full credit to those he led. "My crew was very experienced. I was only an average pilot, but my copilot had fifteen hundred hours of combat in Vietnam. All of my officers and noncommissioned officers were very experienced and absolutely top-notch. It was my sole responsibility to make this decision, but I could not have made the decision I did if I did not trust them completely."[2]

McCutchan may or may not have been an average pilot. But

for certain, the air force recognized that he was a far-above-average leader — a leader of integrity. Today, Clay McCutchan is a full colonel in the U.S. Air Force Reserve.

WHAT IS INTEGRITY?

What exactly is this quality that is so universally prized by people who lead others under the most demanding of circumstances? In simple terms, integrity means adherence to a set of values that distinguishes honesty and freedom from deception. But it is more than honesty. Integrity means doing the right thing regardless of circumstances or benefits to the leader or the organization.

The *United States Air Force Core Values* says integrity "is the willingness to do what is right even when no one is looking."[3] Combat leaders sometimes refer to integrity as "honor." In fact, the *Merriam-Webster's Dictionary* indicates the two words — integrity and honor — are synonyms. Both are closely tied to telling the truth, following moral principles, being ethical, conforming to accepted professional standards of conduct, and doing the right thing.

COMBAT LEADERS SAY THAT IT MUST BE "INTEGRITY FIRST"

Most of the combat leaders I surveyed emphasized the primary importance of integrity in successful leadership in or out of combat. Kermit Johnson was an infantry platoon leader in combat in Korea. He eventually resigned his commission, got a master's degree in divinity from Princeton, and reentered the army as a chaplain. When he retired from the army, he was a major general and chief of army chaplains.

General Johnson noted, "When I attended Army War College, one individual made the statement, 'Ethics never won a battle.' My other classmates took him apart, piece by piece. Every one of them had been in battle, and they knew better. Integrity is an essential component for success in leading."[4]

Charles Kennedy is currently manager of Systems Safety and Human Factors at the B-2 Division of Northrop Grumman. He flew in combat as an air force lieutenant and captain in Vietnam. He says: "Depending on the skills a leader brings to the table, he may be weaker in some areas than others. However, integrity stands alone. Someone possessing integrity will be forgiven other less important attributes he or she may lack. But a lack of integrity will never be forgiven."[5]

HISTORY CONFIRMS "INTEGRITY FIRST"

I found numerous examples stretching into antiquity that confirm these views. In his *History of the Peloponnesian War*, Thucydides writes that Pericles, one of the leading Greek generals and statesmen, "by his rank, ability, and known integrity was enabled to exercise an independent control over the multitude — in short, to lead them instead of being lead by them."

More than a millennium later, Benjamin Franklin, who was a colonel in the Pennsylvania militia, concluded that through his integrity and lack of dogmatic expression, he led his fellow citizens despite the fact that he was "a bad speaker, never eloquent, subject to much hesitation in my choice of words, hardly correct in language."

Maj. Gen. John Grinalds, a Rhodes Scholar, U.S. Marine Corps combat leader, and West Point classmate told me: "The most important action a leader must take to be successful in or out of combat is to keep his integrity. The leader must always maintain integrity first, no matter what." After he left the marine corps, General Grinalds carried on his philosophy as headmaster of Woodberry Forest School in Virginia.[6] Last year, John was selected to become president of the Citadel, the military college of South Carolina. The Citadel chose him because they sought a leader of great integrity during a period of challenge and transition.

Shortly after his inauguration, he wrote a letter to Citadel friends and alumni. In it he said, "Leaders who have the intellectual power to understand and solve society's needs and also have the leadership skills to translate their solutions into actions are of questionable value if they have no moral basis for their solutions and their actions. For that reason, the cadet Honor Code remains fundamental to a Citadel education. The commitment to one another not to lie, cheat, or steal nor tolerate those who do, leads to a commitment to keep one's word, the essence of every lasting relationship in human society: leader to follower, parent to child, employer to employee, spouse to spouse, colleague to colleague."[7] The Citadel can count on John Grinalds.

WHAT GEN. COLIN POWELL
SAYS ABOUT INTEGRITY AND VIETNAM

Perhaps the strongest indictment of violation of integrity in Vietnam comes from Gen. Colin Powell, who was a combat leader there. General Powell said: "Our senior officers knew the war was going badly. Yet they bowed to group-think pressure and kept up pretenses, the phony measure of body counts, the comforting illusion of secure hamlets, the inflated progress reports. As a corporate entity, the military failed to talk straight to its political superiors or to itself."[8]

Recently army major Herbert R. McMaster, Ph.D., wrote a meticulously researched book about Vietnam. The title says it all. His book is called *Dereliction of Duty: Lyndon Johnson, Robert McNamara, the Joint Chiefs of Staff, and the Lies That Led to Vietnam* (Harper Collins, 1997). I recommend this book to anyone who wants to understand fully the terrible price that is extracted when leaders, military and civilian, fail to maintain absolute integrity.

Many of our current senior military leaders believe that in knowing the Vietnam War could not be won as fought, members of our Joint Chiefs should have retired rather than continue to serve. I count myself among these. Since active military officers are prohibited from speaking out against the policies of their superiors, resignation or early retirement is the only recourse they have. The feeling is that had they taken this step, perhaps the publicity over their early retirement might have raised questions and caused the war to end much sooner.

In the same Vietnam War, there were strict Rules of Engagement (ROE) limiting the targets and the conditions under which they could be attacked. One rule stated that aircraft could not attack enemy antiaircraft artillery or missiles unless threatened. While limiting, this restriction was acceptable because warning gear installed in many aircraft indicated when radar singled them out prior to a missile being fired. However, in 1971 the North Vietnamese improved their defense system so that they could launch missiles without being detected. American aircraft began to be shot down because of the limiting rule of the ROE.

Air force general John D. Lavelle was in charge of the air war in Southeast Asia at that time. He made repeated attempts to get the ROE changed. Not only was he unsuccessful, but he was criticized by Washington and the Joint Chiefs of Staff for lack of aggressiveness in fighting the air war.

General Lavelle was between a rock and a hard place. The sixth universal law of leadership is take care of your people. How could he do this while unduly risking his troops because of the lack of warning when missiles were launched?

General Lavelle decided on a questionable interpretation of the ROE. Later he testified before Congress that the enemy's air defense system was constantly activated against his crews, and this was ample rationale to launch planned protective strikes against the launch sites and their controlling radar. He ordered these attacks. His air crews knew that by the ROE, they were required to be directly threatened first. Not knowing how to respond during debriefing, many lied and said they had received a threat indication. The upshot was that General Lavelle was fired and forced to retire with two stars instead of the four he wore as commander of Seventh Air Force. He was accused of encouraging his crews to lie and running his own war by not following the ROE. There were other consequences, including months of investigations and a congressional hold on air force promotions.[9]

While we can all sympathize with General Lavelle's dilemma and his decision, he did have an alternative solution — to retire early and thus refuse to send his crews into combat under the conditions demanded by the ROE and his superiors.

In my opinion, if a leader cannot support the actions of a superior and he has the right to retire or resign, he or she should do so. Integrity means having the moral courage to stand up for what you believe.

An Admiral from the "Silent Service" Speaks

Rear Adm. Dave Oliver, Jr., served in the "silent service." He was a submariner and did months of duty beneath the sea in nuclear submarines. In his book, *Lead On!*, he explains the need for integrity:

> *Truth sells itself. Truth gets you through situations nothing else will. Looking dumb is oodles better than lying. The risk of false accusation is one of those risks that accompany success and senior leadership positions. The only way to ensure yourself against this risk is to be publicly,*

privately, and deliberately squeaky clean. Integrity ensures you solve and do not ignore real problems. It acts as a forcing function for needed improvements. Lack of integrity on the part of an individual is often a key indicator of a deeper problem in an organization or unit.

Integrity is the only product Congress or the Pentagon is interested in buying from a professional warrior.[10]

Make no mistake about it, this is the only product that superiors, subordinates, associates, and your customers are interested in buying either.

A MAJOR STUDY SHOWS THAT LEADERS WITHOUT INTEGRITY FREQUENTLY LOSE OUT

In 1983 the Center for Creative Leadership in Greensboro, North Carolina, began a groundbreaking study to identify traits or behaviors associated with eventual success or failure of top executives in civilian life.[11] The researchers surveyed top managers and senior human resource executives. They gathered descriptions of twenty-one junior managers who advanced into the ranks of middle or top management but at this point, failed to perform successfully. These executives had been on the fast track, but they had derailed. These "derailed" managers were fired, opted for early retirement, or simply were never promoted again.

The researchers also obtained descriptions of twenty managers who made it all the way to the top. They analyzed the two sets of descriptions to identify the similarities and differences. Then they analyzed the extent to which various flaws were likely to derail a promising career. One major difference they uncovered was that those managers who were extremely successful were much more likely to have demonstrated strong integrity. For example, derailed managers were far more likely to try to advance their own careers at the expense of others. They were more likely to betray a trust or break a promise. An example given in the original study was an executive who didn't implement a decision as promised, causing conflicts between marketing and production that affected four levels of frustrated executives below him.

"Jim," a former combat leader, gave me this example: "I was the director of new product development. At an annual marketing meeting of the top corporate staff, the president asked me about the development plan for a new product and how it was going. I had never heard of it before and said so. The president turned to one of the division managers who was a vice president and said, 'Joe, I thought I told you to ask Jim to develop a plan for that product for this meeting?' Joe answered, 'I did boss,' and reached in his briefcase. He pulled out a sheet of paper and began to read from the paper, 'Informed Jim that president wants new product plan for the annual marketing meeting. Jim agreed.'

"I was so shocked that acting purely on reflex, I jumped up and grabbed the paper out of Joe's hand. It was blank. Apparently, he had forgotten to pass on the information from the president to me and lacked the moral courage and integrity to admit it.

"I never trusted this man again, and I doubt that anyone one else who was there that day did either. His lack of integrity made working with his division very difficult for all of us. I know I tried to avoid dealing with him whenever I could. There is no doubt we could have accomplished much more if he had our trust. Before long, sales in his area began to decline. I don't know whether this happened due to the specific instance with the blank paper, but it seemed to begin at about that time. Eventually, he was eased out of his line management position, and he left the company. To the best of my knowledge, he never became a corporate officer again."

A PROFESSOR TEACHES FUTURE BUSINESS LEADERS TO LIE

Unfortunately not everyone agrees that you should do what you believe to be right regardless of the cost. Some years ago, a professor at one of our most prestigious business schools taught a different brand of integrity. In his graduate course, he made no bones about his recommendation to lie. He said it was necessary in business. In fact, he even dignified lying by teaching it as a management technique. He called it "strategic misdirection."

What a horrible notion! Is it any wonder that some of today's CEOs, presidents, and managers think nothing of lying or cheating to get ahead? That they treat workers and employees as so much corporate fodder to be sacrificed without a second thought? That they do all this with apparently few feelings of guilt, to the detriment of their colleagues, workers, and customers . . . even their companies? Far better that our teachers and leaders listen to men of integrity, such as Thomas Jefferson who gave us the following warning: "He who permits himself to tell a lie often finds it much easier to do it a second and third time, til at length it becomes habitual; he tells lies without attending to it, and truths without the world believing him. This falsehood of the tongue leads to that of the heart, and in time depraves all its good dispositions."[12]

PETER DRUCKER'S VIEWS

Peter F. Drucker has been given the titles "the greatest management thinker of our time," "the greatest management writer of the century," and similar tributes. They are all arguably accurate. He shares one thing with the individual who teaches lying. Peter is also a management professor. But after that the similarity ceases. Twenty years ago, he was my professor at Claremont Graduate School, now the Peter Drucker Management Center at Claremont, California. Peter has given considerable thought to leadership and what makes it work. He says, "Leaders in an organization need to impose on themselves that congruence between deeds and words, between behavior and professed beliefs and values, that we call 'personal integrity.'"[13] When he and I discussed the eight universal laws, he told me, "You know, you are undoubtedly correct about these laws. But there is one thing you should also understand. The first, 'maintain absolute integrity,' covers each of the other seven. One cannot, for example, agree to be leader of an organization when one does not have the necessary competence. 'Maintaining absolute integrity' is the root law."[14]

WHERE DO "WHITE LIES" FIT IN?

A white lie is an innocent lie that does not take advantage of anyone. In fact, it could be to someone else's benefit. On one of the television shows in the "JAG" series, a retired marine corps general has a son who was under the influence of alcohol while on duty. Calling erroneous map coordinates for an artillery barrage, another marine is killed. The general's son cares for no one but himself. He lies repeatedly and shoots another marine when he is caught trying to escape. After being mortally wounded in his attempt to escape punishment, his final words are, "Why me?"

The TV series hero was the only one who heard those last words. When the old general asks what his son said before he died, he tells him, "Tell my father I'm sorry." This is a white lie told for the father's benefit, not for the benefit of the hero. In the same manner, a leader could tell a white lie to his followers without compromising his integrity as long as it was for their clear benefit and not his own.

"Fred," an executive in corporate relations, told me the following story. He had only been out of college for a couple of months when his boss called him into his office. "'Tomorrow, representatives from the media — newspapers, TV, and radio — will come to our offices to get information about our new product,' my boss said. 'I was scheduled to give this interview, but I have to leave for Canada first thing tomorrow morning. I know you've never done anything like this before, but I've gotten to know you in the short time since you've been here. You've seen me give interviews before. I've got all the information you'll need right here. Study it tonight. I have full confidence that you will do a great job for us tomorrow.'

"I was very much afraid of doing the interview, but I was proud that my boss had so much confidence in me. I was determined to justify it. I worked long into the night preparing. I had never been so scared of anything in my life. But the next day I met with the media representatives and did a credible job.

"Years later, after I had been promoted several times, I had occasion to have dinner with my old boss, who was now a senior executive at corporate headquarters. I recalled the incident and asked how he came to have so much confidence in me even though I was so inexperienced."

'I was more scared than you were,' he told me. 'But we had no choice. You were absolutely the only one available to do the interview.'

Fred's boss had told a lie, but the lie had not been for his own benefit. It was for Fred's. The boss didn't violate his honor by telling it.

YOU DON'T HAVE TO CHEAT TO WIN

Two world-famous authors got together to write what they considered a very important book. Both these men had previously written best-sellers, which had had a tremendous effect on the way managers manage and even on the way people think and achieve. One author was Kenneth Blanchard. His best-known book, coauthored with Spencer Johnson, was *The One Minute Manager*. The other author was Norman Vincent Peale. His book

The Power of Positive Thinking was one of the best-sellers of all time, selling millions of copies.

These two well-known authors collaborated on *The Power of Ethical Management* because they felt that ethics was the most urgent problem facing America. Moreover, both believed that ethical managers were winning managers. The subtitle of their book proclaimed: "Integrity Pays!" Does it?

A FAILURE OF INTEGRITY HURTS THE LEADER AND THE ORGANIZATION

Marine lieutenant Tony Garcia flew helicopters in Vietnam. One hot and sticky day, he was sent to rescue five marines trapped behind enemy lines. Arriving in the area where they were supposed to be, Tony could see five figures in marine uniforms lying motionless on the ground. He attempted to make radio contact with them, with no success. Were they wounded, or had they been killed? In any case, radio contact was essential for the rescue. Standing orders forbade marine helicopters to land in a combat zone without making radio contact with friendly forces on the ground in that zone.

Tony reported his inability to establish radio contact to his commander back at headquarters. Not wanting to be known as a leader who abandoned wounded men, the commander lied. He told Tony he had been in radio contact with these men previously. As Tony came in to land, the "marines" stood up and began firing at the helicopter. They were not marines at all but North Vietnamese wearing captured marine uniforms.

Fortunately, Tony still had enough airspeed to lift off and escape. However, his tail rotor was disabled and his medic wounded. It had been a very close brush with disaster. It was difficult for this commander to regain the trust of Tony and others who were aware of what had happened. This lack of trust hurt the commander's ability to lead and therefore hurt his organization as well.

No one wanted to leave wounded marines to the enemy. The commander might have said, "You and I both know the orders on landing without radio contact. However, if you think the situation looks okay, go ahead in under my orders. I'll take the responsibility. If things don't look right, don't go in, and I'll back you on that, too." But you cannot lie as Tony's commander did and expect to retain the confidence of those you lead, no matter how well-intentioned. You must maintain absolute integrity, even when it hurts.

Unfortunately, Tony had a similar experience as a civilian. Shortly after becoming the program manager for a company, a contractor from another company asked whether he could make a change to the requirements documentation for one of Tony's programs. He asked the contractor why he wanted to make the change and how it would affect the contract. The contractor said, "No real effect other than clarifying the language." Not long after the contract went into effect, the contractor used the change he had made to his advantage to modify the work he was doing.

Tony says, "Since there was no inherent bond in trust, I could never trust the individual again, and made my feelings clear to his management. He was replaced shortly thereafter."[15,16] Had this individual not been replaced, there is little question that the lack of trust would have affected the ability of both companies to work together to complete the project.

As a director with Litton Data Systems in Agoura Hills, California, Tony is acutely aware of his lessons on trust. At Litton, an annual award has been established, which is presented yearly "to the employee whose leadership qualities of competence, integrity, and concern for fellow workers inspire others to exceptional performance."

ONE WHO MAINTAINS HIS INTEGRITY IS ALWAYS HONORED

When the Civil War began, Robert E. Lee was only a colonel, but he was held in such respect that he was offered command of the entire Union Army.

However, when his state, Virginia, seceded from the Union, Lee searched his soul and found he had a serious problem. He did not believe in slavery. He did, however, believe that a state had a right to leave a union it had voluntarily entered. There was another important question. Did a citizen owe primary loyalty to his state or to a distant central government? Today allegiance to one's state is not an issue. But prior to the Civil War, it was a question of burning importance and controversy to many Americans.

After pacing his room during a sleepless night, Lee came to a decision. "I cannot draw my sword against my friends and neighbors," he decided. He resigned his commission in the U.S. Army and soon thereafter was commissioned in the Virginia militia.

Becoming commander of the Union Army would have been the pinnacle of a long and successful military career. Lee didn't reach the equivalent position in the Confederate Army until three months prior to the end of the war. Until then, he was only commander of the Army of Northern Virginia. During the first year of war, Lee held no command at all, serving instead as military advisor to the president.

On one occasion, Jefferson Davis, president of the Confederacy, summoned Lee and asked him for his opinion regarding a certain general's fitness for high command. Lee answered that the general was an able and competent officer and should be promoted. Another officer who was present was astonished but kept quiet. When Jefferson Davis left the room, he asked, "General Lee, how could you give this officer such a glowing recommendation? He has never said anything good about you." General Lee paused and then responded, "President Davis did not ask for this officer's opinion of me, but my opinion of him."

Robert E. Lee was a man of impeccable integrity. His men loved, honored, and followed him during the war and afterward. Though he fought against the United States, Americans honor Robert E. Lee today. But as we will see, history does not honor leaders who lack honor themselves.

THIS DESPISED GENERAL WAS ONCE A HERO

During our War of Independence, one combat leader stood out above the others. He was known for his daring and aggressiveness. Through force of personality and competence, he rose through the ranks to become a brigadier general. After serving as the commander in several battles, he thought he deserved, and probably did deserve, promotion to major general. The Continental Congress unfairly promoted less able and deserving men who had more political clout. General Washington interceded and, finally, the combat leader was promoted to major general.

But this leader lacked integrity. He felt wronged in not being promoted when he thought he should have been, and generals who were not as capable as he were now his seniors. When the British secretly offered him a pardon, and a commission as a general in their army, he was ready to commit treason and switch sides. He knew what was right, but he didn't take that path. He conspired with the British to surrender the strategically important fort at West Point. Fortunately the plot was uncovered before his treason was consummated. He barely succeeded in escaping to England.

In the old Cadet Chapel at West Point, plaques put there in the 1820s line the walls. Each plaque honors a general in our War of Independence. The plaque has the honoree's rank, name, date of birth, and date of death. One plaque has only the rank of major general plus the two dates of birth and death. That plaque "honors" former major general Benedict Arnold. Everyone knows that Benedict Arnold is a synonym for the word "traitor." Few know that this man once played an important role as a combat leader in gaining America's independence.

MEN OF INTEGRITY CAN LEAD SUCCESSFULLY UNDER TERRIBLE CONDITIONS

Vice Adm. James B. Stockdale was a prisoner of war in North Vietnam for eight years. Repeatedly tortured, beaten, and kept in isolation, Stockdale never gave in. And most of his fellow prisoners didn't break either. He led his men under conditions that many would say were worse than combat. His conclusion after this forced "education" was that leaders under pressure must keep themselves absolutely morally clean. In his words, "They must have earned their followers' respect by demonstrating integrity. . . . The necessary leadership attributes under pressure are bedrock virtues all successful leaders must possess, under pressure and otherwise."[17]

FOUR WAYS TO DEVELOP INTEGRITY

1. Keep Your Word
2. Chose the Harder Right Over the Easier Wrong
3. Guard Your Principles
4. Do the Right Thing

KEEP YOUR WORD

If you say something, make certain it is the exact truth. If you later realize you have misspoken, correct yourself. If you say or promise you will do something, make certain you do it, no matter what.

Keeping His Word Costs
Arby's CEO His Job

Leonard Roberts became CEO of Arby's, Inc., at a time when the business was doing very poorly. He turned the corporation around when sales had been falling 10 to 15 percent a year. He did this by promising service, support, and money to Arby's franchisees. He delivered, and the franchisees supported him in turn. Sales soared.

Eager for more profits, Arby's owner threatened to withdraw the help Roberts had been giving to franchisees and did not pay bonuses earned by Roberts's staff. Roberts had been appointed to the board of directors. The first meeting he attended lasted fifteen minutes. The board was simply a rubber stamp for the owner. Said Roberts, "I knew what I had to do. I had to take a stand, so I resigned from the board." Roberts also took steps to rectify the situation both with his staff's bonuses and with the franchisees. "I had promised to shield them," he says. Roberts's boss considered this insubordination. He fired him for supporting the franchisees.

At the time, business researcher Richard Poe said, "Roberts's sacrifice was not in vain. The integrity that he showed only increased his renown in the franchise world; in the end, it will benefit the organization he left and his own career."[18] To the benefit of his career or not, Roberts kept his word. No one said maintaining absolute integrity would be easy.

What happened to Leonard Roberts afterward? Did this finish his career as a CEO? Not quite. In fact, he stumbled right into another situation that challenged his integrity to the fullest. Through a headhunter, Roberts was offered the position of chairman and CEO of a chain of two thousand Shoney's restaurants headquartered in Nashville, Tennessee. The situation looked right, so Len Roberts accepted the offer. Only afterward did Roberts learn, much to his dismay, that Shoney's was the subject of the largest racial discrimination lawsuit in history. Questioned by the *Wall Street Journal*, Roberts promised that the suit would be settled without long-term impact on the company.

Unfortunately settling the suit was more easily said than done. It was not simply a misunderstanding. The policy of the former chairman was not to hire African Americans. In fact, his official policy was to fire any restaurant manager who did! "The settlement of that suit was the thing I am most proud of in my life," says Len Roberts. "The former chairman agreed to pay up and settle. This saved the company. But I had to agree to resign after he did so. This was my second time out of work in almost as many years. My stand on integrity was getting kind of hard on my wife and kids. However, I knew it had to be done. There was no other way."

Fortunately, Leonard Roberts became the CEO of Radio Shack after leaving Shoney's. A year after that, he took on the additional job of CEO of the entire Tandy Corporation. Last year *Brandweek* magazine named him retail marketer of the year.

Roberts says, "You cannot fake it. You must stand up for what is right regardless. You cannot maintain your integrity until it hurts your pocketbook or risks your job. You cannot maintain your integrity 90 percent and be a successful leader. It's got to be 100 percent."[19]

CHOOSE THE HARDER RIGHT

As a leader, you will have plenty of opportunities for decision making. Frequently you'll be faced with a choice of right or wrong. No matter what your boss thinks, no matter what the stockholders think, no matter if you will lose your job, choose the right. The right may be hard to do, the wrong much easier. If you want to develop your integrity, choose the right anyway.

Carol Barkalow graduated in the West Point class of 1980 — the first class to admit women as cadets. As a young captain, she commanded the Fifty-Seventh Transportation Company at Fort Lee, Virginia.

Even when military units are not at war, they are constantly training and being tested. One of Barkalow's most difficult tests as a commander was the ARTEP, or Army Readiness Training and Evaluation Program. This important exercise replicates actual combat conditions and measures a unit's performance over a four-day period. It is pass or fail in every area measured.

In one required maneuver, the entire unit has to move to another location after a nighttime drive of fifteen miles. Captain Barkalow's soldiers told her that other units frequently "simulated" the combat move. That is, they really didn't move at all. They just declare that they did. If Barkalow's unit actually moved, it would be particularly complicated because they were in an area of heavily wooded roads and soldiers who had pitched their camouflaged tents nearby. They would have to travel at snail's pace. They sure wouldn't get much sleep or be ready for the next day's tests. Why make things difficult? Why risk a failing grade? Why not just "simulate" the move? There was only one reason. An actual night-driving maneuver was a requirement of the ARTEP.

"I told them I wanted nothing to do with simulation; we moved the unit that night," said Capt. Carol Barkalow. A failure would have been a major factor on her officer's effectiveness report. That would have affected her future chances for promotion. But she knew that and accepted it. Captain Barkalow was lucky that night. Even with the additional problems, her company completed the night move with nothing more serious than some sprained ankles.[20]

In the larger scheme of things, did the fact that Barkalow refused to compromise her integrity and chose the harder right have any impact on the U.S. Army and national defense? You would think not. But let me tell you about what happened to another young officer, and you be the judge.

HE CHOSE THE HARDER RIGHT AND IT AFFECTED THE REST OF HIS LIFE

As a young air force lieutenant in 1960, "Herb" was a new navigator on a B-52 crew. Among his responsibilities was the programming of the two air-to-ground "cruise" missiles nicknamed "Hound Dogs." The missiles were also new, and many problems with them hadn't yet been solved. The few crews in Herb's squadron that had flown with them had got mixed results. Sometimes they hit right on target. Sometimes they weren't even close.

The crews didn't actually launch the missiles. That would have been too expensive, as each missile cost millions of dollars. The crews programmed the missiles while they were flying to the launch point. That took several hours as Herb repeatedly updated each missile's computers on its location. When about fifteen minutes from the target, the crew would put the missile into a "simulated launch" mode. Herb then instructed the pilots to follow a special needle indicator on their consoles. If the needle turned right, the pilots turned the aircraft right. If the needle turned left, they turned the aircraft left. When they did this, the aircraft followed the course to the target according to information in the missile's inertial guidance system.

Two minutes from the target Herb turned on a tone signal. On the ground, a Ground Control Intercept (GCI) site tracked Herb's aircraft on radar. At the point where the missile would dive into its target, the missile would automatically interrupt Herb's tone signal. The course the missile would take to the ground once it started its final dive was based on predetermined factors — the weight of the missile, its shape, etc. This unpowered flight path from the air to the target on the ground is known as the missile's ballistics. So by tracking the aircraft's tone signal on radar and knowing the missile's ballistics when the tone signal stopped, it was easy for the GCI site to calculate where the missile would impact if it had actually been launched. This was the same way that the aircrews practiced making bomb runs without actually dropping any bombs. The only difference was that the needle the pilots followed was wired to the bombardier's bombsight.

These practice runs had a major impact on the crews' careers. Crews that received good scores were promoted. Those that did not were held back. Woe to a unit commander when one of his crews got a "bad bomb" or, now, a "bad missile."

Herb's crewmates were all far more experienced than he. His aircraft commander was a lieutenant colonel. Before going to flying school during World War II, the commander had been a first sergeant. He was still tough, and, at six foot two inches, he looked the part. The commander's copilot was a captain. The electronic warfare officer was also a captain. The senior navigator, who was also the bombardier, was another lieutenant colonel and veteran of World War II. Finally, Herb's crew had one noncommissioned officer. That was the gunner. He was a master sergeant and a Korean War veteran. Herb was a lieutenant and fresh out of flying school.

Herb's crew had never flown with missiles previously. However, while on seven-day alert, their aircraft commander called the crew together. "We have missiles for the first time," he said. "I don't want to discuss it. We're going to cheat to make sure we get good scores. All I want to know is how we're going to do it."

Herb was shocked and speechless. The bombardier spoke up. "That's easy. Don't follow the missile needle. I'll figure out an

28

adjustment for the ballistics, and I'll 'bomb' the target using my bombsight. All you have to do is follow the bombsight's needle as we normally do. The GCI site will not know that we're actually 'bombing' the target. It will be easy."

The aircraft commander dismissed the crew immediately afterward and they were released from their duties. They had three days of crew rest before getting together to plan the mission which would involve the twelve-hour flight with the missiles. The mission would include the simulated missile launch, some bomb runs, and an aerial refueling.

The three days were absolute hell for Herb. He was new to the crew and the squadron, but he had heard that this type of cheating was not unusual. Now he was being ordered to do it with the very missiles with which he was entrusted. He talked it over with several friends. They told him not to rock the boat. They told Herb that this sort of thing was routine and that everybody did it. If he didn't cheat, they said, it would be the end of his career.

Herb had worked long and hard for his career. He had worked long and hard to enter one of the academies and make it through four years there. He had spent a year in navigation school, six months in bombardier school, and many weeks in air force survival training and B-52 ground and air training. It had been six years altogether, not counting three years he had been in the U.S. Reserve Officers Training Corps (ROTC) before that. How could Herb let it all slip away for this one little lie that apparently nobody cared about anyway?

"But I had been taught integrity," says Herb. "I was taught 'integrity first,' that this was the essential law of being an officer. This lie was contrary to everything I had been taught and believed in."

When Herb's crew met to plan the mission, he asked to speak to his aircraft commander privately. As soon as they were alone Herb told him, "If you want to cheat on these missiles, that's up to you. But get yourself a new navigator, because I'm not going to do it." Herb's commander was furious and berated him for quite a long time. Then he slammed the door to the room and left. Says Herb, "I was plenty scared, and I thought it was the end of my career."

An hour or so later, Herb's commander was still angry when he said he wanted to see Herb alone. Once alone he said, "Okay.

We'll do it your way. And this won't affect your performance report. But those missiles better be reliable." "I'll do everything possible to make them so, but I won't cheat," answered Herb.

Herb heard later that this commander told someone, "I don't know whether Herb's a good navigator or not, but I trust him. He's honest, and he's got guts."

The missiles were reliable. To this day Herb tells me that he doesn't know whether he was skilled or lucky. But here's something Herb does know. He knows how far he would go for what he believes to be right. And the answer is: all the way. Herb, who later became a general and is currently a company executive, says, "I believe that knowledge has helped me immensely over the years, and I believe that I owe whatever success I have achieved in part to it. In fact, it still affects my thinking today. Had it ended my career then and there, it still would have been worth it for this priceless piece of knowledge about myself."

That's what Carol Barkalow gained by choosing the harder right rather than the easier wrong, too. She knows how far she will go to protect her integrity: all the way.

You're in the same position. If you haven't met this test yet, you will. If you already have and passed it, congratulations. You're on the right path. If you failed, don't make the same mistake twice. You don't have to. The past does not equal the future. Chose the harder right beginning now. Then you'll know that you're willing to go all the way, too.

GUARD YOUR PRINCIPLES

As we saw earlier, integrity doesn't only mean being honest and talking straight. It means being trustworthy and principled. Many leaders in business state that integrity is important. Yet these same corporate executives don't blink at discharging thousands of loyal employees. If asked, they would probably say that the firings "go against their principles," but they had "no choice." They offer little or nothing to most of their employees to ease the pain of dismissal. Yet many of these employees worked for these organizations their entire lives. Moreover, in many of these corporations, CEOs took big bonuses and salary increases even as they fired employees. That's because their profits went up as they cut the human resource costs.

There is only one acceptable reason for massive layoffs, and that is not profitability alone. Firing people to raise profits is a very short-term solution. The only acceptable excuse for massive layoffs is survival of the firm. In this case, if the layoffs did not take place, everyone would lose his job. However, even when layoffs are necessary for corporate survival, there are two cautionary notes for company executives who want to maintain absolute integrity. First, the leadership should share the pain through cuts in salary, bonuses, etc. Second, everything possible should be done to ease the hardship of those who must be dismissed.

ONE CEO FINDS GUARDING YOUR PRINCIPLES PAYS OFF

Others may compromise their integrity in business, but not Michael Armstrong, former CEO of Hughes Electronics. For Hughes's survival, Armstrong cut his workforce by 20 percent. But Armstrong didn't abandon his integrity when he did this. He gave a "golden parachute" severance package to each worker. It included five thousand dollars for training or tuition, six months of health-care benefits, and up to forty weeks of severance pay. Moreover, while many companies are fond of including a pink termination slip along with a paycheck giving two weeks' notice, Armstrong insisted on far more. "We instituted a sixty-day warning, with a ninety-day warning preferred. Above all, people need time to prepare," he says.[21] One Hughes manager said, "It was something that had to be done, but he did it well and fairly."[22]

"A leader doesn't really have a choice," says Armstrong. "Any leader has to earn the respect of others by showing respect for every individual. Sometimes cuts must be made. When they are, they must be done with respect, sensitivity, and consideration. If I hadn't done this at Hughes, I wouldn't have had the support of the Hughes employees that remained."[23]

On the face of it, Armstrong's actions were a negative drain on the corporation's dwindling treasure. In the long run, the cost of integrity bore positive results. Morale and productivity rose among Hughes employees still on the job. Far from hurting the company's bottom line, Hughes's profits increased. Over a four-year period, Hughes Electronics became one of the hottest consumer-electronics and communication companies around. Sales skyrocketed 28 percent to $14.7 billion while operating margins almost doubled. Maintaining your integrity is the right thing to do even though it may cause temporary problems. Over the long haul, Mike Armstrong proved it could positively affect productivity and profits.

Recently, Mike Armstrong was named the chairman and CEO of troubled AT&T. He replaced Robert Allen, who had dismissed tens of thousands of workers while trying to regain lost profits. Allen's efforts were unsuccessful.

In his first public meeting with Wall Street analysts since taking over, Armstrong presented what the *Los Angeles Times* called a "bold plan." Those in attendance at the meeting seemed to like it. "He didn't deflect any questions, and he's tackling some issues that some of us who have been here for fifteen or twenty years still have a tough time with," said David Otto, a telecommunications analyst with Edward Jones in St. Louis.[24]

Armstrong did announce a layoff of fifteen thousand to eighteen thousand managers to help reduce costs. However, in contrast to the way that cuts at AT&T were made in the past, up to eleven thousand layoffs will come from voluntary early retirements with significantly enhanced pensions, the rest from a hiring freeze and normal attrition. Morale is up because Armstrong has convinced his employees that he can and will do the right thing.[25]

Where did Armstrong learn to guard his principles? "I had the good fortune to be raised with family values to do the right thing," he explains.

"This was reinforced by a strong corporate culture at IBM, where I grew up and developed as a corporate executive. Respect for the individual and the best customer service, as well as excellence in everyday performance, were principles that were revered and followed. To me this is what integrity is all about. It comes down to doing the right thing. You earn respect by showing respect for others.

"Guarding your principles helps to maintain your integrity," Armstrong continues. "It gives you the credibility a leader needs to lead. It must start at the top. If there is pain, you've got to share the pain. You can't delegate it. At AT&T, before we started any general downsizing, we announced a reduction in corporate officers of 25 percent. We greatly reduced corporate perks for top managers. We initiated a salary freeze for the top five hundred executives. We're taking out two layers of management. Only after we started this process did we start to work on our general plan for downsizing. And we're doing everything possible to do this with as great a sensitivity as possible for those of our employees who must leave after good and honorable service with our company. This is the right thing to do, and the right thing from a business standpoint, too."[26]

DO THE RIGHT THING

When you are in a situation in which you stand to lose a lot by stating the complete truth, that is exactly the time to do the right thing. If you do, not only will others treat you with a new respect, you will also treat yourself with a new respect. And why not? Don't you respect others you trust and believe would do the right thing regardless of benefit or cost to themselves?

A FUMBLING NEW PLATOON LEADER DOES THE RIGHT THING

Second Lt. George Brown joined the 377th Infantry Regiment, 95th Infantry Division, as a platoon leader as it advanced into Germany in late November 1944. George Brown had never been in combat before. He was replacing a popular officer who had been not only well liked by his men, but well thought of by his superiors. This officer had a reputation for both courage and quick thinking in battle. George knew that he had big shoes to fill and had to win the respect of both his subordinates and his superiors.

Unfortunately nothing seemed to go right. On his first day in command, a hidden German sniper caught the platoon strung out on the open road and suddenly opened fire. Until then, no one knew of his existence. Eventually, his platoon got the sniper with mortar fire, but they were tremendously fortunate to suffer no casualties. The unwelcome surprise of the sudden fusillade may not have been George's fault, but he was responsible.

A few days later, several Gestapo officers his company sought to capture got away. Then his company commander sent him to lead a night patrol to capture prisoners. As luck would have it, the patrol stumbled into an unsuspected minefield, suffering two wounded and capturing no prisoners. Again, George had done nothing wrong directly, but he was in charge when things went wrong. He knew that he suffered from comparison with his predecessor. He suspected that his boss thought him incompetent. At best, his soldiers probably thought him unlucky. In combat, some feel that being unlucky is just as bad as being incompetent, maybe worse.

The following day the platoon ran into a hidden machine gun. Lieutenant Brown and a private, himself a new replacement, were separated from the rest of the platoon. The machinegun held George's platoon immobilized. They could not even raise their heads without coming under a hail of fire. But George and the private were out of the enemy's line of sight. Moreover, the private carried a bazooka. This weapon fired a rocket with a highly explosive warhead.

George motioned the private to follow him, and they began to maneuver so they could attack the machine gun with the bazooka. As they got closer to their objective, a German rifleman guarding the machine gun spotted them and opened fire with his assault rifle.

George loaded the bazooka from the rear and told the private to fire. Then he rapidly fired a burst from his carbine at the German and started to move forward. He missed. At almost the same time, he was temporarily blinded from the blast of the rocket as the private, who was now somewhat in front and to his right, fired the bazooka. Apparently, the private had been hit by the German rifleman. He fell to the ground immediately after firing, mortally wounded.

As George continued forward, the bazooka rocket that the private had fired struck near the machine gun and exploded. Without thinking, George scooped up the bazooka from the fallen private. The surviving Germans were confused and demoralized. They immediately stood up and raised their arms in surrender.

George's men saw the rocket explode. Then they saw their lieutenant charge the position and capture the Germans. He had the bazooka slung over one shoulder and his smoking carbine held at the ready with his other arm.

His men left their positions of concealment and joined him. Before George could say a word, they enthusiastically congratulated him. "Way to go Lieutenant!" "Wow — better than Sergeant York!" "He's a one-man army!"

Almost immediately, the company commander arrived. George's men gave the commander a dramatic account of the incident, giving George credit for destroying the enemy position by himself after the private who had been with him was killed. George's company commander congratulated him on his feat. He told George he would be recommended for a high decoration, the Distinguished Service Cross. George knew that if he said nothing, not only would he be a hero, but he would have completely erased any bad impressions made during his first few days with the unit. No one knew the truth. Even the surviving Germans thought that George had fired the bazooka which destroyed their position.

After all of George's earlier problems, it was very difficult for him to choose to do what he knew to be the right thing. That's the real test of integrity — to do the right thing when no one is looking. He did.

"That's not what happened," he told his platoon and his company commander. He then went on to give an accurate account of the incident. George stated he was recommending the private for the posthumous award of the medal that the company commander wanted to give him.

George Brown went on to become a very effective combat leader. Everyone respected him. It did not matter that he didn't fire the rocket that destroyed the gun emplacement. What did matter was that George was a leader whom both subordinates and superiors could trust absolutely. They knew he could be counted on to do the right thing even when no one was watching.

Maj. Gen. Perry M. Smith is a former combat leader who was formerly commandant of the National War College in Washington, D.C. He has written several books of his own on leadership. Says General Smith: "It's particularly important to be honest in military organizations because trust in combat is so essential. Trust in combat is so essential that military institutions must generate a mentality of trust and honesty in peacetime. The role of the leader is very, very important. I find that integrity will go downhill fast if the leader isn't on top of that issue and doesn't set very high standards for himself. Leaders have to be squeaky clean in this area."[27]

Let's see how these high standards of integrity in battle leadership carried over into civilian life for George Brown.

PROFESSOR GEORGE BROWN DOES THE RIGHT THING AGAIN

I met George Brown before he retired from his civilian career.

After World War II, he went back to school under the G.I. Bill. Eventually he got his doctorate and became a university professor. As I got in the "professor business," George was getting ready to retire. In the university, his leadership skills and integrity were tested in one of the most trying of environments other than combat: the college classroom. And George excelled. He won numerous awards for teaching. He was popular and respected equally by students, faculty, and administrators.

As a new professor just starting out and a fellow former "warrior," George took me under his wing. He told me the story of his days in combat as well as the story that follows.

During George's first year at the university, it was rumored that some professors were cutting their night school classes and letting students leave as much as an hour early. Evening classes were supposed to start at 6 P.M. and continue until 10 P.M. with a twenty-minute break at the midpoint. Apparently the chancellor's office had got wind of what was going on from student complaints. The chancellor told the deans that he would send someone around to monitor the classes unannounced. Professors not teaching their full class periods would be disciplined. Professors who were not yet tenured, like George, would be dismissed.

George's dean sent warnings to all professors teaching night classes. George had been following the rules and so wasn't worried. However, only days after the dean's warning, George ran into a problem.

For one of his night classes, he had invited a guest speaker to speak for an hour, followed by a half-hour question-and-answer session. After a short break, George would lecture for the final two hours and ten minutes.

Unfortunately, George's guest speaker did not show up. Several years later, this would have been no problem. With more experience, the professor would have enough material to cover another couple of hours from the following week's lesson. However, as a new professor, George was only slightly ahead of the students. He had two hours and ten minutes of lecture for them that night, perhaps a few minutes more, but that was it.

THE MAN IN WHITE MAKES IT
AN INTEGRITY ISSUE

Normally, George would have dismissed the class early, learned his own lesson from what had happened, and moved on.

However, he remembered the dean's warning. And sure enough, on this one night, there was a stranger dressed in an all-white suit with a black tie. George knew it had to be the monitor from the chancellor's office.

He reviewed his options. He could drag his lecture out and think up some time-wasting activities. With a little luck, dragging the break out a little longer, etc., he could probably stretch things to 10 P.M. His alternative didn't look so good. George knew that he stood an excellent chance of losing his job if he let his students out early. It had been hard to secure his position. There weren't many professorial openings the year he completed his graduate degree.

As George continued to lecture, he wrestled with his options. He knew that the right thing to do did not include wasting forty students' time because of his own inexperience and lack of preparation.

At the lecture's halfway point, he announced the twenty-minute break. He told me, "I really hadn't admitted to myself that I was going to let them go early, what with 'the man in white' there and everything. But I guess in my heart of hearts, I knew. Any leader, in the classroom or out, must do the right thing or he will lose his self respect."

At the end of his lecture, George told the class what had happened and took full responsibility. He announced they would be leaving more than an hour early, and he recommended they use the time to study. The students applauded. "The man in white" wrote something down in a book. George Brown's heart sank.

That night he told his wife, "Well, I screwed up, and I may get fired." She told him not to worry, that it would all work out.

The next day one of his female students came to his office. "I enjoy your lectures so much that I invited my fiancé to attend last night," she said. "I hope you didn't mind. I didn't have an opportunity to introduce him to you, but he was the one in the white suit and black tie. He's a host at a restaurant and came right from work."

"I never felt so relieved and so foolish all at the same time," George told me. "I was relieved that I wouldn't be losing my job, but I think I was even more relieved when I realized how close I had come to wasting more than forty man-hours simply because one of my students brought her fiancé to class!"

Lt. Gen. Winfield Scott flew F-51 fighters in Korea and F-4

fighters in Vietnam. General Scott is a West Pointer who served as superintendent of the Air Force Academy. After retirement from the air force, he became the superintendent of New Mexico Military Institute in Roswell, New Mexico. General Scott says, "The leader must demonstrate complete honesty and integrity in all dealings with people — boss, peers, and subordinates. Then he or she must have the courage to do what is right. Forget the 'look-good' syndrome. Results tell the story of success."[28]

Maj. Gen. B. J. Ellis of Sumter, South Carolina, flew one tour of combat in Korea and an amazing three combat tours in Vietnam. He knows something about leading people in difficult circumstances. General Ellis says, "Honesty is crucial. Don't let your staff or even higher headquarters seduce you into doing something wrong. You know what's right. Do it!"[29]

HOW TO GET YOUR ORGANIZATION TO DUPLICATE YOUR INTEGRITY

As a leader, your followers won't always do what you say, but they will always do what you do. After more than thirty years of leading others in a wide variety of roles, that's the conclusion of retired air force lieutenant general Jay Kelley. He should know. His last assignment was commander of Air University, the organization responsible for the professional military education of senior officers and noncommissioned officers. Kelley was able to share experiences with hundreds of other successful leaders in the air force.

"It's just like raising kids," says General Kelley. "You can tell your kids what to do all you want. Everybody does that. But they're going to do what you do, regardless of what you say. So if you want your kids, or those in your organization, to do the right thing, you must do the right thing as well."[30]

Gen. Alexander Haig, Jr., is one of the most distinguished American leaders of our time. He led our troops in both Korea and Vietnam, winning high decorations for valor in both wars. He rose to the rank of full general. Then he retired to become chief of staff to the president of the United States. During the difficult days at the close of the Nixon administration, Haig's role was crucial in maintaining our democracy during one of the severest periods of stress to befall the United States. Afterward, during the height of the Cold War, he returned to active duty to become Supreme Allied Commander in Europe, where he led troops from many nations. Retiring from the armed forces a second time, he first served in industry as president of United Technologies and then as secretary of state to President Ronald Reagan before returning to the fields of international business and education. The breadth and depth of his leadership experience is unique and rare.

General Haig states unequivocally, "In an era marked by at least the appearance of questionable integrity and moral courage by many contemporary leaders, the demonstration of absolute integrity by a leader is the most important principle that any leader must follow."[31]

HOW TO MAINTAIN THE BOTTOM-LINE RULE

Maintaining absolute integrity is the bottom-line rule for any leader if he wants his subordinates to follow him under all conditions — to hell and back. You can develop your integrity if you will:

1. Keep Your Word
2. Chose the Harder Right Over the Easier Wrong
3. Guard Your Principles
4. Do the Right Thing

If you do this, others in your organization will do it, too. You will build the foundation if you:

MAINTAIN ABSOLUTE INTEGRITY

ENDNOTES

[1] Kelly, Orr, *From a Dark Sky* (New York: Pocket Books, 1996), 280.
[2] McCutchan, Clay, telephone conversation with the author, October 1, 1997.
[3] *U.S. Air Force Core Values* (Washington, D.C.: U.S. Air Force, 1997).
[4] Johnson, Kermit, letter to the author, July 26, 1993.
[5] Kennedy, Charles, letter to the author, May 28, 1996.
[6] Grinalds, John, letter to the author, October 12, 1993, and telephone interview, February 10, 1998.

[7] Grinalds, John, "Letter to Friends of the Citadel," October 22, 1997.

[8] Powell, Colin, *My American Journey* (New York: Random House, 1995), 149.

[9] DeRemer, Lee E., "Leadership Between a Rock and a Hard Place," *The Airpower Journal* (Fall 1966): 87–94.

[10] Oliver, Dave, *Lead On!* (Novato, California: Presidio Press, 1992), 205–6.

[11] McCall, M.W., Jr., and M.M. Lombardo, "What Makes a Top Executive?" *Psychology Today* (February 1983): 26–31.

[12] Jefferson, Thomas, August 19, 1775, as quoted in Robert A. Fitton, ed., *Leadership: Quotations from the Military Tradition* (Boulder, Colo.: Westview Press, 1990), 297.

[13] Drucker, Peter F., "The Mystery of the Business Leader," *Drucker Management* (Spring 1993): 2–3, previously published in the *Wall Street Journal* (September 29, 1987).

[14] Drucker, Peter F., meeting with the author, November 7, 1997.

[15] Garcia, Anthony, letter to the author, April 4, 1996.

[16] Garcia, Anthony, letter to the author, June 10,1996.

[17] Stockdale, James B., "Machiavelli, Management, and Moral Leadership," *U.S. Naval Institute Proceedings* (1980).

[18] Poe, Richard, "A Winning Spirit — It Takes Integrity To Lead Franchises to Victory," *Success* 37, no. 6 (August 1990): 60

[19] Ibid.

[20] Barkalow, Carol, with Andrea Raab, *In the Men's House* (New York: Poseidon Press, 1990), 256.

[21] Armstrong, C. Michael, telephone interview with the author, March 1, 1998.

[22] Schine, Eric, "Lift Off," *BusinessWeek* (April 22, 1996): 142.

[23] Op. Cit., Armstrong, C. Michael

[24] Kaplan, Karen, "AT&T Lays Out a Bold Plan for Its Future," *Los Angeles Times* (January 27, 1998): D1, D19.

[25] Elstrom, Peter, with Kathleen Kerwin, "New Boss, New Plan," *Business Week* (February 2, 1998): 124–126.

[26] Op. Cit., Armstrong, C. Michael.

[27] Smith, Perry M., "Leadership and Ethics: A Practitioner's View," in *Moral Obligation and the Military: Collected Essays* (Washington, D.C.: National Defense University Press), 1988, 137.

[28] Scott, Winfield W., Jr., letter to the author July 23, 1993.

[29] Ellis, B. J., letter to the author, July 28, 1993.

[30] Kelley, Jay, conversation with the author, Air University, Maxwell Air Force Base, Alabama, July 18, 1996.

[31] Haig, Alexander M., Jr., letter to the author, February 6, 1998.

KNOW YOUR STUFF

A competent leader can get efficient service from poor troops, while on the contrary an incapable leader can demoralize the best of troops.
— GENERAL OF THE ARMIES JOHN J. PERSHING

One of the most celebrated cases of American battle heroism in this century is that of Sergeant Alvin C. York during World War I. Many do not realize just how much his story illustrates the second universal law of leadership.

York was a soldier in Company G, 328th Regiment, 82nd Division of the U.S. Army. No one noticed anything particularly unusual about him when he was drafted into the army until he filed to avoid military service as a conscientious objector. However, the paperwork took some time, and he was assigned to a unit and began training as an infantryman. With considerable effort, his new company commander convinced him to remain in the army. York withdrew his request to avoid service and went overseas to France with his unit.

There was one other item of note in his background — one that made him very attractive as a combat infantryman. It may also help to explain why his company commander tried so hard to keep him in the army. York was an expert shot. He had been a champion marksman in his home state of Tennessee before the war. As a rifleman, he really knew his stuff. His company commander felt York's knowledge and skill in marksmanship would be very handy to have on the battlefield. As it turned out, this expertise became more important than anyone could have imagined.

By 1918 York was a corporal. One day in late October he was

sent on a patrol in the Argonne Forest with sixteen other men under the command of a sergeant. The patrol managed to surprise a German headquarters and took several prisoners. As the patrol moved on, the soldiers stumbled on a hidden nest of enemy soldiers with machine guns and were themselves surprised. The soldiers opened fire with deadly effectiveness. Only York and seven privates survived the first volley. Corporal York was suddenly in command of seven frightened subordinates facing an entire machine-gun battalion. This was World War I. York hadn't been to leadership school. He hadn't graduated from a noncommissioned officer academy. He was a young man thrust into the role of leader in a very perilous situation.

The seven privates wanted to surrender. York asked them to wait while he "tried something." He told them to keep under cover and guard their prisoners. York began to look for a position from which to fire at the Germans. You can imagine what must have gone through the minds of those young privates. Was York going to take on a German machine-gun battalion by himself? What chance did he have? York had only one thing going for him. These privates knew that York was an expert marksman. In this respect, he knew his stuff.

Corporal York found a good spot. He could see the enemy clearly, but they could not see him. He fired several shots and then moved to a new position. He kept repeating the process. By the time a machine gun began to fire at him, York had already moved. At each point, he was able to get a couple of shots off at the Germans manning the guns. He rarely missed. The enemy felt helpless against his relentless sniping. They thought they must be facing many Americans.

The Germans sent a squad of eight armed infantrymen to reconnoiter. York had a clear view of them as they approached. He fired, working the rifle's bolt as rapidly as he could. He shot all eight. Then York moved to another position where he could start shooting at the machine-gun crews again.

More enemy soldiers began to fall. The German commander seemingly could do nothing. Thinking a large force must surround him, he offered to surrender. With only the seven privates helping him by guarding the prisoners they had captured earlier, York captured another 132 prisoners, including three officers.

The Supreme Allied Commander, the French marshal Ferdinand Foch, saw hundreds of situations in which courageous leaders performed heroic deeds. Yet Foch called York's feat the greatest individual action of the war. General Pershing, the overall American commander, immediately promoted York to sergeant and recommended him for the Congressional Medal of Honor. This is America's highest decoration for valor, and Sergeant York received it shortly thereafter.

Now let's look at the facts of York's exploit from a leadership perspective. York was a very brave man and a highly skilled marksman. However, he had to persuade his men not to surrender before he could accomplish anything. Unguarded, the former prisoners would have soon informed the German commander that only one man opposed his battalion. Do you think that commander would have surrendered to York then? He and his men would have been encouraged to attack in overwhelming numbers. York's privates obeyed his plea not to surrender even though they faced overwhelming odds only because they knew that York was such an extraordinary marksman. York may have been their leader for only a few moments, but they knew that this leader knew his stuff.

My West Point classmate Lt. Col. William "Bill" Schwartz led two Vietnam combat tours as an infantry officer. Today he is director of international marketing for Litton Applied Technology in San Jose, California. Bill says, "I am most proud of the fact that no one lost his life under my command because I didn't know my stuff. Job competence is crucial because leaders lacking it waste lives and frequently still fail to accomplish the mission."[1]

During World War II, the U.S. Army conducted a study to find out what soldiers thought about their leaders. It was the first time any army had ever done this. The best and the brightest did the research, including professors from Harvard, Princeton, and the University of Chicago. They surveyed tens of thousands of soldiers and asked: "What are the most important factors associated with good leadership?" The most frequent answer these researchers received was: "That the leader know his stuff."[2]

KNOWING YOUR STUFF IS AS IMPORTANT IN BUSINESS AS IN BATTLE

You'd think that the importance of knowing your stuff would be obvious in either military or civilian life. Yet unfortunately, some leaders don't know their stuff to the extent that they should. This is because their emphasis is more on getting ahead than on becoming an expert and "learning one's trade." Their focus is on office politics rather than office expertise. Moreover, a number of management books fall into this same trap in advising their readers. They fail to emphasize that a leader becomes the real leader of his organization when those who follow recognize that the leader knows what to do when he gets ahead, not because the leader knows how to get ahead.

Followers don't follow leaders because leaders are good at office politics. They follow leaders because they are good at what they do.

A leader must invest time into becoming an expert. As *Fortune* proclaimed recently: "Forget about fighting over titles and turf — it's what you know (and how you use it) that really counts."[5]

In 1994, Gordon M. Bethune took over as CEO of an ailing Continental Airlines that had twice filed for bankruptcy. In a little more than a year, he built a $650 million cash reserve and took Continental from last place in on-time takeoff performance to number two. Not bad for a leader who spent twenty years as an enlisted man in the navy and had to go to night school to graduate from high school. However, Bethune knows his stuff and how to use it. He attended five colleges and finally got his bachelor's degree from Abilene Christian University in 1982. He learned aircraft mechanics in the service. Today he is both a licensed pilot and mechanic and sometimes flies the company's jet aircraft. It is perhaps because Bethune knows so much about the working level of airline operations that they say he has brought a new flavor to employee relations.[6] He really knows his stuff, and as Fortune proclaimed, "it does count."

Retired air force lieutenant general Thomas H. McMullen, who flew in combat in both Korea and Vietnam and went on to direct the development of such important weapons systems as the A-10 says, "You've got to understand your organization and your people, both strengths and weaknesses. Then you've got to understand the mission, both short- and long-term."[7]

When you know your stuff and how to use it, it constitutes a unique power. What academic researchers call "expert power" can work miracles. It can even make you the richest man in the world.

HOW BILL GATES BECAME
THE RICHEST MAN IN THE WORLD

Bill Gates is the chairman and CEO of the Microsoft Corporation, with $8.6 billion in sales and twenty thousand employees in forty-eight countries. Moreover, with a personal fortune estimated at $18.5 billion (that's billion with a "b"), Gates is probably the richest man in the world. Amazingly he achieved much of his success while he was still in his twenties. He became a billionaire when he was only thirty-one.

What do you think? Was he just there at the right time and the right place? Was Gates just lucky? Did people lend him money and did others of ability acknowledge him as a leader and help to build his giant corporation because of his academic education? Because of his Hollywood-handsome looks? His influential parents? Hardly. Bill Gates went to Harvard, but he dropped out after only two years. He wears glasses. Some say he looks almost nerdish. His father was a Seattle attorney and his mother a schoolteacher.

If you look at Gates's career, you can see that he took the time to learn his stuff. His secret was not office politics, but the expert power he acquired. Gates started learning how to program computers when he was thirteen. By the time he entered high school, he knew enough to lead a group of computer programmers in computerizing his school's payroll system. Then, while still a teenager, he started a company that sold traffic-counting systems to local governments. When he entered Harvard, he was already an acknowledged computer expert. He spent his freshman year preparing the language for the world's first microcomputer. His second year was more of the same. Then he decided to drop out so he could develop computer software full-time. Not long after that, he founded the Microsoft Corporation. Others followed Gates because in this new field of computer programming, he was top gun. They didn't care how old he was. They didn't care that he wasn't six foot five inches or who his parents were or whether he had a college degree. Gates knew his stuff.

Almost every day, newspapers and magazines carry news of Gates's latest exploits. He usually doesn't make the news because he may be the world's richest man, but because he still knows his stuff. Says Edward Rogers, head of Canada's largest cable system on Gates's recent foray into the cable business, "We're dealing with the smartest man in America."[8]

A LEADER WHO WAS NEVER IN COMBAT LED THE LARGEST INVASION IN HISTORY

It is what you know and can do that is important, not anything else. It isn't wealth or connections, whether in the military or in civilian life. You will see this important point crop up again and again.

In the military, combat is considered one of the important way stations for higher command. They call it "getting your ticket punched." After all, isn't fighting what the military is all about? Combat is important as a credential for military leadership. Yet depending on the job, it may represent only a small part of knowing your stuff.

Gen. Dwight Eisenhower never served in combat. He graduated from West Point in 1915, and he volunteered repeatedly for combat duty during World War I. However his superiors considered him too valuable in his stateside job. Despite his lack of combat experience, he rose to become one of only a handful of U.S. officers ever to wear the five-star insignia of general of the army, admiral of the fleet, or general of the air force. Moreover, he led the largest invasion in the history of the world. He commanded hundreds of thousands of men who were in battle. Not only were they combat troops from all services of the U.S. armed forces, but from other armed forces as well. Since Eisenhower had no combat experience, how was this possible? Doesn't this violate the universal law: know your stuff?

Eisenhower's secret was that he dedicated his life to learning his profession. He became an expert. He may have not have had combat experience, but he did know his stuff. He had that expert power that academicians talk about. Before World War II, he was a relatively junior officer. Yet he was considered one of the army's best planners. He graduated only in the middle of his West Point class, but he graduated number one from the Army's Command and Staff College at Ft. Leavenworth, Kansas. He volunteered for and graduated from the Army Industrial College in Washington, D.C. During the growing U.S. Army first large-scale maneuvers in Louisiana in 1941, Eisenhower played a prominent role and performed extremely well. Then he was selected to lead the first American offensive in the European Theater during World War II — the North African landings called Operation Torch in November 1942. Again, he was successful. He was an outstanding leader of the largest invasion force in history because, quite simply, he knew his stuff. The other "stuff" he knew was more important than the combat experience he lacked. Building on the same principle, Eisenhower became a successful president of Columbia University. Later yet, he became a very competent president of the United States even though he had not been a politician.

Other well-known military leaders who never served in combat also reached the top because they knew their stuff. These included Henry "Hap" Arnold, the five-star commanding general of the U.S. Army Air Force during World War II, and Gen. George C. Marshall, Chief of Staff of the Army during the same war and later the secretary of state after the war.

So you can successfully lead a manufacturing company without having worked on the assembly line if you are an expert in other important aspects of the business.

THE TWO IMPORTANT COMPONENTS OF EXPERT POWER

The experiences of tens of thousands of military leaders show that there are two important components to expert power. These are:

1. Technical expertise
2. Leadership expertise

As a leader, you must develop expertise in both components. General Sir John Hackett, experienced as a battlefield commander as well as principal of Kings College, London, and author of the international best-seller, *The Third World War,* says: "The leader, besides being a competent manager, must be known to possess a high degree of competence in some specific skill or skills closely relevant to the discharge of the organization's primary task."[3]

A TEENAGER BECOMES A FIGHTER ACE AND A COLONEL

Some say we can't learn much from the young, but that simply isn't so. A nineteen-year-old American wanted to join the air corps and become a pilot back in 1940. This was shortly before the United States entered World War II. Unfortunately Chesley "Pete" Peterson could not pass the army's eye exam. One day he learned that the British were looking for volunteers for the Royal Air Force. England was already in the war and was short on pilots. The RAF decided to form a squadron made up entirely of Americans. Because they needed pilots badly, the visual standards weren't as high as in the United States.

Peterson took the flight physical for the RAF and passed. They sent him to Canada for pilot training. Before long he was a fighter pilot in one of the two American Eagle Squadrons flying Spitfires against the best pilots in the German Luftwaffe. What happened afterward shows how having both technical expertise and leadership expertise is important.

Peterson's squadron was in combat over England almost every day. Needless to say, there was considerable danger. Losses were high. When not actually flying, many pilots lived pretty wild lives on the ground. Peterson could party with the best of them. But, during periods of combat operations, he didn't waste his time partying. Instead, he took the time to become an expert fighter pilot. He read everything he could about air combat and sought out other pilots with whom he talked at great length.

He also went through a lengthy ritual every night. Before going to sleep, he went over every minute of the fights he had with the enemy during the day. He reviewed what went right and what went wrong. He thought about what he had done that worked and what he had done that had not worked. He analyzed his mistakes and considered how he could avoid them in the future. He planned what he would do differently the next day. Before long he shot down his first enemy aircraft. And then another. It wasn't long before he had shot down five enemy aircraft. This earned him the designation "ace." Peterson was now an expert fighter pilot. Would it surprise you to learn that, although he was one of the youngest pilots in his squadron, when the Royal Air Force needed a new squadron commander, it chose Peterson?

Squadron Leader Peterson continued to strive for excellence. This time he worked at becoming an expert as a squadron commander. He followed the same routine, so he learned fast. When the Royal Air Force needed a new wing commander, again it selected Pete Peterson. He stuck with his plan. When it needed a group commander . . . well, you can guess the rest.

By 1943, the United States was very much in the war and needed experienced pilots. The U.S. Army Air Force asked

Peterson and other Americans serving in the RAF to transfer to our air force, even giving Peterson the rank equivalent to the rank he held in the RAF. At the age of twenty-three, Peterson became the youngest colonel in the U.S. Army Air Force. He remained in the U.S. Air Force after World War II, and twenty years later, he was promoted to general. He was still only in his early forties. I'm certain that much of Peterson's success had to do with the fact that he always took the time to learn his stuff. I don't know whether Peterson knew anything about office politics — I rather think he did not.

John Hummer, who today is a corporate director with the Lockheed Martin Corporation, commanded in nuclear attack submarines and later in a shore training establishment in the navy. He retired from the navy as a captain. Says Captain Hummer: "You've got to know your job, including the barriers to success, and know your people."[4]

HOW GENERAL PETERSON HELPED PROMOTE ME TO MAJOR AT AGE TWENTY-SEVEN

I like to tell Peterson's story because it impacted my own career in a very positive way. When I entered the air force, it no longer had very young colonels. As a matter of fact, it took eleven years of service just to be promoted to the rank of major. But one day I found a book about the RAF Eagle Squadrons.

Until I read about General Peterson and how he got to be a leader, I was about average. I led no one. I was a lieutenant with four years of service as the navigator of a B-52 in the 26th Bomb Squadron, 11th Bomb Wing, flying out of Altus Air Force Base in Oklahoma. I had recently been teamed up with a senior navigator, a lieutenant colonel by the name of John Porter. He taught me navigation, but he could only do so much. I decided to try to implement Peterson's methods. "What do I have to lose?" I thought.

I read everything I could about navigation. I became an expert. I started to write articles on navigation. I became the informal leader of a group of navigators who wanted to try out new methods. Before long, I was asked to be an instructor and not long after that to join the senior instructor crew in the squadron. Three days after my new assignment, I was promoted to captain as part of the normal promotion cycle.

Seven months later, I was asked to join one of the wing's

three standardization-evaluation crews. These were the folks who evaluated and gave flight checks to everyone else in the squadron. Now I had really hit the big time. Some months later, and three days after I became eligible, I was promoted to major. I was twenty-seven years old.

There were two other majors who were B-52 navigators in the wing's standardization-evaluation division. They had nine and ten years' service respectively in the air force. I only had about five and a half years' service, and for six months, still not enough time in grade as a captain to be promoted to major.

Thank you, General Peterson! You showed me the importance of knowing your stuff.

WHAT KNOWING YOUR STUFF REALLY MEANS

To know your stuff means that you:

1. Know Your People
2. Learn from the Bottom Up
3. Learn from Every Experience
4. Learn from Your Subordinates
5. Never Stop Learning

YOU'VE GOT TO KNOW YOUR PEOPLE AS INDIVIDUALS

Carol Barkalow was in the first class at West Point to accept female cadets. She entered West Point in 1976 and graduated four years later. At the time of this writing, she is a major and remains on active duty as a career army officer. As a young lieutenant in the antiaircraft artillery in Germany, she noticed that her new battery commander was tough but very caring with each of his soldiers. He treated each as an individual. He even met with the counselors of those undergoing drug rehabilitation. Neither of her two previous commanders had done this. "When I asked him about it," she recalled, "the captain would quote the philosophy of General Omar Bradley, 'The greatest leader in the world could never win a campaign unless he understood the men he had to lead.'"[9]

Capt. Scott O'Grady spent six agonizing days and nights in hostile territory after his F-16 fighter was shot down by a surface-to-air missile over Bosnia. He says, "In a combat environment, you need to trust people, to predict their reactions and rely on their snap judgments. But before you trust people you have to know them. You have to live and work — and laugh — together."[10]

More than two hundred years ago, the Marshal Comte de Saxe of France said, "There is nothing more important in war than the human heart. In a knowledge of the human heart must be sought the secrets of success and failure of armies."[11]

Gen. Edward C. "Shy" Meyer saw combat in Korea and Vietnam and became the youngest chief of staff the army ever had. Regarding combat leadership, he says, "Competence is critical. You've got to learn the trade and spend considerable time studying at all levels to understand your soldiers."[12]

PEOPLE ARE ALL DIFFERENT

World-class leaders treat those they lead as individuals, not as cogs in organizational machinery. People are all different. This fact constitutes one of the most fascinating yet challenging aspects of being a leader. Every follower thinks differently and may be motivated to action by different stimuli. Psychologist Carl Jung found that, faced with the exact same situation, each of us have different preferred ways of acting, of decision making, or of getting a job done.

Isabel Myers and her mother, Katherine C. Briggs, organized Jung's theoretical work into a conceptual framework and a psychometric questionnaire called the Myers-Briggs Type Indicator. Based on a preference for alternatives in decision making and the answers to a battery of questions, individuals are classified into one of sixteen personality types. Amazingly these sixteen personality types determine much about how each individual lives, loves, and works. The Myers-Briggs Type Indicator, or MBTI, has become one of the world's most used research survey tools, with one's MBTI score being correlated with everything from job preference to finding a mate.

The MBTI is not a success indicator. There are outstanding leaders and successful people in every single one of the sixteen categories. The main lesson for any leader to learn from MBTI is that those who follow are human beings. They have different experiences in life and have different beliefs and values. To get them to perform at their maximum potential you must know and understand those differences that motivate and affect your people.[13]

To Know Your People Is to
Maximize Their Productivity

While rummaging through old bookstores, marine corps colonel Jim Toth found a little ninety-nine-page book written after World War I by Capt. Adolph von Schell, a German infantry officer. Von Schell was highly experienced. He had served in combat throughout World War I, first in command of an infantry platoon and later in command of a company. He wrote the book *Battle Leadership* while attending the Advanced Class of the U.S. Infantry School at Ft. Benning, Georgia, from 1930 to 1931.

The book related von Schell's observations on leadership from the vantage point of a junior officer in the Imperial German Army. Toth realized the collection of lessons from von Schell was as valuable in the present as on the day Toth recorded it. Toth contacted the Marine Corps Association, which agreed to reprint the book. In a preface, marine corps major general D. M. Twomey said that the book "should be required reading for all combat leaders," and it is read by many.[14]

Captain von Schell's lessons on battlefield psychology show the age-old importance of knowing and understanding your subordinates. Says von Schell, "As commanders we must know the probable reaction of the individual and the means by which we can influence this reaction."[15] To do this, von Schell suggests estimating the psychological aspects as well as the technical aspects of a situation.

He cites a classic example of this art practiced by a brigade commander in the year 1917:

This general said, "Each of our three regimental commanders must be handled differently. Colonel A does not want an order. He wants to do everything himself, and he always does well. Colonel B executes every order, but he has no initiative. Colonel C opposes everything he is told to do and wants to do the contrary."

A few days later the troops confronted a well-entrenched enemy whose position would have to be attacked. The general issued the following individual orders:

To Colonel A (who wants to do everything himself):

"My dear Colonel A, I think we will attack. Your regiment will have to carry the burden of the attack. I have, however, selected you for this reason. The boundaries of your regiment are so and so. Attack at X hour. I

don't have to tell you anything more."

To Colonel C (who opposes everything):

"We have met a very strong enemy. I am afraid we will not be able to attack with the forces at our disposal.

"Oh, General, certainly we will attack. Just give my regiment the time of attack and you will see that we are successful," replied Colonel C.

"Go, then, we will try it," said the general, giving him the order for the attack, which he had prepared sometime previously.

To Colonel B (who must always have detailed orders), the attack order was merely sent with additional details.

All three regiments attacked splendidly.

The general knew his subordinates; he knew that each one was different and had to be handled differently in order to achieve results. He had estimated the psychological situation correctly. It is comparatively easy to make a correct estimate if one knows the person concerned; but even then it is often difficult, because the person doesn't always remain the same. He is no machine; he may react one way today, another way tomorrow. Soldiers can be brave one day and afraid the next. Soldiers are not machines but human beings who must be led in war. Each one of them reacts differently at different times and must be handled each time according to his particular reaction. To sense this and to arrive at a correct psychological solution is part of the art of leadership.[16]

Von Schell's example shows us how important it is to know your people in battle. Failing to do so can have serious consequences. In 1779, at the siege of Savannah during the Revolutionary War, Franco-American forces faced heavy English fire. Col. Arthur Dillon offered his men of the LXXX Infanterie of the Franco-American force a hundred guineas to the first man to plant a flag in the British position. Not one man came forward. The colonel grew angry and called his men cowards. A sergeant-major stepped forward and said, "If you hadn't offered money as an incentive, every man would have been willing to go." The sergeant-major took the colonel's position, and to a man the LXXX Infanterie followed him and advanced, even though they suffered heavy losses.[17] The importance of knowing your people can't be underestimated in battle, or in business.

A PRIVATE LEARNED FROM THE BOTTOM UP AND BECAME A FOUR-STAR GENERAL

Frederick Kroesen has to be one of the most unusual generals ever to serve in the U.S. Army. I had the privilege of meeting him in 1989 while attending the Industrial College of the Armed Forces in Washington, D.C. One of the elective courses I took was in top-level leadership. Six outstanding military leaders, retired generals and admirals from all services, came in to speak to us at different times as a part of this course.

My army classmates said that they called General Kroesen "John Wayne." And sure enough, General Kroesen looked and spoke a little like the famous actor. But that's not why he was so unusual. General Kroesen had served in every rank in the U.S. Army, from private through four-star general. Four stars is the most any general has worn since General of the Army Omar Bradley, of World War II fame, retired.

General Kroesen had been drafted as a private and then promoted through the ranks of private first class, corporal, sergeant, staff sergeant, technical sergeant, and master sergeant. At this point, he won a battlefield commission of the rank of second lieutenant. He was then moved through the officer ranks of first lieutenant, captain, major, lieutenant colonel, colonel, brigadier general, major general, lieutenant general, and full general. Quite an accomplishment!

As a major general wearing two stars, General Kroesen had served as commander of the army's recruiting command. At that time, this was considered a final assignment prior to retirement. But Kroesen had been promoted to lieutenant general with three stars and given command of a corps. One of my fellow students asked Kroesen how this had happened.

Said General Kroesen: "I think one of the reasons for my success was that no matter what job I held in the army, I became intensely interested in it and resolved to become an expert. So when I was appointed head of army recruiting, I did the same thing. I became an expert, maybe the world's best recruiter. As you might imagine, because I was now an expert, army recruiting improved dramatically. Up until then, some senior army leaders thought in terms of my retirement. But then they said, 'Wait a minute. If this guy can take even an unglamorous job like recruiting and make such a success of it, we better take a second look before we let him go.' They did, and I was promoted to three stars and went on from there."

What Peter the Great
and General Kroesen Had in Common

Peter I, the seventeenth Russian tsar, was called "the Great" for a reason. He not only was a great administrator and a great military leader, he founded the Russian empire. He changed what had been a backward country into a modern Western state. Like General Kroesen, Peter the Great served in every rank in the Russsian army from private on up. Previous rulers had been given senior rank in an elite regiment or fleet even before they were teenagers. Peter refused to accept any rank he did not earn. He enlisted in the Preobrazhensky Regiment as a drummer boy because that was the very lowest position. He allowed himself to be promoted only when he felt he had merited the promotion. When on garrison duty or in the field, he permitted no distinction between himself and others. When it was his turn at guard duty, he served it. He slept in the same tents as his brother soldiers and ate the same food. When ordered to dig, he dug, and when the regiment paraded, he stood in the ranks, undistinguished from others.

Like General Kroesen, he eventually won an officer's commission. His refusing to serve in military positions other than what he earned was a lifelong policy. When he went with his army or sailed with his fleet, it was always as a subordinate commander. He believed that leaders had to know their stuff, and to do this, they must learn their business from the bottom up.[18]

How Steven Spielberg Became
an Award-Winning Director

Steven Spielberg is arguably the most successful movie-maker of our time. His career demonstrates the same concept that Private Kroesen used to become a four-star general. Steven Spielberg was only in his twenties when he directed *Jaws*, but he didn't stop with one big hit. This is the man who made science fiction thrillers such as *Close Encounters of the Third Kind*, sensitive movies such as *ET*, adventure thrillers such as *Indiana Jones*, serious movies including *The Color Purple* and *Schindler's List*, and movies of spectacular technical effects such as *Jurassic Park*.

How did Spielberg accomplish so much, starting at such an early age? Wealthy parents with connections in the movie industry? Not quite. His father was an electrical and computer engineer and his mother a concert pianist.

Maybe Steven went to a great graduate film school like the University of Southern California (USC) in Los Angeles, then was hired immediately into a high-paying director's job? Right? Wrong! As a matter of fact, Spielberg applied to USC twice. And he got turned down twice. USC probably regrets that decision dearly.

No, Spielberg's secret was that he took the time to become an expert at what he wanted to do. When only ten, he got his hands on an 8mm movie camera and began to turn out home movies starring relatives and friends. He decided right then on his life's goal: he wanted to make movies.

A year later, he actually won a prize for writing a fully scripted war movie. At the age of sixteen, he made a two-and-a-half-hour science fiction movie. It cost five hundred dollars. He persuaded a local theater to run it as a favor. It must not have been great because they only ran it once. But that didn't bother Spielberg because he was already almost an expert.

While he was waiting to receive the second of the rejections from USC, Spielberg took a tour of Universal Studios. Lots of people take that tour. I've taken it myself. But Spielberg wandered off on his own. He found an abandoned trailer and decided to set up shop in it. On the trailer's side he painted, "Spielberg Productions." He looked and talked as if he knew what he was doing. In fact, since he knew his stuff, he did know what he was doing. By now, he was an expert. It had been just a few years since he started making those home movies.

Thereafter, he began going "to work" every day in his trailer. Despite the strictness of studio security, no one stopped him. The guards assumed he belonged there. He was able to go anywhere on the studio lot. He learned a lot about how movies were made and made lots of contacts.

At age twenty-two, Spielberg borrowed $15,000 from a friend and made a short film. His contacts brought it to the attention of the president of Universal Studios. It must have been pretty good because the president immediately recognized Spielberg's talent and expertise. He hired Spielberg as a director on a seven-year contract. Spielberg knew his stuff, and his many successes followed.

You Can Become an Expert in Anything in Five Years

Earl Nightingale, the famous motivational speaker, spent a lifetime researching and interviewing highly successful leaders. These individuals came from many different fields, from medicine to business. According to Nightingale, these successful men and women unanimously agreed that you could become an expert in just about anything in five years or less — if you made the effort.

That is surprising information, but it certainly was true about then Col. Chesley Peterson, the ace fighter pilot. You would also have to say this applied to Bill Gates. He started learning computer programming at age thirteen, and by the time he was eighteen, he was president of a computer programming company. I have looked into the careers of many well-known authors, doctors, attorneys, entrepreneurs, and others. In almost every case, the individual appeared to have become an acknowledged expert within the magical five-year period.

YOU MUST LEARN FROM EVERY EXPERIENCE, AS WASHINGTON DID IN WAR

Every experience as a leader can teach us something, the failures perhaps more than the successes. In fact, you may be able to make an argument that the more and bigger failures you have, the greater your potential for success — so long as you learn from your experiences.

George Washington began as Commander-in-Chief of American forces with no top-level command experience. Previously he had been a major in the British army. Consequently he blundered badly at first — so much so that his mistakes could have ended the American Revolution less than two months after our Declaration of Independence was signed.

What did he do wrong? First, he ignored the Continental Congress's direction to defend New York, even though he knew that to do so threatened the very existence of his army and therefore American independence.

Once having made this decision, he split his army, putting one-third under the able Maj. Gen. Nathanael Greene on Long Island and retaining the remainder under his personal command on Manhattan to prevent the British from attacking up the Hudson River. The selection of Greene was a good choice, but splitting his army was dangerous. The two forces were not mutually supporting, and the British could have concentrated first against one, then against the other, and easily defeated both.

When General Greene fell ill, Washington blundered again. He chose an unknown quantity, Maj. Gen. Israel Putnam, as Greene's replacement. Unfortunately General Putnam was a general who needed to be on a very short leash. Washington should have kept him on one until he better knew Putnam's capabilities. Instead he trusted Putnam in this critical assignment and provided little supervision.

But that wasn't all. Washington didn't make the command relationship between himself and Putnam clear. Putnam didn't know whether he had an independent command and could do as he saw fit, or whether he should try to function under Washington's immediate direction.

Washington's opponent, British general Howe, shifted the bulk of his forces to Long Island. He discovered that Putnam had made a basic error. The American left flank was not secured along the Brooklyn Heights. Howe easily brought ten thousand men around Putnam's left flank and encircled his army. Putnam's defense collapsed.

Washington then compounded his earlier errors. He took reinforcements to Long Island. This had the effect of moving additional troops into the trap. The river couldn't be forded and so couldn't be supported or reinforced easily. Washington's army was in the perfect position to be totally destroyed. He was saved only because Howe failed to attack. Howe's decision was so bizarre that historians can only speculate that perhaps the British commander deferred in the hopes that the Americans would rejoin the mother country with minimum bloodshed. In plain fact, we came very close to losing the war. On the night of August 29, 1776, Washington wisely evacuated his troops and withdrew.

Eventually Washington was pushed out of New York proper and reestablished a defensive position near White Plains. Here again, he split his army, placing half under the command of the ambitious and incompetent Maj. Gen. Charles Lee. The only thing that prevented the loss of Lee's entire command was that Lee managed to get himself captured by the British, thus removing top-level incompetence from American ranks.

On December 26, Washington won a small but important victory at Trenton, New Jersey, by crossing the Delaware River. You've probably seen the famous painting of the event. Soon after his victory, however, Washington realized that he had erred again. He had left his right flank unprotected, just as

Putnam had done. If that flank was attacked by the British, he would have no place to go but back toward the sea.

Yet with all these mistakes, Washington was learning his trade. He learned from every experience. Washington didn't dwell on his errors. He analyzed the situation, drew conclusions, and noted what he had done wrong and what he had done right. He planned how he would react in the future.

Washington slipped around the British secretly by using icy backroads. He made a forced march to Princeton, where he had numerical superiority over the enemy. He surprised, attacked, and defeated three British regiments. These were part of General Cornwallis's army. Washington couldn't take on the British general's army head to head. It was much larger than Washington's. But he entrenched his forces alongside Cornwallis's line of communications and forced the British to evacuate all of central and western New Jersey. This ten-day campaign beginning with Washington's crossing the Delaware has been called "one of the most brilliant in military history" . . . and that despite the mistakes.[19]

WITH A LITTLE LEARNING, ABE LINCOLN FAILED HIS WAY TO SUCCESS

Learning from your experiences also applies on a personal level. In this way, you can actually fail your way to success. Perhaps one of the greatest examples of this comes from another of our country's foremost leaders.

In 1832 Abraham Lincoln lost his job. He learned and moved on. He ran for the state legislature of Illinois the same year. He was badly defeated. He learned and moved on again. He started his own business in 1833. He went broke. But he learned from the experience. In 1838 he ran for Speaker of the House. He lost again, but again he learned. He learned more from a failed bid for nomination to Congress in 1843, a rejected appointment to the U.S. Land Office in 1849, a defeat for a U.S. Senate seat in 1854, and another defeat for nomination to U.S. vice president in 1856. He finally learned from yet another defeat for the Senate in 1858 before becoming president of the United States in 1861 — whereupon he saved the Union, abolished slavery, and left his mark as one of our greatest presidents. Although not referred to much today, Lincoln had combat experience from the Black Hawk Indian War.

Self-made millionaire Wayne Allyn Root actually organized the idea of failing your way to success into a formalized structure with this book *The Joy of Failure*. In it, Root describes how his application to law school was rejected, how he lost a political election, and how he then drove his real estate business into the ground. Says Root, "I failed at twelve careers and businesses."[20] But like Lincoln, he learned from every failure and went on to great financial success.

Learning all the while, John Macy failed at founding seven department stores before he established the one that caught on. It is said that Thomas Edison failed at more than a thousand attempts to invent the lightbulb. It seemed that every material he tried for filament burned up. While many of us would call each attempt another failure, Edison had it right. America's most versatile inventor declared: "I have not failed. I have learned yet another material that will not work as a filament."

HOW A SOCIAL SECURITY RECIPIENT BECAME A MULTIMILLIONAIRE

"Colonel" Harland Sanders got his first Social Security check after retirement and decided it wasn't enough to live on. He went on the road and spent two years trying to sell owners of fast-food restaurants on the idea of using his recipe for his "Kentucky-fried" chicken. He didn't ask for any money up front, only that the owner try his recipe, and if successful, give him a few pennies from each sale. Every single owner he approached turned him down. But Sanders learned from each rejection. He improved his presentation. He did more research. He learned to handle every possible objection. Finally, after two years, he got an acceptance. And then another, and another, and another after that. Like Lincoln and other great leaders, he never stopped learning.

No wonder governor of Kentucky John Y. Brown, Jr., who was also a former owner of a Kentucky Fried Chicken franchise, wrote about him: "Sanders took a bunch of people, most of whom had never been successful in their lives, and made them something of themselves. . . . In my lifetime I have had the opportunity to meet and know nine Presidents, most of the political and business leaders of our time, but the Colonel still stands as one of those great men you can count on one hand."[21]

Norm Brodsky, president of CitiStorage, an archive-retrieval business in Brooklyn, New York, and a past *Inc.* 500 business owner says, "You will never stop making mistakes. We hope that the new ones won't be the same as the old ones, but I promise you they'll be just as painful. . . . But, as upset as you may get, it's important to bear in mind that failure is still the best teacher. You'll do fine as long as you're open to the lessons it's trying to teach you."[22]

YOUR SUBORDINATES CAN TEACH YOU

You can learn a lot from your employees on a daily basis. Why not structure this learning experience? One of the biggest innovations in teaching over the last twenty-five years is the teaching evaluation. When I attended school for my B.A.,M.A., and Ph.D. degrees, we evaluated no one. Even the thought would have been revolutionary. What do students know? If they knew anything, they wouldn't be students, would they? What can a professor possibly learn from a student?

I recall the time in 1967 when one of my professors at the University of Chicago half-jokingly corrected one of my classmates, Capt. Charles Melenyzer, U.S. Air Force. Melenyzer asked innocently, "Professor Brownlee, why can't you do it this way? You get the same answer."

With a twinkle in his eye Professor Brownlee immediately responded, "Mr. Melenyzer, I do not object to your question, it is a good one. However, I do object to your right to ask it."

One didn't ask such questions in those days. Too bad. Professor Brownlee was brilliant and well liked. He was a good professor. However he could have been a better one. Without feedback, it is impossible to learn from your subordinates and to improve. You do not know your stuff to the extent that you could.

Thank goodness someone broke the paradigm and changed all that. Today, students confidentially evaluate their professors at almost every university. We learn a lot from these evaluations. We improve our courses. We improve our presentations. We improve as leaders. We improve as professors. Evaluation helps us to know our stuff.

LEARNING FROM SUBORDINATES
IN THE MILITARY

Some years ago, I was selected to attend the Industrial College of the Armed Forces at the National Defense University in

Washington, D.C. At the time I was department chairman at my university and an air force reservist. The Industrial College of the Armed Forces is a school that prepares selected military officers and civilians for senior leadership positions. Most of the students are active duty officers, but I was selected as one of three air force reservists in my class of two hundred or so officer-students.

Prior to my departure to the school, I received a package of leader evaluation forms from the college. I was instructed to give them to my subordinates, colleagues, and superiors. The evaluations were then mailed directly to the college without my having seen them. Later we were shown our scores and those for the entire class. I learned a great deal about how I was perceived as a leader by those I led, those with whom I associated, and those who led me. Some of this information I could have learned in no other way. Yes, we can learn a great deal from those around us.

A COMPANY FINDS A WAY
TO LEARN FROM EMPLOYEES

There are many ways leaders can learn from those they lead. Dana Corporation of Toledo, Ohio, makes auto parts. CEO Woody Morcott found quite a unique way of getting important feedback from a rather mundane, sometimes much maligned, source — the suggestion box. In one year, Dana Corporation received on average 1.22 ideas a month from each of its 45,500 employees. If employees are writing on average more than one suggestion a month, they must be getting something out of this exercise. They are.

More than 70 percent of the suggestions are used. How suggestions are handled is left to each Dana Corporation location. But whatever the location, the managers make a big thing out of taking the suggestions seriously.

There are awards and luncheons for those who generate ideas. They even have a class on how to generate ideas. One plant in Chihuahua, Mexico, gives employees $1.89 for every idea, and another $1.89 if the idea is used. At Cape Girardeau, Missouri, Dana managers divide their employees into thirty-two teams that meet weekly for a half-hour to work on ideas costing five hundred dollars or less. More costly ideas are covered at a monthly meeting. In Reading, Pennsylvania, ideas are submitted on anything from napkins to scraps of paper, but they are logged into a computer by a coordinator. And so it goes. Steve Moore, a Dana plant manager, says: "We drill into people that they are responsible for keeping the plant competitive." CEO Morcott says: "It's a core part of our value system."

The benefits? Some are tangible. With one tiny weld saving a few cents, one plant reassigned six workers and saved $250,000 a year. Another employee found a way to stagger work schedules and saved the construction of a $110,000 parking structure.[23] No doubt the suggestion system gives every employee greater ownership in the company. Most important, listening to employees helps Dana leaders know their stuff.

NEVER STOP LEARNING

Leaders who think they have learned all they'll ever need to know for their careers are making a big mistake. New ways of doing things are always being developed. Technology changes. The business environment is constantly changing, especially as the leader becomes involved with new companies, industries, or geographical areas.

Peter F. Drucker once told me, "A successful organization that continues to do what made it successful in the past will eventually fail." Why is this? Because of change. It makes what an organization knew or did to achieve success in the past irrelevant or even wrong. So leaders of organizations must constantly learn just to keep up with change. They must constantly consider new approaches and new techniques with every task or project they are assigned.

Lt. Gen. Richard G. Trefry is a retired army officer. He commanded combat operations in Vietnam and Laos and later served as military assistant to the president and was director of the White House Military Office. General Trefry notes, "This is a profession that requires a lifetime of service to teach yourself that you never know everything. As a matter of fact, when you stop learning and teaching, you stop growing."[24]

WHAT GENERAL SCHWARZKOPF DID THAT NO COMMANDER HAD DONE BEFORE

Gen. Norman Schwarzkopf's victory against Saddam Hussein during Operation Desert Storm was unique. The losses suffered by coalition forces were extremely small considering the large numbers of troops and the huge amount of firepower used to attack the world's seventh largest army. What made all the difference was not the "Hail Mary" left hook during the ground campaign. This was an excellent strategy once the ground war started, and it worked to cut off much of Saddam's army and to defeat it. However, in my judgment, the real difference was the way in which airpower was used before the ground campaign even started.

And what makes this early use of airpower so impressive is that it was a new approach for many leaders from all the services. They did not learn the strategy from past wars. In fact, they had to put aside what they had learned from their experiences in order to support this new air campaign.

Airpower theorists have long maintained that airpower is decisive in warfare. Some claimed that airpower by itself could win a war. Yet while few military experts doubted the impact of airpower, it had always fallen short of claims made by air force generals. In World War II, German production of airplanes actually increased, even though U.S. and Royal Air Force bomber crews maintained around-the-clock bombing, night and day. The war in Korea ended in stalemate despite American air superiority. In the Vietnam War, a laundry list of targets in North Vietnam was struck sequentially until few remained. Still, it was North Vietnam that prevailed. From these experiences, army generals came to be leery about some of the claims of what airpower (not including nuclear weaponry, of course) could do.

So after Vietnam, the army evolved a concept known as the Air-Land Battle. In this doctrine, the air campaign was relegated to a secondary role in supporting the ground assault, while both were to be initiated simultaneously against an aggressor. When Saddam Hussein invaded Kuwait and refused to withdraw, this seemed to be a perfect case for the implementation of this type of warfare.

There was one person who did not agree. He thought there were other possibilities. He was an air force colonel by the name of John Warden. Colonel Warden was a brilliant air strategist and the author of a book on planning air campaigns. In 1990 Warden was assigned to the Pentagon as Air Force Deputy Director for War-fighting Concepts and head of a directorate in air force plans known as "Checkmate."

When the Iraqis invaded Kuwait, Warden was vacationing with his wife in the Caribbean. He hurried back to the Pentagon and got his team to work immediately on giving the air force something that did not exist at the time: a concept for offensive action using airpower. Plans did exist for deploying an air force in defense of Saudi Arabia. However no plan existed for attacking Iraq strategically by air. Working at a feverish pace, he and his team put together a proposal for a strategic air campaign, which they called Instant Thunder.

The selection of this name in itself was significant. During Vietnam, the campaign called Rolling Thunder was supposed to steadily increase the pressure on North Vietnam by sequentially destroying important targets over a period of time. It failed to accomplish its objective. Warden's plan was to cripple Saddam's ability to wage war by simultaneously destroying targets critically important to his regime right at the start of the war. Then the bombers could be turned against the Iraqi army entrenched in Kuwait in more direct support of a ground campaign. When the ground campaign started, demoralized Iraqi forces would already be weakened and cut off from resupply, intelligence, and even orders from the dictator in Iraq. It would paralyze Iraqi war-fighting potential and make the ground assault far easier.

Warden was able to present his plan to the commander in chief, General Schwarzkopf. But how would the general receive it? Colonel Warden's group was operating off its turf. The Checkmate organization was set up in the Pentagon as a think tank within the U.S. Air Force Directorate of Planning. Schwarzkopf commanded Central Command or CENTCOM. Normally CENTCOM's air component, commanded by Lt. Gen. Charles Horner, would plan the campaign. Within CENTCOM, Air-Land Battle doctrine gave priority to destruction of the Iraqi army, not a separate strategic air campaign.

Warden briefed his new concept to General Schwarzkopf. General Schwarzkopf responded immediately and without hesitation, "That's exactly what I want! Do it! You have my approval — 100 percent! This is absolutely essential! I will call the chairman today and have him give you a directive to proceed with detailed planning immediately . . . This will lower losses."[25]

Later General Horner and his own planner, Brig. Gen. Buster Glosson, modified Warden's initial plan extensively. Nevertheless they remained true to his basic concept. When Colonel Warden retired from the air force in 1996 as commandant of the Air Command and Staff College, he received a special letter from another retired officer. Gen. Norman Schwarzkopf wrote thanking him for his contribution and his important role in attaining the decisive victory in the Gulf with minimum allied casualties. However, it was Schwarzkopf himself who immediately grasped the opportunity that Warden presented. To do this he had to overcome the biases not only within the air force, but within his own service. Schwarzkopf was successful because he didn't try to refight past wars, especially the war in Vietnam. He learned from them, but he never stopped learning. He knew his stuff.

UNTIL THIS MAN BECAME CEO, THE AVON LADY ALMOST QUIT CALLING

Traditionally men ran Avon. They held all the senior management positions. When the environment started changing in the 1970s, men almost ran Avon into the ground. Avon sells its cosmetic products through independent saleswomen. These were mostly part-time housewives who were not working in companies as part of the regular workforce.

The company's research showed that women were entering the workforce in greater numbers. So when Avon Ladies called, fewer and fewer women were at home to buy. Moreover, it was getting harder and harder to recruit Avon Ladies because women now had other work options. Avon's stock plummeted from $140 to $20 a share. Operating margins fell from 21.7 to 11.4 percent.[26] Avon operated in a woman's world. But what would Avon's men decide to do?

Avon could have followed the market into the workplace. Instead, Avon's male leaders first denied the trend and then sought refuge through acquisition. Acquisition was considered a very macho thing to do. It was a disaster. Afterward there were no less than three takeover attempts. Surviving all three, Avon was able to boast only a horrendous debt and a product line that was dying of neglect.

Then Jim Preston took over as CEO. Unlike other Avon leaders, Preston had never stopped learning. Said head of human resources Marcia Worthing, "We really filled the pipeline with women." Avon did diversity training. They set quotas. When they analyzed performance reviews, they found out that men were hesitant about criticizing women subordinates. They corrected that. Then Avon found there was a difference in what it took to get promoted within the company. Men were promoted on potential, but women were promoted solely on past accomplishments. It was almost as if they had to accomplish some figure set in the mind of their bosses, or they got a performance evaluation that read, "She's not quite ready yet." Preston began looking at that phrase as a sure sign he should give a woman a shot at a bigger job. He did. Most were successful.

Preston also changed executive perks. He did away with the annual hunting trips where the routine was for male executives to while away the night drinking and playing cards. Season tickets to the Knicks and Yankees disappeared in favor of tickets to the New York Ballet and the New York Philharmonic. Women were given showers and lockers in their bathrooms just like the men.

A new image of the Avon Lady made an appearance in an advertising campaign. In one ad, former Olympic athlete Jackie Joyner-Kersee said, "I throw a nine-pound shot put 51 feet. I bench-press 155 pounds. I have red toenails."

Because Preston never stopped learning and took action on what he had learned, he was able to positively affect those he led. Did his new emphasis on women for a woman's product and market have any positive quantifiable results? Look at this. After Preston's changes, sales were $4.8 billion, up 7 percent. Profits were $318 million, up 11 percent. Avon stock shot up 52 percent last year. Including dividends, the stock has produced a 30 percent compounded annual return for stockholders since 1989.

When Preston retired, four of the six candidates to replace him as CEO were women. Even though a woman didn't end up with the top job, this was revolutionary for Avon and set a new course for the company. Times they are a' changing, and because Preston never stopped learning and knew his stuff, Avon has prospered.[27]

John Haas flew combat in Vietnam and retired as an air force colonel. Today he is director of operations research for BDM Federal in McLean, Virginia. John Haas says: "The desire may be there, but unless a leader is qualified, capable, and proficient, his leadership will suffer. If you can't find the target and deliver your ordnance accurately, you shouldn't be leading."[28]

FIVE WAYS TO DEVELOP EXPERT POWER

1. Know Your People
2. Learn from the Bottom Up
3. Learn from Every Experience
4. Learn from Your Subordinates
5. Never Stop Learning

That way, your people will follow you because you:

KNOW YOUR STUFF

ENDNOTES

[1] Schwartz, William L., survey form and letter to the author, May 3, 1996.

[2] National Research Council, with the collaboration of the Science Service, *Psychology for the Fighting Man*, 2d ed. (New York: Penguin Books, 1944), 307.

[3] Hackett, Sir John, *The Profession of Arms* (New York: Macmillan Publishing Company, 1983), 217.

[4] Hummer, John Jay, survey form and letter to the author, May 13, 1996.

[5] Fisher, Anne, "Six Ways to Supercharge Your Career," *Fortune* (January 13, 1997): 46.

[6] Zellner, Wendy, "The Right Time, The Right Place," *Business Week* (May 27, 1996): 74–75.

[7] McMullen, Thomas H., survey form and letter to author, July 26, 1993.

[8] Lesly, Elizabeth, Amy Cortese, and Ron Grover, "Bill Gates, The Cable Guy," *Business Week* (July 14, 1997): 22–24.

[9] Barkalow, Carol, with Andrea Raab, *In the Men's House*, (New York: Poseidon Press, 1990), 194.

[10] O'Grady, Scott, with Jeff Coplon, *Return With Honor* (New York: Doubleday, 1995), 71.

[11] Op. Cit. Hackett, 215.

[12] Meyer, Edward C., survey form and letter to the author, November 10, 1993.

[13] For those who want to know more about these Jungian concepts, the MBTI, and how it is used, I can recommend the following

books: *Gifts Differing*, Isabel Briggs Myers with Peter B. Myers (Palo Alto, California: Consulting Psychologists Press, 1980); *Please Understand Me*, David Keirsey and Marilyn Bates (Del Mar, California: Prometheus Nemesis Book Company, 1984); *Type Talk*, Otto Kroeger and Janet M. Thuesen (New York: Dell Publishing, 1988).

[14] von Schell, Adolph, *Battle Leadership* (Quantico, Va.: Marine Corps Association, 1982). Originally published (Ft. Benning, Georgia: *The Benning Herald*, 1933), as the foreword.

[15] Ibid., 9.

[16] Ibid., 11–12.

[17] Lawrence, Alexander, "139," in Hastings, ed., *The Oxford Book of Military Anecdotes* (New York: Oxford University Press, 1985), 174–175.

[18] Massie, Robert K., "96," in Hastings, ed., *The Oxford Book of Military Anecdotes,* 139–140.

[19] Dupuy, R. Ernest, and Trevor N. Dupuy, *Military Heritage of America* (New York: McGraw-Hill, 1956), 86–91.

[20] Stuberg, Robert, "An Interview with Wayne Root," *Insight* 175 (Niles, Illinois: Nightingale-Connant Corporation, 1997).

[21] Pearce, John Ed, *The Colonel* (New York: Doubleday & Company, 1982), dustcover, vi.

[22] Brodsky, Norm, "Failure Can Be the Best Teacher You'll Ever Have — Provided You're Ready To Learn," *Inc. Magazine Archives, Inc. Online* (November 1996): 31.

[23] Teitelbaum, Richard, "How to Harness Gray Matter," *Fortune* (June 9, 1997): 168.

[24] Trefry, Richard G., survey form and letter to the author, August 2, 1993.

[25] Reynolds, Richard T., *Heart of the Storm: The Genesis of the Air Campaign Against Iraq* (Maxwell Air Force Base, Ala.: Air University Press, 1995), 56–57.

[26] "Avon Tries a New Formula to Restore Its Glow," *Business Week* (July 2, 1984): 46.

[27] Morris, Betsy, "If Women Ran the World," *Fortune* (July 21, 1997): 74–79.

[28] Haas, John J., survey form and letter to the author, June 24, 1996.

DECLARE YOUR EXPECTATIONS

If a man does not know to what port he is steering, no wind is favorable.
— SENECA, 4 B.C.– 65 A.D.

You may have learned the name John Paul Jones in school . . . but you may have forgotten why. His is a story worth retelling because it strikes at the very heart of the power of the universal law of declaring your expectations.

John Paul Jones was a young Scotsman with significant sea experience. He asked for and was given a commission as a lieutenant in the Continental Navy during America's War of Independence. He soon gained command of a newly commissioned ship purchased from France. In honor of the French, and in honor of Benjamin Franklin, Jones named his ship the *Bonhomme Richard*. In French, that means "Poor Richard," which was the name of the almanac Franklin published in Philadelphia.

Jones was highly successful right from the start. He captured seventeen English merchant ships on his first patrol. On September 23, 1779, he located a convoy of British merchant ships escorted by two ships of war. He immediately attacked the larger warship, the HMS *Serapis*. Jones lashed his ship to his larger enemy so it could not escape and began to fire into her. However he had failed to reckon on the efficiency of the Royal Navy. The *Serapis* fired broadside after broadside into the *Bonhomme Richard*. Soon, the American vessel was on fire and in danger of sinking.

The British captain demanded that Jones surrender. Jones's answer, given more for his own men than the British, set a course for all time in the fledgling U.S. Navy. It was an outstanding example of a leader declaring his expectations. "I have not yet begun to fight," he declared. Jones's crew rallied, and they rose to the occasion. They sunk the *Serapis* and won the battle.

FOLLOWERS EXPECT LEADERS TO SET THE STAGE

Peter Drucker has spent years working and consulting with Japanese companies. Drucker maintains that it wasn't so much "quality circles" or some other unique technique used in Japan that improved the poor quality of Japanese goods in the 1970s. Rather, it was that when Deming, Juran, and other management experts made Japanese leaders aware of the problem, the Japanese business leaders declared their expectations regarding a focus on quality. This redirected the emphasis in their companies to a subject that had previously been ignored or thought unimportant. "Quality circles" and other techniques that became Total Quality Management in America simply supported that effort.

Says Drucker, "The foundation of effective leadership is thinking through the organization's mission, defining it and establishing it, clearly and visibly. The leader sets the goals, sets the priorities, and sets and maintains the standards. . . . What distinguishes the leader from the misleader are his goals. Whether the compromise he makes with the constraints of reality — which may involve political, economic, and financial or people problems — are compatible with his mission and goals or lead away from them determines whether he is an effective leader. And whether he holds fast to a few basic standards (exemplifying them in his own conduct), or whether 'standards' for him are what he can get away with, determines whether the leader has followers or only hypocritical time-servers."[1]

CHRYSLER'S FIGHTER PILOT DECLARES HIS EXPECTATIONS

Chrysler, America's number three automaker, suddenly took off in the early 1990s. It doubled its revenues and grabbed five points of market share. Was this sheer luck? Hardly. You didn't need to look very far to find a leader declaring his expectations. Coincidentally, this leader, like John Paul Jones, wore the navy uniform as an aviation cadet, although he came from the marine corps enlisted ranks and took his commission in the marine corps.

Former marine fighter pilot, Robert A. Lutz, then president and chief operating officer of Chrysler and now vice chairman, challenged his company with these words: "Where is it written that Chrysler has to be permanently number three in the American market?"[2]

Lutz explained, "'Becoming number two' is not Chrysler's long-term goal; I use that expression merely to communicate the limitless possibilities. . . . Our real, clearly enunciated goal is to 'be the premier automobile company in the world by the year 2000.' . . . 'Premier' is hard to communicate; I liken it to winning the decathlon; you don't have to be first in every event, but when all the points are added up (low cost? highest quality? best return to shareholders? best reputation? most audacious? fastest growing? most exciting new products?) you must have the highest total.

"I believe deeply in the need for communicating the goal, or the overarching vision, effectively. . . . The better a leader is able to communicate the goal, the more it becomes shared and ingrained in the company's associates, the more easily the leader can bring about positive change while empowering subordinates. He doesn't have to push, because they know where the team is headed and they want to get there, too. But, communication must not be 'hollow' and later let down by obvious character flaws in the leader, such as a lack of integrity. In other words, the leader must be able to 'talk the talk.' But, to be successful over time, he'd better 'walk like he talks,' too, or disillusionment and cynicism will set in with the troops."[3]

Highly successful leaders declare their expectations every chance they get and in every way they can. These expectations may include their visions, missions, goals, ideas, and values. Such leaders excite and motivate us. Soon, their expectations become ours and together we go on to achieve what these leaders declared.

THERE ARE TWO CLASSES OF EXPECTATIONS

The leader is concerned with two categories of expectations. The first tends to be tactical and of shorter term. These expectations have to do with immediate tasks and short and intermediate goals and objectives. The second set of expectations has to do with the leader's vision for the organization. The word "vision" calls up an image of the leader seeing a picture of the organization in the future . . . what it will become and how it will look. Both sets of expectations are equally important. If the leader's vision of the organization is fuzzy and vague, the firm will probably be unsuccessful in the long term no matter how well the shorter-term tasks, goals, and objectives are formulated and executed. This is because these expectations may be taking the firm to a less than optimum future. On the other hand, a clear, sharp, well-thought-out, and worthwhile vision may never be reached should the shorter-term class of the leader's expectations be neglected.

AN AIR FORCE SQUADRON COMMANDER SOLVES A DIFFICULT SHORT-TERM PROBLEM

During the Vietnam War, Ted Crichton was given command of a squadron flying four-engined C-130 transports out of Danang, Vietnam, and later Ubon, Thailand. Ted's squadron had an unusual and difficult mission, and his job was to accomplish that mission with an aircraft intended for combat support, not combat flying. The lumbering C-130 transport was to be used as a controller of fighters attacking heavily defended targets over North Vietnam and Laos at night.

Ted soon learned that his huge C-130s had to make rapid high "G" maneuvers called "jinking" to avoid the fire of antiaircraft guns. But the C-130 was built as a transport aircraft, not a fighter. Transports were not designed to take the high stress of jinking.

With the addition of a flare dispenser to hold the flares used to illuminate targets on the ground, the lower door of the C-130 could be locked but not the upper one. The high stress of jinking could cause the upper door to open. With the door open, the top safe speed was 150 knots, or 172.5 miles per hour. Above this speed, the additional stress could cause the structural integrity of the aircraft to fail. For effective jinking, the C-130 needed to fly at 250 knots, or 287.5 miles an hour. To jink at a lower speed would not be as effective and could cause the aircraft to stall.

Ted and others informed higher headquarters of the problem. They contacted the Lockheed Aircraft Company that built the aircraft. Meanwhile, Ted and his squadron had to jink their aircraft every night with the danger of structural damage to the airplane. Ted credits his squadron's solution to this problem to the third universal law. He didn't mandate a solution because he had none to offer. Instead, he declared his expectation of solving the problem to everyone in his squadron at every chance he got. Eventually someone came up with the idea that worked. Every time a C-130 jinked, the crew made certain that maximum hyraulic pressure was exerted on the door to hold it closed. They did this by working a hand pump designed to restore hydraulic pressure if it were lost in an emergency. This additional hydraulic pressure on the door in effect raised the stress limit by increasing the force holding the door closed. This was not a solution that higher headquarters liked. Lockheed wouldn't certify Crichton's solution, and it wasn't certified by the air force either. But there was nothing else available, and it worked.

After retiring from the air force as a brigadier general, he became president of American Nucleonics Corporation. Ted Chrichton credits his success partly to the same universal law of leadership. "Constant discussion with your people of your expectations . . . what you are trying to do and how you are doing . . . is always the key," he says.[4]

THE ROBOT COMPANY REACHES A LONG-TERM $2 BILLION GOAL AND GOES FOR MORE

Casey Cowell dropped out of graduate school at the University of Rochester to found a futuristic company. He chose the name, U.S. Robotics, taken from Isaac Asimov's science fiction classic *I Robot*. In twenty years of manufacturing modems, he built U.S. Robotics to $20 million in sales. How did he do it?

"In 1990, when annual sales were $56 million," says *Business Week*, "he began exhorting salespeople to reach '5 by 5,' meaning $500 million by 1995. Now he's aiming for '5 by 2' — $5 billion by 2000."[5]

Can it be that easy? There is always more to it than a leader's simply stating his goals. But doing exactly that seems to be basic to good leadership both in and out of combat. U.S. Air National Guard general Hugh L. Cox, who led combat missions in Southeast Asia, says that the first and most important action that a combat leader should take is to define the objective.[6] Maj. Gen. Clyde W. Spence, Jr., who saw combat as an artillery officer in both Korea and Vietnam and then became the president of Marion Military Institute says, "First and foremost you've got to issue orders in as simple terms as possible so that they are understood by everyone."[7]

WHAT I LEARNED FROM
THE PROCESSIONARY CATERPILLAR

You can't get "there" until you know where "there" is. Vision, goals, and objectives are your "there." These have to be big enough, important enough, and clear enough to be compelling. If your "there" has these qualities, and you are committed, those who follow you will break their necks to help you and your organization get "there." And well they might.

Do you think that you can learn anything about a leader's vision from an insect? I did. Here's the story. A professor at a large midwestern university is an entomologist. That's a fancy way of saying he studies insects. He became curious about a strange insect called a processionary caterpillar. What makes this species of caterpillar so unusual is the way it travels. A family of these caterpillars moves as a physically connected unit. They actually "hook up," one behind the other, and move in a long, undulating, connected line. The leader knows where they are going. The others simply hang on and have a rather spectacular view of the rear end of another caterpillar.

This professor wondered what would happen if there was no leader and hence no vision of where they were going. He designed a little experiment. He took a family of these caterpillars that was already connected and hooked the leader up to the caterpillar who was last in line, so that there was no leader. Then, he placed the circle of caterpillars on the rim of a flowerpot with a circumference that exactly matched the size of the circle of caterpillars. He placed water and mulberry leaves at the bottom of the flowerpot. Mulberry leaves are the processionary caterpillars' favorite food. What he wanted to know was how long the caterpillars would continue to travel around in a circle going nowhere. How long would they continue without a leader and no vision of where they were going before they changed tactics, or at least stopped for a coffee break?

As the leaderless caterpillars began to travel around the flowerpot's rim, the professor pressed the start button on his stop watch and waited. He planned to calculate to the millisecond how long the caterpillars would continue their trek.

The professor never pressed the button to stop his chronograph. Why? Because the caterpillars kept going round and round until they fell unconscious for lack of sustenance. Yet food and water were always only a few inches away. "Where there is no vision, the people perish," says Proverbs 29. That appears to apply to caterpillars also.

WHAT IS A VISION, ANYWAY?

A vision is an all-encompassing picture of the way you want an organization to look in the future. Without a vision, your organization is as helpless as the leaderless caterpillars. Without a vision, you'll never get "there" and neither will your organization. Just like the song sang by Bloody Mary in the Rodgers and Hammerstein musical *South Pacific*, "If you don't have a dream . . . if you don't have a dream, how you gonna make a dream come true?"

THE MAN WHO KNEW HOW TO TAKE ADVANTAGE OF DEREGULATION

As a naval officer, Ph.D. economist Kenneth Lay devised a modern accounting system for military purchases and later served as Deputy Undersecretary in the Interior Department for energy matters. He became CEO of Enron, the Houston energy company in 1985. He has built the company into a $13.2 billion colossus by taking advantage of regulation in the gas business. He has been the leading advocate for deregulating electricity and expects his electricity business to almost triple in 1998 to $3 billion.[8]

How does he do it? Let's listen to Lay: "We put a great deal of emphasis on vision. In the twelve years since Enron was formed with the merger of two large integrated natural gas companies, we have successfully achieved two of our visions and are now into our third. Our first vision was to become the premier integrated natural gas company in North America. Our second vision was to become the world's first natural gas major. Our third and current vision is to become the world's leading energy company. . . . The primary characteristic of each of these visions at the time they were set is that they were very ambitious, and at the same time sufficiently exciting to get our people to rally around achieving a common goal."[9]

CAN A VISION BE SUSTAINED?

A leader's vision can be so strong that it can continue long after the leader himself is gone. Even in the businessworld. P. T. Barnum was a nineteenth-century businessman and showman. Some say it was he who said, "There's a sucker born every minute." Whether or not he spoke these words, his vision was not that of an organization that cheated the public. Rather, it was of an organization that amazed the public. Barnum put together a show of the most unusual people imaginable. These included Tiny Tim, whose height was only 18 inches, a man so hairy he was termed "the Wolf Man," and a woman who was thought to be 150 years old. He took them on tours all over the world, and their amazed audiences included even the crowned heads of Europe. His show eventually grew into the world-famous Ringling Bros. and Barnum & Bailey Circus. Barnum succeeded because he had a vision, but it was a nineteenth-century vision. It was to bring live entertainment not only to the wealthy but also to the masses.

By the mid-twentieth century, television, movies, and the fact that it became increasingly difficult to pitch circus tents near the big cities changed everything. As a result, sales plummeted. John Ringling North sold the circus to Irwin Feld in 1967 for $8 million in cash. Feld turned the business around by abandoning tents and using convention centers.

However, it was his son Kenneth Feld who recognized that while business conditions, demographics, and technology had changed, Barnum's original vision for the business was still a good one. He took over the company in 1994 on the death of his father. "My goal was to have the largest live entertainment company in the world," he announced. He succeeded. In ten years, he owned not only the circus, but Walt Disney's *World on Ice*, *Siegfried & Roy* at Las Vegas's Mirage Resort, and George Lucas's *Super Live Adventure Show*. Today, his shows play to almost thirty million people a year, and annual sales are estimated at about a half a billion dollars.[10] P. T. Barnum would have nodded in approval and understood the success. Barnum's vision of entertainment for the masses marches on under Feld's leadership.

GREAT VISIONS ARE ALWAYS POWERFUL

The vision held by the successful leader is extremely powerful partly because it is always before him. Dr. Norman Vincent Peale, who wrote the best-seller *The Power of Positive Thinking*, found that with great visions, "You have it, because it has you." Such a vision is so strong that it can even appear in the subconscious to make things happen.

A Vision Helps Elias Howe Invent the Sewing Machine

Elias Howe is the inventor of the modern sewing machine. He had a strong vision as to how such a machine would work — that of a needle moving in and out of the item to be sewed. But, instead of the needle being worked by hand, it would move one hundred times as quickly because it would operate mechanically. There was just one problem. Howe couldn't get his machine to work. The point would penetrate the cloth and drag the thread down with it. But when the needle was withdrawn on the upstroke, it either got entangled in the cloth or tore it.

Howe tried everything. He sharpened the needle at both ends. It still got entangled. He used a curved needle. Still no luck. But his compelling vision of a sewing machine wouldn't go away.

One night he woke up after a strange dream. In his dream, cannibals on a South Sea island had captured him. As they made ready to cook Howe, they danced around him brandishing their spears. Howe noticed that their spears were very unusual. Each spear had a hole in its head where it was sharpened to a point. Through each hole was a length of rope.

When he awoke, he remembered his dream. In an instant, he realized the solution to the problem of the sewing machine: put the hole in the head of the needle and allow the needle to sew without extracting fully on the upstroke. With his compelling vision of his sewing machine, Elias Howe may have eventually hit upon a solution without the help of the savages. But don't discount the power of the subconscious. What is a dream, but a vision?

Compelling Visions Change the World

In his famous speech, Dr. Martin Luther King, Jr., told us, "I have a dream." King went on to describe a very different kind of America than existed at that time . . . one in which a person wasn't to be judged by the color of his skin but the content of his character. Dr. King's vision changed America forever.

Sam Walton built a spectacular retail chain because he had a vision of providing quality goods to people in geographical areas that major retailers were not serving. He felt so strongly about his vision that he risked his personal future and well-being and left a well-paid, executive position at J. C. Penney in order to implement it. Wal-Mart was the fruit of his powerful vision.

All successful organizations, whether small businesses, *Fortune* 500 companies, athletic teams, combat units, or even countries, must be built on a clear and compelling vision. This vision provides direction for everyone. It guides all action and tells everyone exactly where the organization is going. Properly involved in this vision, members of the organization willingly work toward it. Almost miraculously, the organization usually attains the vision that the leader sees, sometimes in every single detail.

THE LEADER SEES THE VISION FIRST

When the EPCOT Center opened in Florida, a news reporter interviewed Roy Disney, Walt Disney's brother. At one point in the interview, the reporter commented: "It's too bad Walt isn't here to see all this," and asked, "What would Walt have thought about EPCOT Center?"

Roy Disney didn't hesitate in replying, "Walt saw it years ago, before anybody else . . . that's why you and I are seeing it today."

The leader always does see the finished product first, in his or her mind. Then he declares these expectations, promotes them, and motivates everyone to make his vision a reality.

In 1948 Disney took his daughters to an amusement park. He was distressed that amusement parks had become run-down, with unfriendly employees — places that parents no longer wanted to take their children. Walt Disney put out a memo for what he called "Mickey Mouse Park" that very year. It read in part: "The Main Village, which includes the Railroad Station, is built around a village green or informal park. In the park will be benches, a bandstand, a drinking fountain, trees, and shrubs. It will be a place for people to sit and rest; mothers and grandmothers can watch over small children at play. I want it to be very relaxing, cool and inviting."[11] And thus the "Happiest Place on Earth" was created.

HOW DID THE MOST PROFITABLE AIRLINE IN THE WORLD GET THAT WAY?

The airline industry lost $12.8 billion from 1990 to 1994, losing more money than it had made in the previous sixty years! There was only one exception: Southwest Airlines. It has turned a profit every year since 1973. Moreover, its profit margins are the highest in the industry.

Why? Well, there are a number of reasons, but vision ranks right up there at the top. Listen to former CEO and president of Southwest Airlines, Howard Putnam: "Most companies fail in their growth because they don't have a vision. They don't know where to go. When you have a vision and someone comes to you with some convoluted idea, you can hold it up to the vision and ask, 'Does it fit? Does it fly? If not, don't bother me.' A vision must be so strong that it can outweigh the egos of managers that might want to take off in a different direction."[12]

How to Achieve Your Expectations

It doesn't matter whether the expectation is a task, goal, or vision for your organization. The steps in declaring and achieving it are the same. They are:

1. Get Your Expectations Clear
2. Make Your Expectations Compelling
3. Develop a Plan
4. Promote Your Expectations and Implement Your Plan
5. Listen To Feedback and Adjust Your Strategy
6. Be Faithful to Your Expectations

Get Your Expectations Clear

I know this may sound oversimplified, but the truth is some leaders just don't know what they want for their organizations' futures. They only want their organizations to be "successful." But until the leader defines exactly what success means to him and to his organization, there is no hope. Like the processionary caterpillar linked in a leaderless circle with no expectations other than the rear end of another caterpillar, an organization without clearly defined expectations can accomplish no task, reach no goal, attain no object. It will simply perish. Therefore, you must take the time to get your expectations very clear in your mind.

Lt. Gen. Jack V. Mackmull served in combat in Vietnam and has the distinction of having commanded infantry, aviation, paratrooper, and special warfare units. He notes, "You've got to begin by analyzing the mission requirements to determine what tasks need to be accomplished."[13] Again, you can't get "there" until you know where "there" is.

FOCUS YOUR ENERGIES

The basis of all achievement is to concentrate superior resources at the decisive point. Claude Hopkins founded one of the largest advertising agencies in the country in the early 1900s. He wrote two best-selling books, *Scientific Advertising* and *My Life in Advertising*. One day a correspondent asked him to what he owed his success. "Simple," he answered. "I spend more time than any of my competitors on any given project."

Concentrating resources, such as time, requires focus. An American athlete went to Japan to earn his black belt in karate. After several months of daily workouts, his instructor gave him a new routine — one day of very hard work, and then one day of complete rest. A friend convinced him he could work on a black belt in judo, a completely different martial art, on his days off when he was supposed to be resting from karate.

His master instructor at his karate "dojo" knew something was not quite right. He asked why he was not able to put as much energy into his workouts as previously. When he learned the reason, he asked: "Why did you come to Japan?" "To get a black belt in karate," answered the athlete. The master instructor reached into a cupboard where the various colored belts, which indicated levels of achievement in karate, were stored. He grabbed a black belt and threw it at the athlete. "Now you have it. Return to your country," the instructor said. It was with great difficulty, and only after he promised to drop his judo instruction, that the athlete was allowed to continue his karate training. "I learned you cannot devote yourself 100 percent to more than one major goal at the same time," he said.

If you look at Pete Peterson's career described in chapter 2, you will find he focused first on becoming an expert fighter pilot. Only afterward did he concentrate his efforts on becoming an expert leader and then a commander at successively higher levels.

CHOOSE, DON'T JUGGLE

Many leaders are proud of their ability to juggle many different objectives and goals. In some cases, these objectives are even mutually exclusive. For example, the leaders of one company I know set certain short-term objectives in sales and profits. Yet the way they set things up prevented them from reaching their sales goals and from reaching their profits goals. These corporate jugglers cannot understand why they cannot reach greater success in any of their expectations. Peak-performance expert Dr. Charles Garfield says, "Choose, don't juggle!" Choose each expectation very carefully and get it clear in your mind. Is it really worth your and your organization's effort to attain it? If it is, then you can concentrate superior resources at the decisive points, and, like Claude Hopkins, you will succeed where others fail. You can put more effort into any given project by focusing on worthwhile expectations and ignoring those that are less worthwhile.

CLOROX CEO SHOWS HOW IT'S DONE

Clorox Chairman and CEO G. Craig Sullivan made clear some major expectations when he took over the company in 1992. With more than twenty-five years at Clorox after starting out in sales in 1971, he had had time to think through his goals for Clorox with crystal clarity. He knew exactly what he wanted to do. Soon after taking over, he set up ambitious but reachable growth targets and demanded new product introductions across the board. Some senior managers balked at these expectations. Sullivan suggested that those who didn't want to participate had best move on. Almost half his old staff of senior executives did.

"I think I had the advantage of being 'an observer' in the company for a long time so I had a pretty good idea of what needed to be done. Also, since I'm not smart enough to do complicated things, I tried to keep things simple and focused. That seems to have worked out pretty well."[14] Indeed it did. Earnings have increased more than 10 percent every year. Sales in 1997 exceeded $2.5 billion, up 14 percent over 1996.[15] Glenn R. Savage, Clorox's marketing director, notes, "There's power in giving people very clear objectives."[16]

Now that Clorox is doing so well, Craig Sullivan is not resting on his laurels. As Mary Kay Ash, former CEO of Mary Kay Cosmetics who built her company with five thousand dollars and a store front into a half-billion-dollar corporation, says, "Nothing wilts quite so quickly as laurels, rested upon." Many leaders are afraid to voice new expectations for fear they will not reach them, but here are Craig Sullivan's new goals for

Clorox:

To achieve sales of $3.5 billion by the year 2000, requiring average annual growth of 12 percent over the next three years;

To grow the Clorox Value Measure (CVM) at a rate that exceeds 12 percent over time;

To generate total shareholder return over time that places us in the top third of the S&P 500 and the top third of our peer group;

To build an international business that by the year 2000 is 20 percent of total company sales.[17]

ALONE OR WITH OTHERS?

Many leaders get others involved in creating their expectations. Participation and involvement helps get expectations clear and helps get others committed to the expectations. Napoleon Hill was on President Roosevelt's staff as an advisor during the Great Depression. Earlier Hill had been commissioned by the wealthiest man in the world, steel magnate Andrew Carnegie, to discover what leads to a man's success. In his book *Think and Grow Rich,* Hill described a unique phenomenon he had noticed in his research. Highly successful people formed what Hill called "a mastermind alliance" with others. Through this "mastermind alliance, " others shared in helping the successful person fulfill his vision of the future.

You can develop your own "mastermind alliance" with those you lead. That way, you not only utilize everyone's brainpower, but you get everyone's involvement in and commitment to your expectations.

However there are situations when the leader must develop his vision alone. For instance, time may be a major factor. In the early 1960s, I watched a colonel take command of a bomber wing that was flat on its back. By any objective measurement — its bomb scores, on-time takeoffs, aerial refuelings completed, etc. — it was the worst wing in Strategic Air Command. However, this commander came in with expectations and turned the whole situation around in less than ninety days! It actually went from last to first place. A team of individuals representing the wing might have taken that long just to develop a set of expectations.

If you saw the movie *Twelve O'Clock High,* you saw a fictitious commander played by Gregory Peck do the same thing with a B-17 group during World War II. Gen. Bill Creech did the same thing with the very real Tactical Air Command (TAC) in the air force back in the early 1980s. When General Creech took over TAC, the number of missions that an aircraft could fly had been falling over a ten-year period at a compound rate of 7.8 percent every year due to maintenance problems. When Creech took over, it took four hours for a spare part to be sent from inventory storage to the aircraft that needed it. When he left TAC in 1984, the number of missions that could be flown by an aircraft had been rising by 11.2 percent a year. Was getting spare parts out of inventory to keep the airplanes flying still a problem? The time to do this was no longer measured in hours. Now it took just eight minutes! Moreover, all this took place while the budgets for spare parts were falling.[18]

Both the fictitious air force leader and the real ones developed expectations for their organizations without much help or participation from others. General Bill Creech, who *Inc.* magazine named as one of their six-member Management Dream Team for the '90s, says, "It's important to have a clear vision of where you're going — and to share it with everyone in the organization."[19]

As a leader, it is your decision. If gaining commitment is a major issue and you have the time, getting everyone involved makes sense. If time is the main driver, do it yourself. Of course, there may be other factors that argue for one or the other approach. But don't put it off: get your expectations clear. This step is mandatory before you can declare anything to anybody.

MIGHTY CHARLES ATLAS MADE HIS EXPECTATIONS COMPELLING

Whenever I think of compelling expectations, I cannot help but think of Charles Atlas, of whom you may have heard, and Charles Roman, of whom you probably have not. Charles Atlas was a poor Italian boy who immigrated to the United States around the turn of the century. His real name was Angelo Siciliano. As a boy, Angelo was painfully weak — a ninety-eight-pound weakling. After a painful beating by a bully, he cried himself to sleep but swore an oath that no man on earth would ever hurt him again.

He developed his own unique method of bodybuilding, which did not use weights. He had to because he couldn't afford weights. In twelve months he doubled his body weight. He entered bodybuilding contests and won every one he entered. Then he became a well-known artist's model posing for such famous sculptures as Alexander Hamilton in front of the U.S. Treasury Building in Washington, D.C., George Washington in New York's Washington Square, and the "Dawn of Glory" in Brooklyn's Prospect Park. Using the prize money from the contests and his modeling, Atlas developed a physical development correspondence course and began to sell it through the mail. However he couldn't get enough customers with his advertisements, and he began to lose money. With a wife, two children, no income, and a floundering business, Atlas was in serious trouble. Enter Charles Roman.

Charles Roman was a new hire at the Benjamin Landsman Advertising Agency of New York. In desperation, Atlas asked the Landsman agency for help. Roman was a recent graduate of New York University. As the new guy, he was given the account with the worst potential. That was Charles Atlas. Roman read over Atlas's course materials and realized that the ads simply didn't make Atlas's expectations for his potential customers compelling. Roman came up with new ways of doing this. Four months after their meeting, Atlas and Roman became partners. "The Insult That Made a Man Out of Mac," one headline trumpeted. Roman invited respondents to check the kind of body they wanted: "Broader Chest and Shoulders," "Ironhard Stomach Muscles," "Tireless Legs," "Slimmer Waist and Legs," "More Energy and Stamina," the list went on and on. From a few hundred courses sold, the number climbed to three thousand the first year the two men were in business together. Soon sales reached ten thousand. In 1971, the year before Atlas died, they sold more than twenty-three thousand courses worldwide.[20] The course is still selling today.

Now here's the point. Charles Atlas declared his expectations for his potential customers, but until Roman came on the scene, he did not do so in a sufficiently compelling fashion. Once Roman made these expectations compelling, prospects were influenced to buy, and buy in a big way.

Leaders declaring their expectations to influence those who follow them are much like retailers attempting to influence prospects to buy. Successful leaders first make certain that their expectations are formulated in a compelling fashion.

IF YOU WANT EXPECTATIONS TO BE COMPELLING, ASK THE QUESTION "WHY?"

To be compelling, expectations have to provide strong benefits to the organization once they are achieved. John Paul Jones's men knew what the stakes were, or they probably would have asked him, "Are you crazy?" when he told the commander of the British ship that he had not yet begun to fight. What benefits will result once you have turned your expectations into reality? Will your customers be better off? How? Will the members of your organization be happier or achieve more in their careers? Will society benefit? Will your organization be proclaimed number one in its field? Think through and know the benefits of your expectations specifically and in detail.

R. J. "Zap" Zlatoper is a modern admiral in the mold of John Paul Jones. Zlatoper asked the question "Why?" and made his expectation of teamwork compelling in a very dramatic fashion. Admiral Zlatoper flew combat off a carrier during the Vietnam War and commanded major naval combat units during Operation Desert Storm. As a four-star admiral, Zap Zlatoper commanded the entire Pacific Fleet. Then he retired and became CEO of Sanchez Computer Associates, Inc., in Malvern, Pennsylvania. Sanchez Computer Associates offers integrated software solutions and services for financial institutions worldwide.

Says Admiral Zlatoper, "Sanchez was and is a great company with terrific people. But they really didn't understand what it really meant to work together. So, I took my top executives out to the U.S.S. Enterprise aircraft carrier to watch the extraordinary coordination and teamwork necessary to launch and recover naval warplanes at sea. It requires split-second timing and the precise interaction of hundreds of people. One screwup or prima donna can spell disaster, so you can't have any. They saw what I wanted of them, and they did it. I can't help but think this new orientation has contributed to our hypergrowth and our stock's going from five dollars to thirty-two dollars a share."[21]

You will need to know and understand the benefits to communicate your vision to others. You need to have them fixed in your own mind and soul as you progress toward achieving your goals. Without knowing why your goal is important to your organization and its people, you will not be able to convince yourself or others that the sacrifices are worth it once the going gets tough, as it always will. Without knowing why, you will abandon your vision before it is attained. Without knowing why, your expectations cannot be compelling. On the other hand, knowing the specific benefits that will accrue when you complete your task or reach your goal will give you great leverage on yourself and on your organization and that will help you to reach your version of success.

WRITE YOUR EXPECTATIONS DOWN

Once you have your expectations clear and know why you must attain them, write them down. Work on the wording so that it is clear, direct, and compelling. This is where you want your organization to go. This is what you want your organization to be. Keep working with them until they have the impact of a wet rag thrown against a wall. When you think you have written your expectations down perfectly, let them sit for a couple of days and then go back and work on them some more. Once you have your expectations written down so that they are clear and compelling, you are ready to plan how to achieve them.

Mark Victor Hansen, Vietnam veteran and coauthor with Jack Canfield of the *Chicken Soup* series of books, which have sold millions of copies, says: "Write down 101 goals. Put them around your house and office so that you can see them. Then, as you achieve each, don't just down-line through it. Instead, write, 'Victory!'"[22]

YOU MUST DEVELOP A PLAN

There is a very old saying that those who fail to plan, plan to fail. Yet when movie star Paul Newman was asked about future plans for his successful line of food products he answered, "If we ever get a plan, we're screwed."

While I suspect that Newman's answer was somewhat tongue-in-cheek, I have found that even though successful leaders always have a plan to achieve their expectations, the plan is not always documented. However, each and every leader can describe his plan without missing a beat or leaving out a detail, whether it is in writing or not.

Planning is a process of thinking it through. You have established precisely where you want to go and why you must get there. Now you must establish exactly how you are going to do this. Start by scanning your environment. Combat leaders have been doing this for thousands of years. They then come up with something they call the estimate of the situation. They look at alternative courses of action to reach their objective and then decide on the best one. You must do the same.

Maj. Gen. Don H. Payne saw combat in the air force in both Korea and Vietnam. He says, "Plan as meticulously as the situation allows. Generally, the more time and resources available for detailed planning, the more likely are success and reduced losses."[23]

Sometimes reaching your final objective requires breaking the objective or goal into smaller tasks. You can eat an elephant, but only if you eat it one bite at a time. So you may need to break your larger goal down into smaller, doable bites.

Although you can do it in your head, many leaders find it useful to write their plans down with firm dates for reaching each expectation. I like that. It's a way of getting even greater leverage on yourself and your organization to attain what you expect.

HOW ARTHUR MARTINEZ
PLANNED AT SEARS ROEBUCK

Not so long ago, Sears Roebuck & Co. was not in great shape. In 1992, the $30 billion retail business, the very essence of Sears, posted a $2.9 billion loss. Some even thought the corporation would go under. Arthur Martinez came on the scene after heading Saks Fifth Avenue. At his first meeting with executives he laid out his expectations:

1. Focus on core businesses where we know we can win and grow.
2. Position Sears as a more compelling place to shop.
3. Become more locally market-focused in terms of the product and service mix offered to target customers.
4. Accelerate cost and productivity improvements throughout the company.
5. Create a new corporate culture and set of values to lead Sears into the future.

He didn't stop there. He junked more than twenty-nine thousand pages of policies and procedures and replaced them with a couple of simple booklets that promoted his expectations. The booklets were called *Freedom* and *Obligations*. "We're trying to tell our managers what they're responsible for, what freedoms they have to make decisions, and where to turn if they need help," he says.[24]

For planning how to reach his expectations, Martinez would gather his top one hundred executives every month for a planning session. He assigned them plenty of homework. One weekend he had each Sears executive write down the first two paragraphs of the business story that would be written about Sears in 1999. Just a fun way to kill a weekend? Not according to Martinez. "The usual planning processes are expressed in terms of dry financial statistics. We wanted people to come up with a more textured vision of the customer's world."[25]

Did any of this work? Sears has recorded a profit now for fifteen consecutive quarters. Last year's was $1.8 billion. That was the biggest in Sear's history. Sure, Martinez did a lot of right things to bring about a turnaround like this, but planning how to reach his expectations didn't hurt.

PROMOTING YOUR EXPECTATIONS
IS A BIG PART OF IMPLEMENTATION

Promoting your expectations means just that. It means promoting what you want your organization to do, what its values are, where you want your organization to go, and what you want your organization to be. Think about it, use it as a basis of discussion, talk about it, and write about it every chance you get. Tie it in with everything you do. Every time someone takes an action that moves you toward one or more of your expectations, let people know. Give them a pat on the back. As Mark Victor Hansen suggests, just don't just cross a reached goal off your list, declare a victory.

Maj. Gen. Lucien E. Bolduc, Jr., was an infantry officer who survived the attack on Pearl Harbor and went on to lead men in battle in Korea and Vietnam. He considers one of the most important lessons on leadership that he learned from combat to be: "Once you determine the real imperatives of the situation and plan, you must inform and meaningfully convince key collaborators of what must be accomplished, and how."[26]

Successful business leaders also promote their expectations at every opportunity. To communicate his expectations to his salesmen, Elmer Wheeler, one of the most successful sales managers of all time, coined the phrase, "Don't sell the steak, sell the sizzle." His words still live fifty years later.

Kenneth Lay, the visionary head of multibillion-dollar Enron Corporation says, "Setting ambitious visions and goals is just the beginning. It is paramount that the visions and goals be communicated clearly and in such a way that every employee in the organization understands what they are and can mentally grasp what they must do to achieve them. I spend a great deal of my time communicating with not only the leadership level of our company, but also with employees at all levels through floor meetings and other meetings in order to make sure they understand what we are trying to accomplish."[27]

THIS EX-MARINE SAYS YOU NEED TO OVERCOMMUNICATE

Richard Lieb is president of SEI Investment Systems and Services, a $250 million division of a rapidly growing company that develops software and handles mutual funds in Philadelphia, Pennsylvania. Rick Lieb fought as a platoon commander in the Fifth Marine Regiment of the First Marine Division in Vietnam. Before entering the business world, he was in the U.S. Marine Corps Reserve as a major and completed an M.B.A. at Wharton.

"The marine corps gave me a lot of responsibility and a lot of latitude, and then expected results," he says. "That combat philosophy served me well in my career in industry. I treat my people the same way. 'Focus on a common goal and go for it!' I tell them. Then I let them get the job done. But make no mistake about it. You must stay focused on what you want and where you are going. Then, you've got to overcommunicate it to everyone at every level of the organization. And while you are about it you must make sure that fairness, integrity, and honor are integrated in every task, every goal, and every vision."[28]

PROMOTE AND IMPLEMENT YOUR PLAN

Now that you have your plan, you can start working it. When you start implementing your plan, you will see that everything will not work out exactly as originally thought. That's okay. The important thing is to start and stay with it, and adjust your plan as you proceed. Sure, you are going to run into obstacles. That's just normal. The simple fact that your organization is progressing toward its goal will help motivate it to continue.

At giant Boeing Aircraft Company, CEO Phil Condit's defining experience has been the development of the Boeing 777 aircraft, the first jet designed entirely on computer and built to be controlled by electronics rather than hydraulics, making it easier to fly. Everybody seems to love the 777. A book has already been written about it, and PBS aired a documentary entitled "Twenty-First Century Jet." Last year, the National Aeronautic Association awarded the Collier Trophy to Boeing for the 777 for outstanding achievement in aeronautics and astronautics in the United States. For the first time, an airplane was designed with everyone involved in mind — a chief mechanic was on the design team as well as a chief pilot, resulting in a plane that's a lot easier to maintain. The plane is quieter because the Boeing team addressed every individual noise contributor.

How did Condit do it? Listen to Condit: "The first step toward getting everyone at Boeing to pull together is to make sure everyone knows where the company wants to go and how it plans get there. . . . The first thing we did with the Triple Seven was to hold a general orientation session to get the message out to everyone what our goals were with this plane."[29]

A Combat Leader Turns Tenneco Around

Dana Mead began his career as an officer commanding tank units. Elvis Presley happened to serve in the unit in which Dana was an officer in Germany. Later, his alma mater, West Point, asked him to come back to teach. So he did. On the way, he picked up a Ph.D. in political science from MIT. Dr. Mead then served in combat in Vietnam, winning a chest full of ribbons and the combat infantryman's badge. He was selected and became a White House Fellow and returned to West Point to teach and become deputy head of the department of social science. He was promoted to full colonel, and with twenty-one years of service, retired from the army and began a civilian career. Ten years later he was executive vice president and a director of International Paper Company. He came to Tenneco in 1992, first as president. He became CEO in 1994. Today he is chairman of this multibillion-dollar colossus.

When Mead took over, Tenneco was a disjointed conglomerate with many unprofitable divisions and no focus. Overall debt was a mind-boggling $9 billion. Many of its own customers didn't know what business it was in. Even today, the shadow of that time lingers. When Tenneco recently surveyed its customers, 60 percent didn't know its business. Many thought it was primarily oil and gas. Tenneco got out of oil in the late 1980s and gas in 1996. The confusion isn't surprising. Tenneco's portfolio of businesses included everything from shipbuilding to insurance, farm equipment, automotive parts, and more. One division was such a poor performer that the company couldn't even give it away. That was the J. I. Case farm equipment subsidiary. Mead tried to sell J. I. Case off for one dollar back in 1992 and couldn't do it. He simply couldn't give it away.

All that is changed. Not only has Tenneco seen twenty-four quarters of growth, but revenues are 7.2 billion, and Tenneco is profitable. Says Mead, "Four years ago, Tenneco was little more than an aggregate of six divisions, highly decentralized, fragmented, unfocused, and grossly underperforming. We shared practically nothing in common. Since that time, we have become one focused company that happens to be in four different industries, working toward the same goals, using the same management principles and practices and sharing them across business sectors."[30] Today, Tenneco is even more focused in two industries. And J. I. Case? Mead got Tenneco to remove $1.5 billion of Case debt from its own books by establishing Case as an independent company. Then, he sold 100 percent of Tenneco's Case stock for $2.1 billion. Tenneco also received an additional $750 million by capturing tax benefits and proceeds from the sale of other Case debt. So Tenneco received total benefits exceeding $4 billion.[31]

How did Dana Mead accomplish this turnaround? Clearly, some smart management was involved, but Mead says, "We don't even use the word 'management' at Tenneco. We focus on leadership. We concentrated on building a cadre of leaders. Some were already good, but half we trained. We established many new awards, all having to do with leadership. I even wrote, published, and promoted *Behaviors of a Tenneco Leader*. And bonuses? Well, I decided that 50 percent of all annual bonuses would be based on leadership. Many didn't like that at first because they didn't understand it. But now they do, because it worked."[32]

Early on Mead got his expectations clear. Then he made them compelling. Finally he promoted and implemented his expectations. To skeptics and believers alike he proclaimed, "We can grow each of our businesses well in excess of industry averages."[33] The World Wide Web's *PR Central* noted that Mead "understands the importance of communication, both internal and external."[34] Of course! That's how a leader promotes his expectations. Is it any surprise that Mead is known to be more accessible to employees than any previous Tenneco chief, or that he has been known to leave board meetings to return reporters' telephone calls?

But Mead did more. "We established unforgiving emphasis on results. We wanted results, not best efforts, and I told everyone this. I believe accountability coupled with stated goals and objectives is critical. Moreover, we made these goals public. Each senior manager had to stand up every month in front of his peers and state his goals and how he was doing. Of course, the head guy had to stand up, be willing to be held accountable, and do the same thing. And I did.

"Also, I learned a long time ago that you don't make assumptions about what people understand or don't understand, or are doing or not when they are under a lot of pressure. In Vietnam, I was in combat with the First ARVN Division. That was South Vietnam's best division. It didn't make any difference. I learned that I had to repeatedly make my expectations clear when people were under fire. Otherwise, they didn't get the job done. But organizations will respond, if you let people know what you expect, and you hold them and yourself publicly accountable."[35]

TWO OF THE MOST OUTSTANDING EXECUTIVE PROMOTERS I EVER MET

During my forty years in uniform, I was privileged to serve under two of the most outstanding promoters of their expectations I have ever met. A powerful example of how to promote your expectations came from the four-star general who was my boss when he commanded Air Education and Training Command (AETC). His name was Gen. Henry "Butch" Viccellio. General Viccellio was responsible for most of the nationwide education and training in the air force, including flying training, technical training, officers' schools, and advanced degrees.

You might think that an academic like myself, whose "daytime job" was that of university professor, wouldn't need much orientation to a command focused on education. The truth is, until my assignment to AETC, it was the first time I had been in the command since I completed flight training more than thirty years earlier.

General Viccellio suggested I might want to sit in the back of the room during a two-day course for new squadron commanders. "It will be the quickest way to get up to speed," he said. I rearranged my schedule and got to Randolph Air Force Base near San Antonio, Texas, in time to attend the course.

I noticed that General Viccellio himself was on the schedule. That's not unusual. Usually "the boss" kicks off all important conferences with a short introductory speech. Then he disappears. Others usually give the details. This was different. If I believed the schedule, he was going to speak to both the new commanders and their spouses for four hours regarding AETC and his expectations and vision for the command. I did not believe the schedule. I thought there must be some mistake. I overheard several of the attendees talking, and they thought the same thing. How wrong we were.

Along with the squadron commanders, both male and female, and their spouses, I sat riveted for four hours while this four-star commander personally and dramatically told us where the command was going, why, and how it was going to get there. He was totally open, answering questions on any topic. He didn't seem to mind being challenged either, if someone questioned his data. But he knew what he was talking about, and all doubts soon evaporated. It was one of the most impressive performances of a senior executive that I have ever watched. It was worth millions of dollars to the organization and the air force. Those new commanders and their spouses left that conference charged up. They knew exactly where they were headed and why. They knew exactly what their "big boss" expected from them. And they knew it from "the big boss" himself. If leaders of other organizations, in and out of the military, followed General Viccellio's method of promoting their visions, they would find their followers much more enthusiastic about what the leader was trying to do, and there would be much less misunderstanding.

When Gen. Ron Fogleman became U.S. Air Force Chief of Staff, he committed to visiting every single unit in the air force. With hundreds of worldwide locations, many in dangerous, out-of-the-way locations in Eastern Europe and the Middle East, he had set quite a task for himself. No chief of staff had ever attempted this. He started in California at the Space and Missile System Center in Los Angeles. That in itself carried a message and an expectation, because General Fogleman had been a fighter pilot through most of his career. Among the space and missile people, there were few pilots, much less fighter pilots. Most of the people at the Space and Missile System Center were engineers.

General Fogleman spoke for more than an hour, declaring his expectations. Included was that, first and primary, all of us were members of the U.S. Air Force. Only after that were we engineers, scientists, pilots, navigators, missileers, and other specialists. Other great leaders take the same approach. Bill Bartmann, CEO of Commercial Financial Services, Inc., and one of the wealthiest men in America, whom we'll meet in chapter 5, insists that his employees understand that first and foremost they are members of CFS and only secondarily members of a certain specialty.[36]

General Fogleman continued to promote his message at units throughout the air force. Like some of his predecessors, he met with his generals separately. Unlike his predecessors, he met not only with his active duty generals but with his reserve and national guard generals as well. Again, part of the Fogleman message: we were all part of the total air force. No wonder that General Fogleman succeeded in reaching his expectations.

JUMP-START YOUR PROMOTION
THROUGH DRAMATIZATION

Successful leaders following this universal law know that it is important to dramatize their expectations as they promote them. Many combat leaders shorten their expectations into brief messages that have a dramatic impact and are repeated again and again. MacArthur said, "I shall return." Commodore Dewey declared, "Damn the torpedoes, full speed ahead." Capt. John Paul Jones won a battle by telling everyone, "I have not yet begun to fight." General Fogleman declared his strategy for meeting the requirements set by the president and the joint chiefs of staff to be "Global Engagement."

During Operation Desert Storm, a newsman asked Gen. Colin Powell to describe his strategy for defeating Saddam Hussein's army. Powell answered, "First we are going to cut it off, and then we are going to kill it." General Powell's answer reached every soldier in every language of allied forces fighting in the war.

LISTEN TO FEEDBACK

Successful battle leaders know it is just as important to listen as to speak. They demand that followers state their objections to potential courses of action. They consider this a duty. Whenever possible, the good combat leader considers these objections before making his decision. Of course, once the leader's decision is made, everyone must support it as if it were his own. One reason the followers will do so willingly is the leader listens first.

Unfortunately some corporate leaders label subordinates who disagree "insubordinate." They fire them or punish them in more subtle ways. As a result, their companies fall far short of the best they can be. Not all corporate leaders are so foolish. In Watsonville, California, a company called Graniterock is a small business in a niche industry. But it is first rate. Not long ago, Graniterock was a finalist for the Baldridge National Quality Award. At the award ceremony, Graniterock's heroic leader and president Bruce Woolpert, proclaimed, "I believe people can only do their best when they can't lose anything, when they are free to ask, 'What's going to produce stronger service and products for the customer?' We try to create a lot of those situations."

Robert Townsend, who served in the U.S. Navy during World War II, was president of Avis Rent-a-Car during its period of greatest growth. He developed the "We Try Harder" theme, which is still used today. He reported that one of his vice presidents who disagreed with a proposed action sent him a note. It began, "If you insist, it will be my duty to make it so. However, I must respectfully tell you that you are full of shit again."

Townsend never punished a subordinate for speaking his mind. He felt it was all part of the "We Try Harder" philosophy. It is also part of the third universal law of leadership.

TO LISTEN, SOMETIMES YOU'VE GOT TO GET YOUR PEOPLE TO SPEAK UP

Lt. Gen. Gus Pagonis was General Schwarzkopf's top logistician during the Gulf War. When Pagonis left the army, he became Sears Roebuck & Co.'s top logistician as an executive vice president. He found he had a problem. "In my first two weeks here, I was not getting any negative information. I kept asking, "Aren't there any problems?" The answer would invariably be, "No, everything is fine."

Now General Pagonis knew that things are never 100 percent

perfect. But how could he get his people to give him the negatives as well as the positives? He said, "OK, each of you will give me three ups and three downs."

"Initially people had a problem with the downs. They would put up a chart listing their ups but no downs. But when we told them that either they start providing downs themselves or we would start filling them in for them, we began to see downs listed."[37]

THIS MARINE LISTENED
AND ADJUSTED HIS STRATEGY

Lt. Neil Witte was a platoon commander in the Third Marine Division in Quang Tin Province, Republic of Vietnam. Witte had a reputation as an expert in establishing night ambush sites. He prided himself on his ability to place just the right number and combination of men in just the right place to intercept the enemy as they attempted to infiltrate American positions at night. His platoon held the record for both the number of successful ambushes and the number of enemy casualties inflicted. He knew that at battalion headquarters they had a saying, "If you want to stop the bad guys, let Witte do it."

Neil Witte didn't know exactly what made him so adept at this assignment, but he had a pretty good idea. He was raised in the backwoods of Georgia and, during his boyhood, he had spent countless nights with his father and uncles hunting and trapping. He had developed an instinct for just what would work in a nighttime attack and what would not. Consequently when he picked an ambush site, no one questioned him. Not his company commander or anyone at battalion headquarters. Certainly not any of his men. They simply accepted his orders, with confidence that whatever he decided was for the best. And he promoted his expectations. "When better ambushes are made, we'll be the ones that make them," he told his men.

In March 1967, a replacement gunnery sergeant was assigned to Witte's platoon. This man had served for almost a year in intelligence and had volunteered for an additional tour of six months in an infantry unit before returning to the states. Witte felt uncomfortable around him. It wasn't that the new man questioned any of Witte's orders or was disrespectful in any way. However, he could see something in the man's eyes. It was as if he analyzed each of Witte's site selections. Witte got the feeling that if the man ever disagreed with a selection, he would probably say something. Witte didn't like that at all. His selections had always been right. He was the acknowledged expert. He was the guy promoting making better ambushes. He would have resented a superior officer disagreeing with his selection. For a combat-inexperienced sergeant to even think about it was almost too much for him to accept.

One evening, it happened. Witte was positioning some men for a night ambush. He was about to put eight of them on a small knoll overlooking a jungle trail. The new sergeant suddenly paled. "Can I speak to the lieutenant in private?" he asked.

"Sure," said Witte. "Let's go over here." He quickly walked away from the others. He knew what was coming.

"Sir, I don't like to question your orders. But before you make your decision final, would you mind if I made an observation?"

Witte minded very much, but he said, "Go right ahead." He gritted his teeth.

"Sir, I know that knoll seems like a mighty good spot to put the men to ambush the trail. But there is a problem with it. There's another trail that winds behind the knoll. It comes within ten meters of the knoll at one point. If anyone gets on that other trail, they have a clear field of fire on the knoll, but because of the foliage, those on the trail won't know they are there and won't be able to return fire when they do."

Witte felt his anger rising. "Don't you think I know that, Gunny?" demanded Witte. "That trail is old and deserted. No one has used it since we got here."

"No sir, but that was one of the things we noticed at intel the last few weeks. The North Vietnamese are starting to reuse old trails they abandoned years ago. If they happen to choose tonight to use that one, they'll be able to see and bring fire on your ambush team on the knoll before anyone even knows they are there."

Witte didn't like what he heard. He didn't like having his judgment challenged. He didn't like having someone in the platoon who was more of an expert than he. He knew if he told the gunnery sergeant to forget it, the gunny would say, "Aye, aye, sir," and that would be it. However, in his heart, he knew the sergeant could be right.

"What if I put another couple of men guarding the deserted trail as well? Will that make you happy?"

The gunnery sergeant smiled. "Yes, sir!"

"Okay, let's do it."

It was probably the best decision Witte made while in Vietnam. That night, an entire North Vietnamese company attempted to infiltrate using the old trail. There was quite a fire-fight, and Witte had to call for reinforcements just to drive them back. If he hadn't assigned a few men to guard that trail, they never would have sounded the alarm. He would have lost the eight men he placed on the knoll.

For several years in the early 1990s, Witte was the CEO of a major corporation. We'll call it the Consolidated Electronics Company, or CEC. His record as CEO was spectacular. He was known for making quick decisions and taking immediate action. He was always two steps ahead of his competition, and profits were the highest in the company's history.

Over a period of months, Witte became convinced that vertical integration through acquisition of a company supplying a major component of a new cutting-edge product could have a major impact on CEC's success. CEC was going to introduce the product the following year. Witte felt that if CEC moved quickly, it would take the competitors years to catch up. He thought his expectation through. He made it compelling. He planned how a suitable target for acquisition would be identified and wooed. Then he enthusiastically promoted his expectation to his senior executives. A committee was put together to locate and investigate takeover targets.

At a trade show only a few days later, Witte met the owner of Ace Manufacturing Company, which seemed to be exactly the kind of company he was looking for. The owner was very personable, and by what appeared to be the sheerest of good luck, he was planning on retiring and was looking for an opportunity to sell. The owner gave Ace's financial statements to Witte. Witte couldn't believe his good fortune. He decided to call his committee chairman right away and curtail the committee's efforts. He would immediately enter negotiations to buy Ace.

Witte's committee chairman didn't agree. He thought it was worthwhile to continue to look for alternative companies. He also asked Witte to allow the committee to launch its own investigation of Ace. Witte was hesitant. He felt that to develop an advantage over competitors, CEC would have to move fast. He wanted to close the deal now. But he remembered what he learned from combat — listening and adjusting one's strategy was an important part of declaring your expectations.

"I'll start negotiations with Ace, but we won't sign anything until the committee makes a recommendation. However, I need this recommendation within a week."

Three days later, the committee chairman called Witte. "You can buy the company," he said. "However, the whole market is collapsing for these guys. They don't know about our new product and they're all trying to get out. We've got three other companies lined up for you if this guy doesn't cut a deal, and they're all desperate, so you should be able to buy any one of them for a song." By his own calculations, Neil Witte's decision to listen saved his corporation at least $20 million.

Simon Burrow served as a noncommissioned officer in the army stationed in South Vietnam's Delta area. He didn't carry an M-16 rifle. He was in charge of repairing generators for transportable hospitals. Today Burrow is the founder and CEO of Brandon International — a $20 million company which manufacturers products from small die cut tools to sewn finished goods. Burrow's business cards read "Head Coach."

Says Burrow, "What I learned about leadership and vision from the army isn't obtainable in any university. If you clearly define what you want others to do, and tell them what results you expect and when, you are well on your way to getting things done. Really it's amazing. Once we were asked to produce a small tool to meet IBM specs. We only had a couple of weeks. Neither we, nor anyone else, had ever done it before. But, my troops got the job done. Not the first try. I had to listen and make changes based on feedback from their initial experience.

"The successful people in business are first willing to state their expectations and make decisions. Then, they watch and get feedback from those they lead. If things are not going quite as they should, and this is frequently the case, they aren't afraid to modify these decisions. Leaders who aren't willing to risk adjusting their decisions based on what they learn from listening face certain failure."[38]

WHAT FREDERICK SMITH
DOES AT FEDERAL EXPRESS

The story of how Frederick Smith grew FedEx with a marketing plan that earned a C grade from his professor in college has become a part of business folklore. Less well known is Smith's considerable leadership talent. It's not surprising. Frederick Smith served not one, but two combat tours in Vietnam as a marine corps officer. Early on, a battle-hardened marine sergeant took him aside and told him: "Lieutenant, there's only three things you gotta remember: shoot, move, and communicate."[39] Smith carried the communication advice into business. Declaring his expectations and communicating them helped Smith father a new industry.

When employees meet his expectations, Smith follows through with a dramatic form of declaring his pleasure. New employees are taught that the highest compliment that they can get is "Bravo Zulu!" That's marine-corpsese for "Job well done, your performance rose above the call of duty."

During the big UPS strike, FedEx was swamped with almost a million extra packages every day. Thousands of employees came forward at midnight and on weekends to put in extra time. After it was all over, Smith ordered bonuses and took out full-page newspaper ads congratulating his employees. All ended with the phrase "Bravo Zulu!" Some say it meant more than the bonuses to FedEx workers. Smith knows how to both declare his expectations and reward his followers when these expectations are attained.

BE FAITHFUL TO YOUR EXPECTATIONS

Today, Phillip B. Rooney is vice chairman of ServiceMaster Company, a $4 billion provider of management services. But in 1966 and 1969, Phil was a marine corps combat leader, company commander, and convoy commander in Vietnam. "Setting goals and declaring your expectations have been one of the keys to success in everything I do," he says.[40]

"In the marine corps, it was 'Semper Fideles' — always faithful. It wasn't a matter of sometimes we're going to be faithful, and sometimes not . . . and it wasn't depending on 'which way the wind was blowing.'"[41]

If you want your organization to keep driving towards your goals and vision until they are reached, remember the marines and always be faithful.

SIX IMPORTANT STEPS

You can't get "there" until you know where "there" is. To help your entire organization reach your "theres":

1. Get Your Expectations Clear
2. Make Your Expectations Compelling
3. Develop a Plan
4. Promote Your Expectations and Implement Your Plan
5. Listen to Feedback and Adjust Your Strategy
6. Be Faithful to Your Expectations

Others will follow because they know where to go. You will succeed because you:

DECLARE YOUR EXPECTATIONS

ENDNOTES

[1] Drucker, Peter F., "Leadership: More Than Dash," *Drucker Management* (Spring 1994): 3.

[2] Bill Vlasic, "Can Chrysler Keep It Up?" *Business Week* (November 25, 1996): 108.

[3] Lutz, Robert A., letter to the author, October 16, 1997.

[4] Crichton, Theodore P., telephone interview with the author, July 12, 1996.

[5] Elstrom, Peter, "Casey Cowell's Modem Operandi," *Business Week* (November 11, 1996): 104, 107.

[6] Cox, Hugh L., III, letter to the author, August 6, 1993.

[7] Spence, Clyde W., Jr, letter to the author, July 24, 1993.

[8] McWilliams, Gary, "The Quiet Man Who's Jolting Utilities," *Business Week* (June 9, 1997): 85.

[9] Lay, Kenneth L., letter to the author, November 17, 1997.

[10] La Franco, Robert, "The Tightest Man in Show Business?" *Forbes* (November 8, 1994): 67–75.

[11] Thomas, B., *Walt Disney* (New York: Simon and Schuster, 1976), 218.

[12] Freiberg, Kevin, and Jackie Freiberg, *Nuts!* (Austin, Bard Press, 1996), 49.

[13] Mackmull, Jack V., letter to the author, July 30, 1993.

[14] Sullivan, G. Craig, letter to the author, October 22, 1997.

[15] *The Clorox Company 1997 Annual Report*, 1.

[16] Hamilton, Joan O'C., "Brighter Days at Clorox," *Business Week* (June 16, 1997): 62.

[17] *The Clorox Company 1997 Annual Report*, 5.

[18] Peters, Tom, and Nancy Austin, *A Passion for Excellence* (New York: Random House, 1985), 48.

[19] Creech, Bill, *The Five Pillars of TQM* (New York: Truman Talley Books/Dutton, 1994), 455.

[20] Gaines, Charles, *Yours in Perfect Manhood: Charles Atlas* (New York: Simon & Schuster, 1982), 69.

[21] Zlatoper, R. J., telephone interview with the author, January 7, 1998.

[22] Hansen, Mark Victor, speech, Crystal Cathedral, Garden Grove, California, November 10, 1997.

[23] Payne, Don H., letter to the author, July 31, 1993.

[24] "Sparking a Cultural Revolution at Sears Roebuck," *PR Central,* Internet: www.prcentral.com, 4.

[25] Lieber, Ronald B., "Sears Tells the Inside Stories," *Fortune* (June 9, 1997): 165.

[26] Bolduc, Lucien E., Jr., letter to the author, October 3, 1993.

[27] Lay, Kenneth L. Ibid.

[28] Lieb, Richard, telephone interview with the author, Feb. 2, 1998.

[29] McDermott, Michael J., "Boeing's Modern Approach," *Profiles* (September 1996): 41, 44.

[30] "A Conglomerate Seeks a Coherent Identity," *PR Central,* Internet: www.prcentral.com, 5.

[31] Ibid., 3.

[32] Mead, Dana, telephone interview with the author, November 19, 1997.

[33] Palmeri, Christopher, "Back on Course," *Forbes* (August 28, 1995): 48.

[34] "A Conglomerate Seeks a Coherent Identity," PR Central, Internet: www.prcentral.com, 5.

[35] Mead, Dana, Op. Cit.

[36] Bartmann, William, telephone interview with the author, October 28, 1997.

[37] Sharman, Graham, "Nobody Calls Me General Anymore!" *McKinsey Quarterly* no. 3 (1996): 113.

[38] Burrow, Simon, telephone interview with the author, Jan. 13, 1998.

[39] Grant, Linda, "Why FedEx is Flying High," *Fortune* (November 10, 1997): 158, 160.

[40] Rooney, Phillip B., letter to the author, January 30, 1998.

[41] Rooney, Phillip B., quoted in Donlon, J. P.,"No Triumphs, No Drums," *Chief Executive* (December 1997): 69.

SHOW UNCOMMON COMMITMENT

In case of doubt, push on just a little further and then keep on pushing.
— GEN. GEORGE S. PATTON, JR.

George "Pat" Patterson was still a young lieutenant in flying school when the Korean War broke out. After being liberated from Japan at the end of World War II, Korea had been divided into Communist and non-Communist halves. On June 25, 1950, Communist North Korea suddenly invaded South Korea with the aim of unifying the country under its rule. The U.S.-backed South Korean army and air force were little prepared for the onslaught, and American troops were rushed to their aid.

As soon as Pat finished flying school, the air force sent him to the Eighth Fighter-Bomber Group in Korea flying the F-80 Shooting Star, America's first operational jet fighter.

Patterson learned something about the power of showing uncommon commitment on his hundredth mission. He was assigned duties as group lead. "We were to hit the bridges on the Yalu connecting China with North Korea. It was the farthest north in Korea I had ever been," Pat said. He would be leading the entire group of three squadrons over distances and terrain that he himself had never flown. Moreover, the weather was forecast to be marginal, with low visibility on the way to the target and uncertainty about whether they would be able to see bridges at all.

Once they took off, Pat discovered that the weather situation was even worse than forecast. They had no navigational aids, and the clouds were so thick that they saw the ground only infrequently. The thirty-six aircraft in Pat's squadrons sometimes couldn't see each other. Many might have aborted the mission. However, taking out the bridges was critical. Over them flowed the weapons and munitions used to supply a numerically superior enemy. As group lead, it was Pat's call.

"I'm sure at least a few of the pilots would have been just as happy if I had made the decision to turn back," Pat remembers. "The weather increased the risks considerably, and we might get to the target area and still not be able to find the bridges. Still, it was worth the risk because of the tremendous problems our troops faced on the ground." As they flew on, the other pilots realized just how committed Pat was to completing the mission, and it strengthened their own resolve.

"I flew a heading I had already planned on the ground," Patterson continues. "If the winds didn't change too much, and we maintained the airspeed I had previously calculated on the ground, we should get to the target area on schedule. Unfortunately, our navigation was made more difficult because we sometimes had to alter course due to poor weather conditions."

But good fortune smiled on Pat that day. Leading the first four aircraft in the lead flight, he broke out of the clouds not far from the target. "I've got the bridges at eleven o'clock!" shouted Pat's wingman over the intercom.

"I was very much relieved," Pat says. "Now there was no question about whether we had flown all this way for nothing. The bridges were in plain sight, and we could hit them." He led the first of four aircraft in a diving attack. Despite the fire of antiaircraft guns, his flight dropped their bombs accurately on the target and knocked one span down.

Banking sharply to the left and then back to the right as they climbed to avoid antiaircraft fire in a maneuver known as "jinking," Pat thought his lead flight's work was done and they could go home. He was wrong.

"As we began to re-form out of the effective range of the antiaircraft guns, we saw enemy Mig-15 fighters approaching rapidly. We barely had the fuel to return to base and we were no match for the Migs. Moreover, combat maneuvering would eat up more fuel. However, if we didn't fight the Migs, the rest of the group would be in serious trouble. They would attack our guys just as they rolled in on the target. I had to make an immediate decision. If I stayed to fight, I would be betting the safe return of our four aircraft against our ability to fly through the weather and land safely with minimum fuel."

Instead of fleeing, he turned his four airplanes to intercept the Migs. At the same time, he alerted American F-86 Sabres, which were flying top cover nearby. Then he warned his other F-80s that were just entering the target area. Pat's men knew that in delaying their return, their chances of getting back safely were diminished. However, because he was extraordinarily committed, so were they.

"We opened fire while the Migs were still out of range. The Migs scattered and their leader made a very bad decision. They flew straight up . . . right into the waiting guns of the F-86s."

Pat's job in the target area was finally over. However, his problems were not. "I could hardly keep my eyes off the fuel gauges all the way home. I knew it would be a close thing. In fact, my entire flight 'flamed out' from lack of fuel either on the runway or while taxiing in," he said.

Pat couldn't have had a closer call. A "flame-out" means that a jet's engines quit running because there is no more fuel to burn. All four aircraft had to be towed back to the parking area.[1]

What made the entire group follow Pat's lead, despite the risks? Good air discipline — that is, instantly obeying a commander's orders in the air — is only part of the answer. The whole answer is that Pat never wavered in his mission to destroy the bridges and save American lives. When the leader shows uncommon commitment, others will do the same. They will follow.

Napoleon Bonaparte knew this truth. In his *Maxims* he declared: "An extraordinary situation calls for extraordinary resolution. . . . How many things have appeared impossible which, nevertheless, have been done by resolute men? . . ."[2]

DOES THIS UNIVERSAL LAW WORK IN BUSINESS?

"Okay," you say, "if the leader shows uncommon commitment in battle, it motivates. Followers echo the commitment of the leader and the organization has a much better chance of performing the task successfully. But that's not going to work in business where people have distractions, such as their families, earning a living, or just having a good time. People in business have to know they must perform or else! The leader's showing uncommon commitment has nothing to do with it." Well, let's wait and see. It's my contention that uncommon commitment motivates not only followers, but others with whom the leader comes in contact. This includes bosses, associates, moneylenders, and others far removed from the leader's own organization. As we will see, Patterson's uncommon commitment to a project outside the air force helped him achieve what others thought impossible.

GEORGE PATTERSON SHOWS UNCOMMON COMMITMENT IN THE BUSINESS WORLD

Eventually Patterson became a general, retired from military service, and became president of Ohio Precision Castings. The company contracted to supply a new type of fuel pump for the then new B-1 bomber. Several million dollars and many jobs were on the line.

"Molding these new pumps was no easy task," Pat explains. "It had never been done before. No matter how carefully the molders worked, many of the pumps did not meet the specifications. There were so many rejects that we got behind schedule and were losing money. I was pretty worried."

Pat could have renegotiated the contract. He could have asked for a delay. He could have scaled back the number of units he was required to supply. All these alternatives would have meant profitability but would have hurt the company's reputation. It would have delayed production of the B-1. It would also have meant laying off some of his workers.

Instead, Pat put everyone to work as they had never worked before. "I met repeatedly with the production crews and engineers. Everyone got into the spirit of solving the problem. I knew there had to be a solution and we tried all sorts of crazy things."

Pat's employees took note of his commitment. They saw he wasn't going to quit. So they didn't either. As his followers had done years earlier in the clouded skies over North Korea, they stuck with their leader. Finally, Pat's experts found something interesting. Since they were dealing with a single molding material, normally the formula and molding temperature for each part of the pump would be the same for all. Only the shape of the part varied. This time this uniformity wasn't working. What if they changed the formula and temperature to optimize it for each separate part?

This seemed to be the answer. But there was still a problem. It was not clear that developing and simultaneously using so many different casting formulas was possible. It had never been done before. Some of Pat's people thought they could not succeed. One said, "Well boss, I guess this means we've got to renegotiate the contract?"

Pat thought otherwise. He kept at it. Everyone was obsessed with finding a solution. The employees not only worked overtime, they worked night and day. Eventually they discovered the correct formula for each separate casting. "We posted it near the molding production machine for each part," Pat said. Molding each part differently was possible. The number of rejects began to decline.

Then they ran into yet another problem. Pat's engineers found that air contacting the exterior of the aluminum molds caused the molding temperature to vary. Varying temperature caused minor differences in the parts — minor, but out of tolerance again. Consultants said that nothing could be done. They said that air always leaked around the exterior of the mold to some degree. "The specifications required are just too tough," they maintained.

Pat wouldn't give up. Because he wouldn't give up, his workers wouldn't give up. Because he was totally committed, so were his employees. "Finally, somebody came up with the idea of using ordinary plastic Saran Wrap to stop the air from escaping," Pat says. "We tried it, and believe it or not it worked."

Pat's company got back on schedule and delivered the pumps on time. The company not only made a good profit and kept its reputation, but Pat's employees kept their jobs.[3]

Why don't more leaders in business show this kind of determination? Maybe they are afraid of failure or distracted by office politics or an upcoming vacation. The reason for this shortcoming is unimportant. The universal law says "show uncommon commitment," and if you want success, you had better obey it. Jacques Naviaux is Director of Business Planning at Hughes Aircraft Company and a retired marine corps colonel who fought in combat in Vietnam. "In all too many circumstances, civilian leadership has been reluctant to make the extraordinary commitment required for sustained success," he says.[4]

FROM NOWHERE TO NO. 1
IN CYBERSPACE IN SIX MONTHS

Over a six-month period, Dell Computer Corp. became the number one retailer on the World Wide Web. Sales from the Dell Web site are growing at the rate of 20 percent each month and are currently at $1 million a day. In one year, revenues exploded 47 percent to $7.8 billion, and profits soared 91 percent to $518 million.

What's Dell's secret? Founder and CEO Michael Dell says, "Speed is everything in this business. We're setting the pace for the industry."[5] Michael Dell shows such uncommon commitment to what the company calls "velocity" that his competitors simply haven't been able to catch up. At the same time, he's structured speed to translate into lower cost.

First, Dell employs its own brand of just-in-time manufacturing. Dell doesn't even start putting the computers together until an order is booked. And it doesn't begin to order parts until right before assembly. As a result, Dell's components are on the average sixty days newer than those of competitors. Just-in-time manufacturing saves inventory costs and saves money when component prices fall, as happens so often and so rapidly in the computer world.

Next Michael Dell speeds up his distribution channels. He's got many of his suppliers warehousing parts only fifteen minutes from the production line. He doesn't have monitors delivered to Dell to be shipped with the PCs to the customer. Instead, when he gets an order, Dell e-mails the order to the monitor supplier. The supplier ships the monitor directly to the customer, and it arrives at the same time as the computer. More money saved. For high-cost items, he's switched to regional suppliers. That saves more time.

Since customers order over the Internet, Dell not only gets his products to the customer fast, he converts the average sale to cash in less than twenty-four hours. Compaq Computer Corp. sells mainly through dealers. It takes thirty-five days for the company to get its money. Even Gateway 2000, which sells by mail, takes 16.4 days. No wonder Andrew Grove, Intel's CEO, says: "I have bruises on my back from Mr. Michael [Dell] when we can't keep up with them."[6] But Michael Dell doesn't run around converting this cash at the bank himself or driving a truck transporting his product from warehouse to the delivery service. Like any leader, he gets his work done through others. In Dell's case, he has 10,350 employees supporting him. Dell developed the strategy of "velocity" and led its implementation. But it is his absolute commitment to this concept that motivates his employees to an equal commitment to get the job done in a way that has won the respect of customers and competitors alike.[7]

HISTORICAL MILITARY LEADERS
TOOK A "BULLDOG APPROACH"

You don't have to read much military history to see that successful leaders in battle are extraordinarily committed to their jobs. This goes far beyond simple determination to succeed. The successful leader lives, breathes, sleeps, and eats his mission. After the project, task, or mission is completed, the leader can relax. This leadership principle does not require the leader to be a workaholic. As a matter of fact, it is interesting that these extraordinary leaders do have so much time for friends, family, and recreation when not completing an important task.

But, as explained by retired army brigadier general Edward Markham, director of Management Information Systems in Lubbock, Texas: "A leader must take a bulldog approach to accomplish the mission."[8]

In 216 B.C. at Cannae, Hannibal looked at Roman forces outnumbering his own by almost four to one. He took a bulldog approach. "We will either find a way, or make one," he said. He inflicted the most decisive defeat in the history of warfare on the Romans. Almost 80 percent of the formerly superior Roman force was left dead on the field of battle.

Fighting in the Carolinas during the Revolutionary War, Maj. Gen. Nathanael Greene also demonstrated this kind of commitment. "We fight, get beat, rise, and fight again," he wrote. During the Civil War, General Grant wrote Lincoln, "I propose to fight it out on this line, if it takes all summer." Little wonder that Grant was the first Union general about whom Robert E. Lee, commander of the Confederate Army of Northern Virginia, expressed concern.

BATTLE LEADERS POINT THE WAY IN SOMALIA

American forces were sent to Mogadishu, Somalia, as peacekeepers. Master Serg. Gary Gordon and Serg. First Class Randall

Shughart were part of Task Force Ranger and the U.S. Army Special Operations Command. Ranger leaders have a history of showing uncommon commitment going back to the French and Indian Wars of the eighteenth century. An army saying is, if you want a job done, you give it to the Rangers, because their commitment is 110 percent.

On October 3, 1993, two American helicopters crashed and were subjected to intense fire from automatic weapons and rocket-propelled grenades from hostile forces. Sergeants Gordon and Shughart learned that friendly ground forces were not in position to rescue four critically wounded personnel in the helicopter at the second crash site. Both sergeants repeatedly volunteered to go to the aid of the wounded Americans. This was far from easy. A huge and growing number of attackers were closing in on the crash site. There was no way of breaking through directly. The sergeants had to be inserted from the air. They finally received permission, but due to the heavy fire, the first attempts to get the two soldiers to the crashed helicopter failed.

Eventually they successfully landed about three hundred feet south of the downed helicopter. Equipped only with small arms, they fought their way to the wounded Americans and pulled them from the wreckage. They set up a perimeter around the wounded to protect them from the hostile forces firing at them. Because these two leaders were totally committed, so was everyone else.

An American force eventually broke through and rescued the wounded crewmen. Unfortunately, it was too late for the two leaders. They had run out of ammunition and both had been fatally wounded.[9] Their sacrifice was not in vain. Their heroism led other Americans "peacekeeping" in Somalia to adopt a far higher standard of commitment to their mission. When Americans withdrew from Somalia, they had succeeded in intimidating the warring factions and in preventing the starvation of millions of the country's inhabitants.

THE MILITARY'S UNLIMITED LIABILITY CLAUSE

Gen. Sir John Hackett of the British army declared that members of the military profession have an unwritten unlimited liability clause in their work contracts. By this clause they are required to accomplish their assigned mission even if it is necessary to lay down their own lives to do so. No such "clause" exists in the contracts of any other professionals. Businesspeople are not expected to give up their lives for their companies, nor should they be. It is not the physical act of sacrificing one's life that all leaders should strive to emulate. Rather it is the spiritual commitment to do everything ethical that can be done to accomplish a task. With this spiritual commitment, a magic takes place between leaders and followers, and those who follow adopt the leader's determination toward the task as well.

THE MAGIC OF SHOWING UNCOMMON COMMITMENT

What's so special about showing uncommon commitment? Why do others follow a leader who demonstrates this quality both on and off the battlefield? Psychologists have identified two main reasons why showing uncommon commitment yields such dramatic results:

1. It proves that the goal is worthwhile and really important.
2. It proves that the leader isn't going to quit.

OTHERS FOLLOW BECAUSE THEY KNOW THE GOAL IS IMPORTANT

People don't exert themselves for little, unimportant goals. They work hard, take great risks, and let nothing stop them only for big, important goals. That's why leaders who try to play down the difficulty of a task make a big mistake. Successful battle leaders know that it is far better to tell people exactly what is expected of them, no matter how serious the situation or how much effort it would require. "Then, you've got to hold everyone, including yourself, responsible for their own actions, and accept nothing less than their best effort," says Walter "Buz" Baxter, currently president of Baxter Seed Company of Weslaco, Texas, and formerly a major general in the air force.[10] That's the essence of showing uncommon commitment.

During the darkest days of World War II, Winston Churchill told his countrymen, "I have nothing to offer you but blood, sweat, toil, and tears." Churchill was 100 percent committed, and the English people knew it. Showing uncommon commitment is how one proves that the goal is important enough to sacrifice for it.

OTHERS FOLLOW BECAUSE THEY KNOW THE LEADER WON'T QUIT

People won't follow you if they think that your commitment is temporary, or that you may quit the goal short of attainment. Why should they? Why should they invest their time, money, lives, or fortune in something if the leader isn't going to lead them there anyway? Others will only follow when they are convinced that you won't quit no matter how difficult the task looks, or no matter what obstacles you encounter along the way.

There will always be obstacles. Someone said, "There are no dreams without dragons." When you show uncommon commitment, followers know that their investment of time and effort won't be wasted. They know that you won't walk away . . . that you will see the task through to the end. Yes, there may be dragons. But your uncommon commitment gives everyone confidence that with you, they can, and will, slay those dragons.

W. H. Tankersley is vice chairman of the board of directors of Sterne, Agee & Leach, Inc., investment bankers in Montgomery, Alabama. He previously served as Deputy Assistant Secretary of Defense and was a rifle and mortar platoon leader in combat in Korea. He continued to serve in the army reserve and retired as a major general. His advice: "If you want to inspire confidence in those you lead, you've got to have the commitment which expresses itself in physical and moral courage, and display both." Do this, and those you lead will know that you won't quit."[11]

If your followers are convinced that the goal is important and that you are not going to quit until you reach that goal, then watch out! There is nothing they won't do to show you that their commitment is equal to yours, and nothing will stop them until they reach that goal or accomplish that task with you.

HOW TO SHOW UNCOMMON COMMITMENT

No matter what organization you lead, you can show uncommon commitment with these five techniques:

1. Meet with Your Followers Face to Face
2. Make a Public Commitment
3. Keep Going When the Going Gets Rough

4. When the Situation Is Impossible, Think Outside the Box
5. Accept the Risk that Goes with Commitment

GIDEON'S FACE-TO-FACE MEETING GETS THREE HUNDRED MEN TO ATTACK AN ARMY

When the Israelites fought their enemies more than three thousand years ago, Gideon led by showing uncommon commitment. In his battle against the Midianites at the Hill of Moreh, he faced a vast, numerically superior enemy. We don't know exactly how many, but Judges tells us, "And the Midianites and the Amalekites and all the children of the east lay along in the valley like grasshoppers for multitude; and their camels were without number, as the sand by the sea side for multitude." Suffice it to say that Gideon and his troops were greatly outnumbered, because the Bible does tell us that Gideon led but three hundred Israelites into battle.

However, Gideon heard a dream repeated in which the Lord promised him victory. He was committed to that dream and that victory. He did not sit back and issue orders through a chain of command. Instead, he met face to face with his three hundred soldiers himself. He said to his small company, "Arise, for the Lord hath delivered into your hand the host of Midian." By explaining to his soldiers the unique tactics they would use and why they were going to win, he gained their commitment.

Gideon divided his small group into three units and issued a trumpet, lamp, and empty earthen pitcher to each fighter. He told them that they would attack at night with each unit approaching the enemy camp from a different direction. They would use their pitchers to cover the light from their lamps. On his signal, every man would uncover his lamp, blow his trumpet, and shout, "The sword of the Lord, and of Gideon."

When the Israelites completely surrounded the camp, Gideon gave the signal. Completely surrounded by torchlights, shouts, and trumpets, the Midianites thought they had been surprised and surrounded by a large Hebrew army. They panicked. In their confusion they fought and slew each other. You can analyze this famous battle in many ways and describe many reasons for Gideon's victory. But it would be difficult to overlook Gideon's showing of uncommon commitment based on his faith during his face-to-face meeting with his small force.

SHE'S NOT THE GRINCH, BUT SHE GOT THEM TO GIVE UP CHRISTMAS BY MEETING FACE TO FACE

Grace Pastiak works for Tellabs in Lisle, Illinois. Tellabs designs, makes, and markets expensive telecommunications products. When Grace was director of manufacturing, her department won a major contract. The only problem was that it was the holiday season, and the job had to be completed by the end of the year.

Grace always took pride in her group's ability to take on any job and complete it successfully. So did her group. But now, she faced a dilemma. Accepting this job would mean time away from families during the holidays. Yet the contract was very important. She did not want to turn it down. Pastiak knew that she needed the full support of her workers. But how could she get it without arousing resentment?

Grace did something she had never done before. She called her employees together and explained all the facts face to face. She told them the job had to be completed by the end of the year. She told them it would involve time away from home at Christmas and New Year's. They would be able to attend religious services, but that was about it. She said that the job was so important that they were going to take the contract. To this, she was committed. However, because of the extent of the sacrifice necessary, they would help make the decision. There were alternatives. She offered several. They could contract to do only half the order before the deadline. They could bring part-time labor in. Or they could subcontract some of the production to other companies. She told them again that she wanted to take the whole contract and accept the deadline as they had always done. But it was their choice.

Giving her workers a choice on how to do the job proved that this was not a regular job order and was extremely important. Grace's workers voted to take the full contract and not to bring in part-time workers or to subcontract any of the work. The contract was completed during the holiday season without difficulty. Is it any wonder that subordinates and superiors alike call her "Amazing Grace"?[12]

MAKING A PUBLIC COMMITMENT WITH NO POSSIBILITY OF RETREAT SAVES ENGLAND

Many people don't realize it, but Winston Churchill, one of the greatest politicians in history, started out in life as a soldier. In fact, he graduated from Sandhurst, one of England's national military academies, and served in combat during World War I.

For British soldiers and politicians, the situation looked very dark after the fall of France in the early part of World War II. England stood alone and outnumbered against Nazi Germany. Hitler planned to invade England in an operation called "Sea Lion." Many, including Hitler, thought that Churchill would negotiate an end to the war on German terms before this happened.

Prime Minister Winston Churchill then addressed Parliament. Churchill said, "We shall not flag or fail. We shall go on to the end, we shall fight in France, we shall fight in the seas and oceans, we shall fight with growing confidence, and growing strength in the air, we shall defend our island, whatever the cost may be, we shall fight on the beaches, we shall fight on the landing grounds, we shall fight in the fields and in the streets, we shall fight in the hills; we shall never surrender."

Churchill's public declaration allowed no room for retreat. It dramatized his intention to continue regardless of the outcome. Because of Churchill's uncommon commitment, the English came together and faced the future and their hardships with confidence. Hitler thought twice. His confidence was shaken, and he postponed and eventually abandoned his plans to invade England. Churchill's public announcement of his bulldog commitment at this time of extreme trial and danger was one of crucial junctures of the war.

As we will see, making a public commitment from which there is no retreat and which dramatizes your intention to continue regardless of the outcome works in business and other pursuits as well.

THE MAN WHOSE PUBLIC COMMITMENT CHANGED CELLULAR PHONES FOREVER

Irwin Jacobs, chairman of Qualcomm, Inc., cofounded his company to develop products for digital wireless technology in 1985. U.S. industry had adopted a system known as time-division multiple access (TDMA) as its digital standard. It had greater reliability than other systems, and reliability was considered the most important factor.

Jacobs stubbornly developed his products based on a less popular system called code-division multiple access (CDMA), which depended on compression technology. Jacobs was convinced his system had far greater potential because of its increased access capacity. No wishy-washy "definite maybes" for Jacobs. He declared to everyone that this was the way they were going to proceed. He made a public commitment both inside and outside of his company and continued to base his products on CDMA regardless of development setbacks and criticism. He was so committed that his followers stayed with the company, even though some outsiders said that Jacobs was nuts.

Four years later, Jacobs approached the Cellular Telephone Industries Association (CTIA) to present his concepts. He had gotten compression technology working reliably, but his timing could hardly have been worse. The CTIA had just completed its own internal fight over standards and technologies. The main competitor to TDMA was the general standard for mobile communications (GSM), the European standard. Jacobs's CDMA had not even been considered. The fight had been bitter, but TDMA had finally prevailed. That's when Jacobs "wandered in" with his proposal that they now consider CDMA again. CTIA would waste no time listening to Jacobs's presentation. According to Jacobs, "They threw us out on our ears."[13]

But Jacobs didn't quit. He publicly claimed his compression technology would increase a network's capacity many times more than competing systems. He showed uncommon commitment while the entire industry ridiculed him and belittled his development. His supporters didn't desert him.

After two more years of struggle, he convinced the wireless division of Pacific Telesis to put up $2 million to build a trial network in San Diego. The results of the trial convinced the CTIA to do something it had hoped to avoid. It reopened the standards debate. Two years later, CTIA approved CDMA as a second standard.

Contrary to helping Qualcomm's interest, reopening the standards debate almost caused the roof to fall in on Irwin Jacobs and his company. Several corporations had already sunk millions into TDMA. They viciously attacked CDMA as too expensive, too complicated, and susceptible to jamming. Moreover, Jacobs was personally branded a fraud.

However when you show such uncommon commitment,

certain others keep supporting you. Despite everything, two companies, Northern Telecom Ltd. and Motorola, agreed to license Qualcomm's CDMA technology. Actually, their licensing didn't amount to much. They were simply covering their bets in case CDMA was real. However this was a success of sorts for Qualcomm, and with it, Jacobs went to Asia to look for more business. His detractors tried everything to prevent additional sales. Letters were sent to likely prospects warning of CDMA's problems and suggesting that Jacob's claims couldn't be believed and that CDMA be subject to the closest scrutiny.

But objective testing began to support Jacobs's claims. Then came a major sales breakthrough. Major carriers of digital wireless, including PrimeCo and Sprint PCS signed on to use CDMA technology. However even these adoptions created a problem. No one made CDMA handsets, and Sprint and PrimeCo needed tens of thousands. What to do now?

Not to worry. Jacobs didn't falter. He convinced Sony to put up 49 percent of the funds needed for a joint phone-making venture. Qualcomm was now in the cellular phone-making business with a hefty multimillion-dollar order for Qualcomm phones, a product they hadn't even previously considered.

Unfortunately for Qualcomm, success still did not come without problems. There is a learning curve in manufacturing, and companies that have only been in the research development business invariably find they have lots of new challenges.

Jacobs tried desperately to meet a delivery deadline for Sprint. He succeeded, but a Qualcomm shipment of thousands of phones was halfway across the country when someone suddenly discovered that each and every phone had a defective menu screen. The truck had to turn around and speed back to Qualcomm's plant in San Diego for rapid reprogramming.

That wasn't all. Ten days before PrimeCo's national rollout of the phones, someone tried one of the buttons on a Qualcomm phone. An ear-piercing screech nearly deafened him. A second phone yielded the same results. And then a third. Testing uncovered the problem. It was in the software. Every single phone was affected. They all had deafening screeches. With forty thousand phones already shipped, it was too late to ship them back to San Diego. Engineers flew out to PrimeCo's Florida warehouse with a just-in-time fix. It took four days to reprogram all forty thousand phones with help from every set of hands they could find to turn screws, open up the phones, and make changes. Again, they managed, just barely, to make the deadline.

However despite all the problems, showing uncommon commitment has its rewards. Today 57 percent of the new-generation wireless systems built will use Jacobs's CDMA technology. Qualcomm revenues doubled last year to $814 million, with projections in excess of $2 billion this year.[14] Irwin Jacobs, chairman of Qualcomm is still committed to his technology. And because he is, so is everyone else in his company.

ONE GENERAL CONTINUED TOWARD HIS GOAL; ANOTHER IS ALMOST FORGOTTEN

It is interesting to contrast the careers of two Civil War generals. One probably saved the Union. The other general was brilliant, but few who are not historians or have not studied military history know much about him today. That's because when the going got rough, one kept going. He showed those who followed him that he wasn't going to quit, and he did this by continuing toward his goal in spite of all obstacles. The other general barely began any real fighting at all.

The brilliant general was George B. McClellan. He graduated second in his class from West Point. Newspapers in the North called him "the Young Napoleon," and President Lincoln gave him command of the Army of the Potomac, the largest and most important Union Army. But brilliant as he was, McClellan simply could not show commitment. He frequently could not bring himself to attack General Lee and the Confederate Army of Northern Virginia when Lee put up the slightest resistance. McClellan had twice the numerical strength of his adversary on several occasions, but still he refused to attack. He asked for yet more troops. Prior to the Battle of Antietam, McClellan actually received a copy of General Lee's battle plan. It showed that Lee had dangerously split his army into separate parts. It was an almost unbelievable opportunity to attack each wing in sequence and destroy both. However McClellan was more afraid of losing than he was committed to winning. He failed to act. In frustration, President Lincoln removed him from command. Later, he gave him another chance, and when it was clear that he still wasn't sufficiently committed to fight, Lincoln finally removed him permanently.

The other man also graduated from West Point, but he was

only an average student. He left the army and went into the dry goods business. At the beginning of the war, he wrote to Major General McClellan asking for a commission as a colonel. He never got an answer. Eventually he gained command of a volunteer regiment from his home state of Illinois. They sent him west. He did well and was promoted to brigadier general. He continued doing well and won many battles. He was promoted to major general.

Meanwhile Lincoln had tried general after general as supreme commander. Each had fought Lee in battle, lost, and retreated to Washington. Eventually Lincoln called on this general from the West who was so successful. Critics said he drank too much. "Get me the name of his brand," ordered Lincoln, "so that I can send it to all my generals."

Lincoln promoted Ulysses S. Grant to lieutenant general and made him general in chief. Rebel general James "Old Pete" Longstreet had been a good friend of Grant's before the war. He had even been Grant's best man at his marriage.

"What do you think of this fellow Grant?" asked Lee of Longstreet. "Try as I might, I cannot remember him at all from Mexico." (They had served together in the Mexican War.)

Longstreet made a wry face and answered, "General Lee, we're in for some trouble. Grant won't quit."

The first battle between Grant and Lee was the Battle of the Wilderness. General Lee defeated General Grant. When Lee defeated a Union general in the past, he could relax. The Union general always retreated. However General Grant was different. He knew the value of showing uncommon commitment to his troops. To do this, he must assess the situation and be willing to take risks.

The Unusual Route of General Grant's "Retreat"

As the Union troops retreated out of the thick woods from which the Battle of the Wilderness got its name, they followed a road that led to an open area. Here they saw a bearded general, his stars affixed to a private's uniform. He was sitting astride his horse and smoking a cigar. He motioned with the cigar toward another road. Although they took the road that the general indicated, they were amazed, for it led back into the Wilderness again. The bearded general waving the cigar, of course, was their general in chief, General Grant. He continued to press the Army of Northern Virginia without letting up.

Grant showed uncommon commitment over and over again. His troops said that when they saw the example set by him, they were ashamed to do less. A year later, Lee surrendered to Grant at Appomattox. Congress voted to make Grant the first full four-star general since Washington.

HOW RAY KROC BUILT THE WORLD'S BEST-KNOWN HAMBURGER FRANCHISE

Only a handful of entrepreneurs can claim to have actually changed the American way of life. Ray Kroc is one of them. He revolutionized American buying habits. He created such concepts as food service automation, franchising, and shared national training and advertising, and he made the concepts work. From a single outlet started by the McDonald brothers in San Bernardino, California, Kroc built a business with annual sales in the billions of dollars.

Along the way, Ray Kroc did an awful lot right. But as he himself contended, his biggest secret was simply that he was uncommonly committed and kept continuing toward his goal no matter what. In fact, the title of his book says it all. It's called *Grinding It Out*. In it, he states that the key element in the success of McDonald's could be found in his favorite quotation. It comes from former president Calvin Coolidge.

"Press on. Nothing in the world can take the place of persistence. Talent will not; nothing is more common than unsuccessful men with talent. Genius will not; unrewarded genius is almost a proverb. Education will not; the world is full of educated derelicts. Persistence and determination alone are omnipotent."[15]

As we will see, persistence and showing uncommon commitment go hand in hand.

THE $350-A-WEEK MAN WHO GOT EVERYONE TO HELP HIM MAKE $1,800,000

General Grant had the authority of military law to enforce his orders. "Leading in civilian life is a lot different," you may think. An executive in a company doesn't have that kind of authority. Leading informal teams, such as those popular in the quality movement, is especially hard. Most decisions can only be made with the consent of others. Similarly, others lead teams in "matrix organizations." The leader controls the budget for the program, but the people who work on the program don't report to the leader. They report to a functional manager. In both situations, leading is harder because the leader has limited authority.

However, there is a leadership situation that is even more challenging — when the leader has no authority at all — in fact, he doesn't even have a formal organization. Let me tell you about my friend, Joe Cossman. He and I wrote a book together several years ago called *Making It!*

During World War II, Cossman served in the Combat Engineers in Europe. After the war, with no formal education, he got a job working for an import company in Pittsburgh, Pennsylvania. His pay, in today's dollars, was $350 a week. On this small paycheck, Joe supported himself, his wife, and a baby daughter.

Joe was committed to a vision of success. "I bought an old typewriter and used my kitchen table as an office every evening after supper. Every night I studied the newspaper, looking for scarce commodities. Then I offered these products through the mail to prospects overseas."

For a year, he stretched pennies, skipped meals, and worked part time at his kitchen table. "I was beginning to get discouraged," he said. "Then one day I saw a small classified ad in the *New York Times*. It was for laundry soap, which was then in short supply. As I had several times before, I answered the ad, got samples, and sent them to several overseas contacts. Almost by return mail, I got an order with a letter of credit for $1,800,000!"

The letter of credit said that a New York bank would pay him $1,800,000 as soon as he gave them bills of lading. These are documents showing that the product is on a ship bound for the buyer. There was a deadline. The bills of lading had to be presented to his bank within thirty days, or the letter of credit would be worthless.

SHOWING UNCOMMON COMMITMENT GETS AN IMPOSSIBLE LEAVE OF ABSENCE

Cossman went to see his boss and asked for a leave of absence. The boss told him it was impossible . . . this was their busiest season. Recalled Cossman, "I didn't want to quit my $350-a-week job. But somebody had to make a trip to New York to close the deal. I asked almost everyone I knew in Pittsburgh to go for me. I even offered them half of the profits. All said 'no.'"

Finally, Joe Cossman went to his boss again. "You can fire me if you want, but I must have a leave of absence," said Joe. His boss saw his commitment. This time, the boss said yes. Joe withdrew his life savings from the bank. It was less than twenty-five hundred dollars today. Then he left for New York.

UNCOMMON COMMITMENT WINS OVER TELEPHONE OPERATORS DURING A STRIKE

"When I got to New York, I telephoned the man who ran the ad. The man didn't own a single bar of soap! He had put the ad in the paper on speculation and sent samples he had bought in a store." Joe went to the library and got names and addresses of every soap manufacturer in the United States. The next day he locked himself in his hotel room. There was a telephone strike, so it took fifteen minutes before he finally got an operator. He told the operator his story. He had page after page of telephone numbers to call. His uncommon commitment persuaded the operator to help him. The operator promised to keep Joe on the line until he made all his calls.

After fifty calls, Joe fell into bed exhausted. "When the sun came up, I began again. I had to tell my story all over again to the new operator. She also stayed with me to help me make my calls." When a leader is really committed, followers rarely quit.

At noon, he finally hit paydirt. He found a company in Alabama that had laundry soap. Joe had a telephone bill of eighty-one hundred dollars, but he had located the product.

"I was so excited, I told them I would fly to Alabama that afternoon. They told me to save my money. Their corporate offices were only a few blocks away in Rockefeller Center."

UNCOMMON COMMITMENT CONVINCES TWO COMPANY PRESIDENTS

Joe ran all the way to Rockefeller Center. Before long he was telling the story to the president of the soap company. He completed the deal with no cash, but with his inexperience, he made a mistake. Joe took delivery of the soap in Alabama. He had to find some way of getting the soap to New York.

"I began pounding the pavements of New York. I looked for someone that would loan me thirty trucks and drivers on credit. It took two days. I finally found a president of a trucking company willing to take his trucks to Alabama even though I had no money to pay in advance."

Joe no longer had a cent to his name. During the trip he borrowed money for meals from the truck drivers. They finally arrived in Alabama and loaded one thousand cases of soap on the trucks. They immediately turned around and headed back to New York. But time was running out.

Continuing against All Obstacles Persuades a Steamship Line President

"We arrived in New York twenty-four hours before the letter of credit was due to expire. They started loading the soap on the 'lighters,' which took the cargo to the freighters in the harbor. The unions weren't as strong in those days, and I persuaded the longshoreman to let me help." Joe worked all night helping to load the soap and through the next day until noon.

He realized he wasn't going to make it. The banks closed at two o'clock. He wouldn't get his "on-board" bills of lading to give to the bank until it was too late. His letter of credit would be worthless.

The offices of the steamship line were near the docks. Cossman found the president's office and barged his way in. He hadn't washed or changed clothes in a week. "I thought I might have made good use of a case of my own soap," he said. Without preamble, he told the president the whole story.

The president looked him in the eye. He recognized Cossman's uncommon commitment. "If you've gone this far, you're not going to lose the deal now," he said.

The steamship line president pressed a half-dozen buzzers on his desk, and people appeared from nowhere. Within minutes Joe had his bills of lading. The president was accepting a risk, because the steamship line's insurance didn't begin until the soap was on the ship. The president even sent his limousine to take Joe to the bank.

Joe got to the bank just fifteen minutes before closing time. He rushed in and presented his bills of lading. "The teller gave me a check for $1,800,000, and I went outside to get a taxi. Only then did I remember that though I had a check for $1,800,000, I didn't have taxi fare to get back to my hotel." He went back into the bank in time to get checks for all his creditors as well as some cash.

Cossman went on to build a multimillion-dollar corporation. His company sold dozens of unusual products, from 250,000 Fisherman Joe's fishing lures to 1.8 million ant farms for children. His employees, and others outside his company, never failed to follow Joe's lead, for everyone knew that Joe Cossman always showed uncommon commitment. Like General Grant, Joe simply would not quit. So neither would anyone else he became involved with, even though he had no official authority over them at all.

SHE DEVELOPED A PRIMAL SCREAM THAT WOULDN'T QUIT

Nicole Dionne had about eight months' experience in the sound design industry. She was only 26 years old and was happily employed with a well-known company. If you've never heard of the sound design business, you are not alone. These are the folks who create sounds for commercial TV advertisements and movie trailers. She had some ideas for improving the business and so put together a thirty-page marketing plan.

Some months later she was distressed to discover that her boss hadn't even looked at her ideas, much less considered them. Dionne and her sound designer talked about starting their own business to implement the plan. Apparently they talked a little too loudly. Her boss heard about it, and she and her would-be partner were both fired.

Given this opportunity, the two partners started their company. They picked a name designed to attract attention: Primal Scream. Now all they needed was money. Said Nicole Dionne, "I took the business plan that had been ignored, built on it and started approaching investors based on the creative sound design talent of my partner, Reinhard Denke."[16]

She met with dozens of venture capitalists with less than satisfactory results. Nicole found that these investors wanted 60 percent of their profits and total control. As she saw it, it would be just as if she were back working for someone else. But she was as committed as Joe Cossman. She didn't stop trying; she just tried somewhere else.

Nicole sought a small business loan. She approached almost sixty banks from all over the country with no success. Most told her that she had to have been in business for two years and have collateral. She and her partner cashed in their retirement plans, emptied their savings accounts, and came up with about $30,000. It wasn't enough. Some potential lenders told her she should first change the name of the company. "Primal Scream is a terrible name," they said. She ignored them and kept trying.

One day, someone recommended a specific loan officer at a bank. She made a presentation stressing her business plan and her partner's creativity as an artist. She asked for seventy thousand dollars. Based on her uncommon commitment, the bank took the risk. Or at least, part of it. The bank loaned her thirty thousand dollars. It was barely enough to get started, but it would do.

Now Primal Scream had to find a location. After a number of false starts, the two partners found a house located in a commercial zone. The rent was barely within their budget. Then they had to get the sound equipment they needed, which was expensive. It could have swallowed up their entire loan. Fortunately the manufacturer was familiar with their work, and they were able to lease the equipment.

Primal Scream did good work and was an instant success. Within three months, the two partners paid off the loan. Eight months later, they were able to expand their business into a music company with a four thousand-square-foot studio in a good location. Recently, they won two Clio awards. A Clio is the equivalent of an Oscar in the advertising industry. Their annual sales today exceed $1 million, and after only two years, Primal Scream is considered tops in their field.

Nicole Dionne says, "Whenever I start to worry, I press on harder. I always think of a herd of zebras being pursued by a predator. It's not the one that keeps focused and has extraordinary commitment that gets caught and eaten. It's the zebra that starts looking right and left to see whether other zebras are getting ahead, or worse, looking back to see how the lion is doing. The people I approached saw that. Whenever I heard 'no,' I immediately started figuring how to turn it into a 'how.' Others take note of your commitment and behave accordingly. I have the same attitude in dealing with my people, and they know it. I am totally committed to whatever project we're working on. But I am not tied to a particular approach. In fact, I have what I call my 'no' rule. That is, if anyone disagrees about an approach, we find another way. But we stay committed to the outcome. There is always an alternative when you are committed."[17]

THE SITUATION WAS IMPOSSIBLE, SO HE THOUGHT OUTSIDE THE BOX

Thinking outside the box means thinking and doing things in a new way. It means taking creative risks. It means doing the previously unthinkable.

More than a hundred years ago, a scholarly professor found his situation impossible. So he did the unthinkable and taught hard-bitten veterans what showing uncommon commitment could do. This professor's middle name was that of the biblical warrior Joshua. His first name was Lawrence. This, too, was the name of a warrior. His father had named him for Commodore Lawrence, hero of the War of 1812. Lawrence was famous for uttering the words, "Don't give up the ship." The professor's last name was Chamberlain.

Professor Chamberlain was teaching at Bowdoin College in Maine when Fort Sumter was fired on in 1861. He believed strongly in the Union cause and resolved to fight for it. He asked for a leave of absence in order to enlist. His request was not approved. Professor Chamberlain, though only in his twenties, held one of the most important and prestigious chairs at the college, Professor of Rhetoric and Oratory. The college didn't want him to waste his time in nonacademic pursuits.

Professor Chamberlain then asked for sabbatical leave to study in Europe. This was approved. Chamberlain was able to convince Bowdoin's president to let him use his "sabbatical" to serve the Union cause. Chamberlain enlisted as a private in the Union Army. Soon afterward, he obtained an officer's commission from the governor of Maine. Two years later, he was a colonel commanding the Twentieth Maine Regiment in the Army of the Potomac.

On July 2, 1863, the Twentieth Maine was in the little town of Gettysburg, Pennsylvania. The battle fought there was to become known as "the high point of the Confederacy." It is one of the most famous and bloodiest battles in American history.

On the second day of the fighting, the Twentieth Maine was defending a wooded knoll known as Little Round Top. It was located on the extreme left end of the Union line. What the Federals didn't know was that Robert E. Lee had concentrated some fifteen thousand battle-hardened Confederates under Lt. Gen. James "Old Pete" Longstreet to attack precisely on the left end of the Union line. If they could take Little Round Top, they could move their artillery to the knoll and fire parallel along the unprotected Union line. That is called enfiladed fire, and it is deadly. They could then outflank the entire Union line, cutting off the Union troops in the center and on the right from their line of supplies. Many military experts believe this action would have been decisive and the United States would have lost the battle.

Because of previous Union defeats and other problems, the war had already become extremely controversial and divisive in the North. England awaited a single decisive Confederate victory to recognize the Confederate States of America as an independent country. Had Longstreet been successful on that hot July afternoon, it might not only have ended the battle, but the war. The United States might have been permanently divided.

Longstreet's corps attacked with great determination and ferocity. The Twentieth Maine held. The Confederates charged Little Round Top again. Once more, the Twentieth Maine beat them back. However ammunition was running low. Chamberlain hoped that the Southerners would not attack again. Both sides had suffered greatly. Many Confederate dead and wounded marked the route of their previous assaults. But once again, the Confederates attacked. After a gallant effort, they were again forced to retreat.

Few of Chamberlain's troops had bullets left to shoot. They had no hope of resupply. His officers advised him to withdraw at once to prevent capture. Chamberlain looked around at his battle-weary troops. The Twentieth Maine had suffered many casualties. Many of the survivors were wounded. The situation seemed hopeless. Then, Chamberlain showed the uncommon commitment that would change history.

"Tell the men to fix bayonets," he ordered. His officers looked at him incredulously, but they carried out his orders. "Did the Colonel think he could scare off the attackers by merely a show of 'cold steel'?" they thought. "What did he have in mind?" But his officers and soldiers knew that whatever he was planning, he was totally committed. And because he demonstrated such a level of commitment, so did they.

Chamberlain looked down the hill toward the Confederate lines. He could see that Longstreet's men were in the process of forming their ranks for yet another attack. Chamberlain again looked at his men. He pointed his saber at the grouping Confederates and commanded: "Twentieth Maine . . . charge!"

There is and was no tactics manual that advised an action like this. But the Twentieth Maine charged down from Little Round Top with bayonets fixed on their mostly empty rifles. They yelled and screamed like madmen. The Confederates, brave as they were, fell back. Joshua Chamberlain's show of uncommon commitment gave the Twentieth Maine the impetus to do the impossible. It saved the entire battle of Gettysburg at this critical juncture.

Chamberlain was wounded several times during the Civil War. General Grant promoted him to brigadier general on what was thought to be Chamberlain's deathbed. But Chamberlain recovered to finish the war as a major general and help lead the victory parade of the Army of the Potomac, the largest of the Union armies, up Connecticut Avenue in Washington.

After the war, he returned to Bowdoin College from his "sabbatical" and eventually became Bowdoin's president. He died from one of his wounds, but not until he had reached the age of ninety-two. Joshua Chamberlain was a remarkable leader. In very real terms, Chamberlain's spiritual show of uncommon commitment substituted for physical bullets. He thought outside the box, first in finding a way to obtain a leave of absence from his college after he had been turned down, and then in attacking with bayonets when he could no longer defend with bullets. As Nicole Dionne says, "There is always an alternative when you are committed."

A BUSINESSMAN FACES AN IMPOSSIBLE SITUATION AND THINKS OUTSIDE THE BOX

In 1939 W. Clement Stone of Chicago, Illinois, had his own insurance agency with a number of salesmen throughout the United States. He was making a good living, and his agency was growing every year. The vast majority of the policies his salesmen wrote were for a single company, Commercial Casualty Co. of Newark, New Jersey, offering accident insurance.

Not only was Stone a good leader and manager, but he spent an extraordinary amount of time in selecting, training, and motivating his salesmen. So able were Stone's salespeople that they sold far more insurance than the salesmen for Commercial Casualty Co.

One day while vacationing with his family in Miami Beach, Stone received a frantic call from his secretary. She said that the CEO of Commercial Casualty Co. had called. A salesman from the CEO's company had complained about one of Stone's salesmen in Texas taking business away from him. Beginning the following week, Stone's agency could write no more insurance policies for their company, the CEO said.

You can imagine how quickly this message must have spread through the organization, occurring right in the midst of the Great Depression. His salesmen had no product to sell.

Stone immediately flew to the New Jersey headquarters of the large insurance company and negotiated an extension of time that his people could continue to sell Commercial Casualty's insurance. No doubt the CEO was impressed with Stone's commitment. Remember, this was back in 1939 when flying was expensive and not the preferred method of travel for the businessperson.

Stone returned to Chicago. The message he gave his salesmen showed them his uncommon commitment. The unthinkable thing he did saved his company. "We won't be phasing anything out," he told his salesmen. "I'm starting my own insurance company, and each one of you has a place in it."

Until this time, Stone's salesmen had only sold policies for other companies, which were the actual insurers. Stone thought that the business of selling insurance was complicated enough. The government laws and regulations having to do with actual insuring were much more complex. Stone had only a high school education. He couldn't even imagine all the problems to overcome. He would have to keep reserves of cash. How much he didn't know. He would have to pay off accounts when money was due. He would be subject to fraudulent claims. He could get sued. He would get sued at times — it was part of the business! He would have to sue. Becoming a real insurance company and the actual insurer rather than an insurance agency performing the sole task of selling policies was unthinkable. He didn't even know where to start. But W. Clement Stone decided to think outside the box.

Stone founded his new company and called it Combined Insurance Co. of America. Later he started the AON Corp., which included his insurance operation and other businesses. Annual sales have reached $6 billion and AON Corp. employs twenty-seven thousand.[18]

W. Clement Stone kept his company and his sales force by showing uncommon commitment, and when faced with an impossible situation, thinking outside the box. Since he could no longer sell someone else's insurance, he started his own insurance company and sold his own.

THIS MAN TAUGHT COLIN POWELL HOW TO GET THINGS DONE IN GOVERNMENT

One of my most amazing West Point classmates is Frederic V. Malek. Fred Malek saw combat in 1961 while a regular infantry lieutenant attached to the First Special Forces Group advising Vietnamese Ranger companies.[19] He left the army and put himself through the Harvard Business School by selling encyclopedias. Then he rescued a failing company in South Carolina and became a multimillionaire by the age of thirty. Recruited by the Nixon White House, he served as deputy undersecretary of the Department of Health, Education, and Welfare, as special assistant to the president, and finally as deputy director of the Office of Management and Budget (OMB). He left government and joined the Marriott Corp., becoming president of the Marriott Hotels. His business experiences also include being an independent merchant banker and president of Northwest Airlines. Today he is chairman of Thayer Capital Partners. Along the way, he helped President Bush in senior positions in both of his campaigns. Few have accomplished so much or made so many contributions in so many fields.[20]

But back in 1973, Fred had a problem. As deputy director of OMB, he was frustrated. He couldn't get things done quickly because layers of career bureaucrats occupied the key positions in OMB. Early on he spotted White House fellow and army major, Colin Powell. He made Powell his executive assistant.

I'll let General Powell pick up the story. "Fred went about gaining control of the government in a way that opened the eyes of this fledgling student of power," Powell says. "Fred started planting his own people in the key 'assistant secretary for administration' slots in major federal agencies. Let the cabinet officials make the speeches, cut the ribbons, and appear on 'Meet the Press.' Anonymous assistant secretaries, loyal to Malek, would run operations day to day, and to the Nixon administration's liking. . . . I learned much in Professor Malek's graduate seminar."[21]

But bureaucrats already occupied many positions in OMB, and the budget couldn't be increased to add new positions for the young Harvard, Stanford, and Wharton graduates Fred Malek wanted to bring in. He thought out of the box again.

"Thereafter, I started phoning agency officials, explaining that I was calling on behalf of Mr. Malek with good news," Powell says. "Their power was about to be broadened. A function currently being handled by OMB was going to be transferred to their agency . . . music to any bureaucrat's ear."[22]

Powell explained to each agency official that their agency would get the new function and the bodies capable of performing it, but the agency would not receive funding for the positions.

"'Mr. Assistant Secretary,' I would say, 'Fred Malek has every confidence that between attrition and some imagination on your part, you will work something out.' Soon the unwanted OMB bureaucrats were gone, their offices and titles freed up, and Malek's youngbloods moved in. Out of that experience emerged one of my rules: you don't know what you can get away with until you try."[23]

COMMITMENT MEANS TAKING RISKS

Some leaders are afraid to show uncommon commitment because it means taking risks. Let's be frank. Some are afraid to show any commitment at all. Yet risk is a part of life, and your willingness to accept it is part of your responsibility as a leader.

How do battle leaders learn to take risks? Simple. First they analyze the situation. Then they ask themselves, what is the worst that can happen? They assess whether the potential benefits of taking action are worth risking this worst. If they are, they accept the risk and go ahead.

It is amazing how once you accept the worst that can happen, you will have much less difficulty making and showing an uncommon commitment to a worthy goal.

A YOUNG LEADER DESTROYS ALL WAR INDUSTRY IN THE RUHR VALLEY

Guy Gibson was only in his twenties. Yet he had already commanded both fighter and bomber squadrons in combat during World War II. He held the rank of wing commander in the Royal Air Force (RAF). That's the equivalent of lieutenant colonel in the U.S. Air Force. In 1943 he was asked to form a secret squadron from some of the best and most experienced bomber crews in the RAF. So secret was the mission that even Gibson wasn't told what it was at first. They only told him that he must train his crews to fly at night at a precise airspeed and at a very low altitude: 150 feet!

In the midst of training, he was given the full story. The Ruhr Valley in Germany was protected from flooding by giant dams. If these dams could be breached, the flooding would destroy the considerable German war industry in the valley.

These dams were monstrous in size. One was 850 yards long and 140 feet high. It was as thick as it was high. Conventional bombing could do nothing against such dams. It would take special weapons delivered at extremely low altitude to destroy the concrete walls. Then the pressure from millions of tons of water behind the dams would finish the job.

To get enough water pressure, the dams had to be struck when the water level was extremely high, just a few feet from the top, and the weapons had to be delivered only a few feet from that mark. Water reached this level only rarely. One such time would be about three months in the future. They would have only that long to train, and the window for the attack would be only a couple of days before the water level fell again.

There were other complications. A bomb that could do the job didn't exist. It would have to be developed and tested within ninety days. Fortunately only a few antiaircraft guns protected the dams because they were considered invulnerable to bombing. This made extreme secrecy imperative. If the Germans got even a whiff of the possibility of a British attack, they would move in many guns. Then an attack using this tactic would be impossible.

Gibson brought together and briefed a number of highly qualified bomber crews. They were told nothing about the target. They were only told that the mission would be extremely hazardous, but it could have a major impact on the war. If they wanted to go, they had to volunteer.

Flying a heavy four-engined bomber at night at 150 feet was no picnic. The crews did not know they would be attacking dams, but they knew that some of the mission would be flown over water. That made the altitude even more dangerous. Judging altitude over water, especially at night, was very difficult. Just a slight gust of wind or touch of vertigo, and they would fly right into the water. Still, every single man volunteered. They did so primarily because of Gibson. They knew he was extraordinarily committed to this dangerous mission, whatever it was. They volunteered on faith that the extreme risk would be worthwhile based on his commitment. They began to train in earnest until they could consistently fly at 150 feet at night and hit a target within a few feet.

Only a few days before they were to attack, Gibson received an emergency call. The weapon needed to destroy the dams could not be developed in time. The requirements were just too great. They simply couldn't get a bomb to detonate after being dropped from 150 feet. However they could get the bomb to work if they could drop it from a lower altitude. They calculated that the attack could still be made if the planes could release the new weapons at 60 feet instead of 150 feet and at precisely 232 miles an hour.

Gibson thought that he and his boys could do it. But what a risk! He called his crews together and told them the story. He said he was going to do it, but they had to revolunteer. By his willingness to attack at night at an altitude of 60 feet, he demonstrated uncommon commitment to the mission. The risks were now enormous. Flying at 60 feet at night was extremely hazardous. But they had to do it while performing a difficult bombing maneuver and facing enemy defenses. The crews saw that Gibson was still totally committed. If he was, then so were they. To a man, they revolunteered and followed him.[24]

Even after this, many trials tested their leader's commitment. During a "live" practice half the aircraft sustained serious damage due to the tons of water sent into the air when the weapons detonated. The crew found that they couldn't fly at 60 feet consistently due to the limitations of the instruments available in those days. Someone designed a simple manual system so that they knew they were at exactly 60 feet to release their bombs. The very night of their mission, they found that the wrong oil had been sent for their engines. Moreover, none of the correct oil was on hand. Somehow they got it in time.

The attack took place successfully. As a result, the Moehne and Eder lakes were emptied. Three hundred and thirty million gallons of water plunged into the Ruhr Valley. As far as fifty miles away, coal mines were flooded and factories completely destroyed. One of the Luftwaffe's largest airfields was under water. Roads, bridges, and railways disappeared. Canal banks were gone, power stations washed away, foundries had no water for making steel. The Germans estimated that they lost the equivalent of several months' work by one hundred thousand men from the damage caused by this one attack.[25]

This mission was successful because of the great skill and courage of the British airmen. But more than that, it was the uncommon commitment, confirmed by his willingness to accept a risk, demonstrated by the leader, Wing Commander Guy Gibson.

THE NEW GUY AT A $19.8-BILLION PHARMACEUTICAL COMPANY TAKES SOME BIG RISKS

When Ray Gilmartin was brought into corporate giant Merck & Company he knew nothing about the pharmaceutical business. His last job was as head of a company making medical gears. Before Gilmartin's arrival, the mighty Merck was stumbling badly. The company had ventured into new areas of business that weren't paying off. Senior executives were fighting for position because of the former CEO's pending retirement. More than a few had left the company. Merck's most highly acclaimed new drug wasn't making the forecast sales. The company's stock had fallen almost 50 percent in two years.

Gilmartin took some big risks to set things straight. When he arrived, many senior executives were afraid he would make changes that they wouldn't like. They threatened to leave if he did.

Gilmartin wanted to set up a management committee with twelve members. Others advised him not to do it. "That's not the way we operate," they told him. "We'll lose more experienced people." Gilmartin considered their advice, but he established the committee nonetheless.

The many new business areas that Merck had gotten into were losing money, but each had its champion who claimed if they held on a little longer, all would be well. Gilmartin insisted on a revised mission statement committing Merck to its research-driven pharmaceutical roots. Gilmartin underlined that decision by quickly shutting down a generic-drug operation and selling off more than $1 billion in assets outside the area of Merck's defined mission. Some executives left the corporation, but Gilmartin's extraordinary commitment to the mission of Merck as he saw it caused others to renew their own commitment to the company.

Did Gilmartin's risky commitment to Merck's new mission and organizational structure work? Merck's net income is up 29 percent and sales are up 28.7 percent since his arrival. Standard & Poor's also took note. Stock is up 162 percent since the day before his arrival.[26] Showing uncommon commitment may be risky at times, but most people will follow those who demonstrate this universal law.

You never know what you can do until you pull out all the stops and go "all the way." As Gen. Colin Powell says: "It can be done."[27]

FIVE ACTIONS LEADERS MUST TAKE

It makes no difference whether you have formal authority over the people you want to follow your lead. Showing uncommon commitment will help you lead them to any goal. To do this:

1. Meet with Your Followers Face to Face
2. Make a Public Commitment
3. Keep Going When the Going Gets Rough
4. When the Situation Is Impossible, Think Outside the Box
5. Accept the Risk that Goes with Commitment

Never forget your basic purpose in these actions:

> ## SHOW UNCOMMON COMMITMENT

ENDNOTES

1 Patterson, George K., letter to the author, July 26, 1993.
2 Bonaparte, Napoleon, "Maxims of Napoleon," LXVII, published originally in Paris in 1830 and translated into English shortly thereafter in *Jomini, Clausewitz, and Schlieffen* (Department of Military Art and Engineering, U.S. Military Academy: West Point, 1954), 89.
3 Patterson, George K., telephone conversations with the author, April 4, 11, 1996.

[4] Naviaux, Jacques C., fax to author, April 9, 1996.

[5] McWilliams, Gary, "Whirlwind on the Web," *Business Week* (April 7, 1997): 132.

[6] Ibid., 134.

[7] Ibid., 132, 134, 136.

[8] Markham, Edward, letter to the author July 27, 1993.

[9] Congressional Medal of Honor Citation for Gary I. Gordon, Master Sergeant, U.S. Army (www.familyville.com: The American War Library, 1996), Congressional Medal of Honor Citation for Randall D. Shughart, Sgt. First Class, U.S. Army (www.familyville.com: The American War Library, 1996).

[10] Baxter, Walter H., letter to the author, August 3, 1993.

[11] Tankersley, W. H., letter to the author, January 1, 1993.

[12] Glasier, Connie, and Barbara Steinberg Smalley, *Swim With the Dolphins* (New York: Warner Books, 1995), 12–17

[13] Schine, Eric, and Peter Elstrom, "Not Exactly an Overnight Success," *Business Week* (June 2, 1997): 133.

[14] Ibid., 132–134.

[15] Kroc, Ray, with Robert Anderson, *Grinding It Out: The Making of McDonald's* (New York: St. Martin's Press, 1987), 201.

[16] Klein, Karen E., "Sound Approach," *Los Angeles Times* (July 15, 1997), D2.

[17] Dionne, Nicole, interview with the author, October 19, 1997.

[18] Hill, Napoleon, and W. Clement Stone, *Success Through a Positive Mental Attitude* (Chicago: Nightingales-Conant, 1988), tape 3.

[19] Malek, Frederic V., letter to the author, December 8, 1997.

[20] Malek, Frederic V., telephone interview with the author, January 21, 1998, and fax, January 22, 1998.

[21] Powell, Colin L., with Joseph E. Persico, *My American Journey* (New York: Random House, 1995), 167.

[22] Ibid.

[23] Ibid.

[24] Gibson, Guy, *Enemy Coast Ahead* (London: Pan Books, Ltd., 1946), 243–317.

[25] Brickhill, Paul, *Dam Busters* (New York: Ballatine Books, 1951), 75.

[26] Weber, Joseph, "Merck's Mr. Nice Guy With a Mission," *Business Week* (November 25, 1996).

[27] Powell, *My American Journey*, 613.

EXPECT POSITIVE RESULTS

For great aims we must dare great things.
— CARL VON CLAUSEWITZ

Moral forces rather than numbers decide victory.
— NAPOLEON

In 1968 David Donlon was a young lieutenant flying A-26 aircraft with the 609th Air Commando Squadron (ACS) out of Nakhon Phanom Royal Thai Air Force Base during the Vietnam War. The A-26 was an old World War II attack aircraft, which had been brought out of storage and extensively modified for use twenty-five years after it had been built. It was not a jet aircraft. Flown by two crew members, its two piston-driven propeller engines gave it an advantage over jets for the mission it was assigned. It could fly much longer using on-board fuel. Unlike the jets, the A-26 could loiter and remain in the target area for up to four hours. Moreover, it attacked at a much slower speed than jets. As a result, it was far more accurate even without sophisticated targeting equipment.

The slower speed made it more vulnerable to antiaircraft fire, but this wasn't so important because the missions were only at night in areas where antiaircraft fire, though heavy, was not radar-controlled. During the day, the slow-flying A-26, with a dark, camouflaged scene painted on top and black paint below, was a much easier target than the jets for enemy gunners on the ground.

To do its job, the A-26 had eight fifty-caliber machine guns in its nose and eight wing stations that mounted a variety of bombs, finned napalm, and rockets. Additional weapons were carried in a small bomb bay. To acquire targets, the A-26 usually worked with a light aircraft known as a Forward Air Controller or (FAC). One of the FAC crew carried a special device allowing it to see truck convoys even in complete darkness. It would use a flare or other pyrotechnic means to mark the target for the A-26. The A-26 then released its weapons in a steep dive on the target.

The primary mission of Donlon's squadron was night-armed reconnaissance along the Ho Chi Minh Trail. The "trail" was much more than its name implied. It was really a collection of rough roads, with countless concealed bypasses, winding through the mountainous rock formations and jungles of Laos and North Vietnam.

David's squadron struck the trucks that were the enemy's line of supply to their troops in South Vietnam. So successful were they in their mission that the 609th ACS was awarded the Presidential Unit Citation. That's the highest decoration that can be awarded to a unit. The 609th ACS got it for destroying more trucks per mission than any other squadron in the war.

One night Donlon was assigned to fly on the last sortie of the evening. This took off at 2:30 A.M., and left the target area as the sun rose. He was assigned to fly with Maj. Bobbie Jenkins, the most successful pilot in the squadron. But it was a slow night, and the FAC could find no targets for several hours. Just as the sun began to rise, the FAC located a convoy of fifteen trucks. By the time the FAC could direct Donlon's A-26 to the convoy, the sun was up, fully exposing the dark-painted, slow-flying A-26. As Donlon and his pilot dove steeply to strike the trucks, every antiaircraft gun in the area opened fire on them. They flew through it all, though Donlon felt he could reach out and touch each round as the tracers streaked past the cockpit. Involuntarily both he and Bobbie crouched lower in the cockpit, though each knew that if a round struck the fuselage, it would make no difference. It would easily penetrate the aluminum skin of the aircraft. David knew that at any moment the aircraft could be enveloped in flames.

Somehow they managed to drop a well-aimed bomb and pull out while furious enemy fire tore after them. They climbed to a safe altitude and awaited the FAC's report on their strike.

"You've got one of them! The rest are stopped on the road! They can't turn around!" screamed the FAC excitedly over the radio.

"Bobbie looked at Donlon. "Looked like quite a few guns," he commented. David Donlon could barely speak, but he managed with difficulty to answer calmly, "Five ZPUs and seven 37mms."

"It looked like more," said Bobbie grimly. But it was easy for Donlon to make an accurate count, even in battle. The enemy always used tracers and Donlon could count the streams of light. Hundreds of rounds had been fired at their aircraft in that one attack.

Donlon thought maybe Bobbie would decide that one truck was enough and go home. Because of their aircraft's vulnerability during the day, they had all been told to be extremely careful about attacking where the enemy had a clear edge in defending the targets. It was the commander's call. That was Bobbie. "Give me another nape," he ordered. David Donlon complied.

Once again they dived on the target. There seemed to be even more guns firing on them this time. Despite the tracer streams, Donlon could not get an accurate count of their number. The A-26s were rarely fired on while attacking, only during the withdrawal phase because at night they couldn't be seen. This was different. They dived and exited through a hailstorm of fire. Nevertheless they escaped after their attack to a safer altitude despite having twice severely tempted fate.

It didn't end there. Jenkins and Donlon attacked again and again, until, after sixteen passes, all the trucks and several of the guns were destroyed. It was the most daring mission Donlon had ever been a part of.

After they landed, Donlon asked his pilot, "How were you able to do that? I could see that you were scared, but you did it anyway. And of course, because you were willing to do it, I was, too."

"David, when I'm fighting, I expect to win. I knew we could do it, or I wouldn't have tried. I just knew it would be a little tougher and a little more risky because of the daylight and the number of guns that opposed us. But I knew we would get all of those trucks in the end. I always expect positive results."

WHY YOU MUST EXPECT TO WIN

It is true that a leader who expects positive results may not actually get them due to circumstances beyond his or her control.

But it is equally true that a leader who does not expect positive results will not get them. So while expecting positive results may not always lead to success, failing to expect positive results will almost always lead to failure.

WHAT A GENERAL SHOWED US ABOUT EXPECTING POSITIVE RESULTS 2,000 YEARS AGO

More than forty years ago, Peter Drucker in *The Practice of Management* advised us to read "the first systematic book on leadership."[1] The book was *Anabasis*, part of the writings of Xenophon, an Athenian general. One translation of this title is *Expedition Up Country*.[2]

In 401 B.C., Cyrus the Younger, son of Cyrus the Great, enlisted Greek troops to help him overthrow his brother, Artaxerxes, who was king of Persia. At the Battle of Cunaxa, they defeated a Persian army many times their size, but during the battle, Cyrus was killed. Since Cyrus, pretender to the Persian throne, was dead, there was little point to the victory of his troops. In fact, the Persians in Cyrus's former army deserted to Artaxerxes.

Artaxerxes offered the Greeks a truce, which was accepted by the Greek mercenaries. Artaxerses told them they could return to their own country unhindered. To celebrate their truce, he invited all the Greek generals to a great banquet. They were told to leave their weapons outside. Once Artaxerses had them under his control, he murdered them.

Xenophon was a young staff officer. He gathered the surviving officers together, and under his guidance they elected new generals. Some Greek officers wanted to work out some sort of deal with Artaxerses. They were discouraged as they saw no way of marching one thousand miles back to Greece with ten thousand soldiers through unfriendly country, not to mention that they currently faced a numerically superior army.

Xenophon assembled the officers and spoke to them. "All of these soldiers have their eyes on you, and if they see that you are downhearted they will become cowards, while if you are yourselves clearly prepared to meet the enemy and if you call on the rest to do their part, you can be sure that they will follow you and try to be like you."[3]

Xenophon expected positive results. Because of this, he convinced the officers and soldiers they would return to their homes even though they had lost their experienced and proven generals, were numerically inferior to their enemy, had thousands of miles of unfriendly territory to traverse, and had no supplies of food and water. Because Xenophon expected positive results, ten thousand followers expected positive results as well. They escaped from Artaxerses and followed Xenophon on the most amazing march in history. They completed their five-month journey successfully despite countless battles and hardships. No wonder Drucker called our attention to Xenophon's work as containing important lessons for leading in business.

DAVID DONLON LEARNS
TO EXPECT POSITIVE RESULTS

Several years after the Vietnam War, Major Jenkins's copilot and navigator, David Donlon, was the new director of the product development department for a small company. For almost thirty years this company had been trying to win a government contract to produce the U.S. Army's gas masks. This was a lucrative contract because the government needed so many. And the company had the expertise. They produced oxygen breathing masks of various types, including those used worldwide by the airlines. Much of the technology of the company's masks was similar, if not identical to that used by the government.

However this small company faced a major problem. A large company produced virtually all the U.S. Army's gas masks. Not only had this company been the sole source of these masks since World War II, but it had won every single government research-and-development contract for the development of improved features for the product.

David Donlon learned that the army intended to develop an entirely new gas mask. Visiting with army engineers and studying some of the specifications desired in a new mask, he realized that the development alone of the mask would involve a contract of several million dollars. The largest government development contract his small company had ever won was for $250,000.

Convinced that his group had some special advantages to offer, Donlon committed to bid for and win this contract. One of the challenges he faced was to gain the acceptance and commitment of engineers and others who had been in the company for many years. They had been unsuccessful in competing against the larger gas mask–producing company in the past. No one thought they had a chance.

Once he had his plans and answers ready, Donlon gathered everyone. Like Xenophon, he spoke confidently to his group. He clearly expected positive results. "Together we are going to bid for and win this contract," Donlon told them. At first they didn't take him seriously. Then they realized he meant it.

Senior officers of the company considered the cost to bid for the contract. They didn't like the figures. It was more than they had ever invested. They would waste time that could better be allocated to other "real" projects. They would look foolish to the government. They didn't know enough about the product. But David Donlon expected results just as his pilot, Bobbie Jenkins, had in combat. His self-confidence showed it.

By the time he received permission to proceed, all his engineers had heard the story. Because of this leader's positive attitude, they felt the same way. The effort they invested in putting together a proposal for this bid was considerable, much more than they had for other contracts.

It would be nice to be able to say that this great effort, based on their leader's positive expectations, had an immediate pay-off and that they won the contract. Unfortunately they didn't. However their proposal was so good that it caused the U.S. Army evaluators to rethink what they wanted. They didn't award the contract to the smaller company. But they didn't award it to the larger one either. Instead they delayed a year and then invited both companies to bid again, this time against slightly different specifications. Now everyone in the little company realized they could pull this off and win. Not only did their leader, David Donlon, expect positive results. They all did. This time, the government awarded the contract. And Donlon's company won it. The contract was for $3 million, and it changed the little company forever.

How Expecting Positive Results Saved Supercuts

Expecting positive results can work miracles in business. Supercuts, Inc., was a revolutionary concept in the 1970s when it was introduced. It replaced the old barbershop and beauty shop with low cost, no-nonsense, unisex, hairstyling salons. At first, Supercuts was extremely successful. Its franchises expanded across the country. But at some point its leaders grew fearful of losing all they had gained. They no longer expected positive results.

According to Maj. Gen. Hoyt S. Vandenberg, Jr., USAF, retired, all leaders fall into two groups: the hunters and the hunted. Hunted leaders are trying to avoid failure. In their hearts they lack self-confidence and don't expect to succeed. Hunter leaders are enthusiastically hunting success . . . and they fully expect to find it.[4]

From hunters, Supercuts' leaders became the hunted. They feared the worst would happen. As frequently happens, exactly what they were afraid of began to occur. This was probably attributable to their actions. In attempting to protect their profits, they started to save money by cutting corners. Franchisees felt shortchanged in advertising and other support. Relations between the corporation and its franchisees grew cool. The franchisees formed an association to protect their interests. Corporate leaders attempted to restrict them from doing this. The result was a class-action lawsuit against the corporation.

By 1987 Supercuts was in deep trouble. Sales were down. Morale was low. The company was floundering. Some business analysts predicted bankruptcy. At the last minute, an investment firm bought the company and brought in a new CEO. Her name was Betsy Burton.

Burton met with the franchisees even before the deal went through. They were so impressed with her openness and positive expectations that they dropped the lawsuit without her asking. Why? The franchisees had asked to set up a joint council with company management. Supercuts' previous leaders wouldn't even consider it. They knew it was a good idea, but they were afraid to be thought of as agreeing with the franchisees.

Burton not only agreed but offered to hold all meetings at corporate expense. She took these actions because she knew who she was and what she believed in. She expected profits to go up, not down. She was a hunter.

Within sixteen months, profits were up by 10 percent. Within three years, franchisees had double-digit sales increases. Revenue grew from $126 million to more than $170 million. The corporation added more than one hundred new franchisees. Noted one, "My stores are registering record sales and profits. Equally important, people are feeling optimistic about the company. It's nice to be part of something that's heading up again."

Franchisees, employees, and management all expect positive results. Betsy Burton expected them first.

HOW YOU CAN LEARN TO EXPECT POSITIVE RESULTS

1. Develop Your Self-Confidence
2. Become a Positive Thinker
3. Visualize the Results You Want To Achieve
4. Maintain Your Enthusiasm

DEVELOP YOUR SELF-CONFIDENCE

No one starts right out in life accomplishing what we think of as big things. We start as an infant and accomplish "small things," such as learning to walk, talk, read, write, and reason. Even with these things, we began by doing still smaller things and slowly increasing the difficulty of the subtasks until we could accomplish the overall task.

Today you no longer have any doubt that when you stand, put forth one leg and then the other, you are going to walk. As you read these sentences, unless you are just learning English, you have little doubt that you will understand what you have read. You automatically expect positive results.

With the challenging tasks and projects of adults, leaders fail to expect success for one of only two reasons. Either they have been unsuccessful at similar tasks or projects in the past, or they have never tried to accomplish them in the first place. And by the way, those who have never tried usually haven't tried because they feel they will fail if they did.

A BABY MUST LEARN TO CRAWL BEFORE HE CAN WALK

How many infants simply took their bottles out of their mouths, placed them on a nearby table, hopped out of their cribs, and began to walk? I don't know about you, but I haven't heard of any. The correct sequence is that the baby begins to crawl, gains enough self-confidence to stand up, gains a little more self-confidence, and takes a step. Usually the first step ends in disaster, and the baby falls. But the baby knows that at least he made a start, and he eagerly tries again not long afterward. Usually the parents are so elated about the attempt that they are full of praise, even though the baby "did a terrible job" and didn't manage to take even a single step successfully.

It's easy to see why many leaders, and people in general, lack self-confidence later in life. A baby usually has someone cheering him on. But even if he didn't, who's to say that his first step was a terrible attempt or a good one? The problem is, as we get older, others discourage us either with or without malice. Many of these observers are judgmental and are certain to let us know when we do a poor job.

A child wants to help mother but accidently drops a plate. Maybe mother is nervous and irritable. So she yells at the child. Is the child as ready to attempt to help with the dishes, or other tasks, in the future? Maybe and maybe not. Worse, what if in addition to yelling, the mother berates the child for being clumsy. If the child accepts that as the truth, it may have serious consequences later.

As the child gets older and out of the house, things can become worse for his or her self-confidence. Other children are very critical. Some teachers can be even worse. Olympic Decathlon champion Bruce Jenner says that as a child he was deathly afraid of being called on in school to read. His teachers criticized him, and the more he was criticized, the less self-confidence he had. And of course, the worse he did. He was attracted to sports because one day a teacher told him and others to run between two points in the school yard. He was the fastest. For the first time, others were complimenting him. "I didn't know you could run that fast." "Boy are you good at running!" "I bet you could outrun anyone." Jenner's self-confidence soared, and of course it spilled into other areas. In his opinion, this was his first step toward winning a gold medal in the 1976 Olympics.[5]

START WITH SMALL SUCCESSES AND WORK UP

Bruce Jenner was fortunate. What if no teacher had ever asked him to run? Would he ever have developed the self-confidence to compete in sports and go on to win a gold medal in the Olympics? We'll never know. But we can use the same concept to build self-confidence in anything we choose. All we need to do is select a relatively easy goal and then go ahead and accomplish it. Every time you complete a task or goal successfully, celebrate and congratulate yourself. Then set a higher goal or a more difficult task. It's just like working out with weights or running. You build up the amount of weight slowly or run farther as you develop your strength. Before long, you'll be doing things you never thought you could. You will have acquired that self-confidence you need to expect positive results as a leader.

LEADERS MUST DEVELOP THEIR OVERALL SELF-CONFIDENCE

Several years ago I was surprised to read a study showing that a majority of senior executives are more worried about speaking in public than they are of dying! Can you imagine that? Why is it true? I guess because dying is something all of us have reasonable confidence we can accomplish successfully, but the same is not true of speaking in public. What this means for many of us, even for those who are extremely successful in some areas, is that we still lack overall self-confidence. In many areas, we are afraid to expect positive results because we have failed one or more times in the past. Now the question is, what can we do about this?

BUILD UP SELF-CONFIDENCE IN ONE AREA AND IT CAN CARRY OVER INTO OTHERS

The military uses something called a "confidence course" to build self-confidence. It consists of man-made obstacles or events that each participant must traverse successfully. All are designed to be moderately to severely difficult and challenging, but doable. One might require climbing down a one-hundred-foot rope suspended from a cliff. Another might force the participant to jump out to catch a swinging rope suspended over a pool of water. Do it right, and you catch the rope and safely reach the other side by dropping off before the rope starts swinging back. Do it incorrectly, and you end up in the water. Another is called a "slide for life." It consists of a rope drawn across a lake from a ninety-foot tower on one side of the lake to the opposite bank. The participant jumps off the tower holding onto a pulley attached to the rope. As he slides across the lake to the other side, he keeps his eyes on a man signaling with a set of flags. On one signal, you raise your legs so that they are parallel with the water and you appear to be in a sitting position. At the next signal, you drop off about twenty feet above the water. Like a stone, you go skipping across the lake to the other side. If you don't let go and drop off the pulley, you hit the bank of the lake with some force and can get injured.

The military also encourages parachute training for all army officers and gives it to almost anyone who applies for it, for the same reason: confidence building. I knew an executive who got most of his sales force to do a parachute jump when sales were lagging.

Tony Robbins runs around the country leading firewalks for the same reason. Yes, I mean walking on a bed of white-hot coals for a distance of twelve feet or longer. Robbins calls this seminar "Fear into Power" and makes it quite clear that he isn't teaching party skills, but rather using the firewalk as a metaphor. "If you could do this which you thought was impossible, what else can you do that you also think is impossible?" Before you put this down as pure quackery, I should tell you that Robbins has been to Camp David and helped the president and other senior executives do a firewalk.

A variety of confidence-building means are available, some commercially, and they will work to raise your overall self-confidence.

PHYSICAL FITNESS AS A CONFIDENCE BUILDER

When we are fatigued, our resistance is down. We make poorer decisions. We are more fearful. We cannot handle stress as well. We don't feel as well, and we are much less likely to expect positive results. This is why all the military services emphasize physical fitness for everyone, whether your job is that of an office clerk, or a Navy Seal, or an Army Ranger. If you are sitting in a missile silo, responsible for the launch of a nuclear-tipped missile, your most physically demanding task may be pressing a button. The physical demands don't seem to justify spending time, energy, and resources on physical fitness. But those who serve in such a capacity know that physical fitness is crucial to the mental performance and the responsibility that goes along with "just pressing a button."

If you are physically fit, you look better, feel better, and have more self-confidence. Some years ago, I watched a TV movie about young men trying to get through Harvard Law School. In one scene, there was to be a debate between two teams of two students. One team consisted of the two top men in the class. The other team was made up of a self-confident West Point–trained army officer and a brilliant but fearful and slovenly introvert.

The West Pointer expected to win. He expected positive results. His partner kept focusing on why they couldn't win. Finally the West Pointer realized he had to build up his partner's self-confidence before he did anything else. So he put his partner on a regime of physical fitness — push-ups, sit-ups, everything. The brilliant introvert said, "We don't have time for this. We've got to prepare our arguments and legal briefs. What has this got to do with winning the debate?"

"Everything!" his army partner told him. After several weeks, the introvert got fit and self-confident, and they won the debate. I don't know who wrote the movie, but he was right on the money. When I was in combat, a friend started working out furiously every day. In about a month, he was beginning to look like Arnold Schwartzenegger. "I'm not as afraid anymore," he told me.

So if you want to develop your self-confidence, I recommend you consider working out. Start slowly at first. Jog from one mailbox to the next. Every day add another mailbox. Or you can slowly start working with weights.

BE REAL

Self-confidence comes from being yourself. You can't be someone you are not. You're stuck! We all are. But it makes no difference. We're all different, but we all have the potential to be competent, even outstanding, leaders.

A. L. Williams was an $18,000-a-year high school football coach in Georgia in 1977 when he founded a life insurance company based on a new concept. Most insurance companies make their largest sales through ordinary life insurance. Williams pointed out that you can buy a lot more insurance for less money with term insurance and build your savings by investing the difference.

Williams had no MBA and no corporate business experience. But his company became one of the largest of its kind in the world in less than ten years with more than $81 billion in individual life insurance policies. Williams wrote a book called *All You Can Do Is All You Can Do, But All You Can Do Is Enough!*[6] What Williams is telling us with this title is it that what we think we lack makes little difference. We still have enough to reach unimaginable success and to become a highly respected leader.

Too many leaders try to be what they are not. They may be kind and thoughtful and yet are afraid to display these qualities. They read a management book somewhere that extolled a tough leadership style. So they want to be seen as tough. Or maybe they heard that "the new leader" always has a participatory style. So they strive for follower participation even when it is inappropriate. Or maybe they try to be over-friendly when by nature they are more reserved.

One senior vice president told me this story back when Total Quality Management was all the rage as the latest management fad. "We hired a team to come in and teach us 'TQ.' They got all the senior and middle managers together for four days. They told us we should all be more open and, as a part of this, call each other by our first names. They made us wear big name tags that read 'Bob' and 'Bill' and 'Joe.' That's never been the style in our company, and it certainly wasn't the boss's style. Then we were supposed to spend three days coming up with a strategic plan. It was one of the worst experiences I ever had and I suspect that the same was true for others, including our middle managers. We had to call the president 'Bob.' It was terrible. I never felt so much tension in relationships with senior leaders in the company.

"We came up with a plan, but we all knew it was awful. Fortunately, 'Bob' recognized it, too. We threw it out and redid the whole thing about four months later. This time, we got real and were ourselves. What a difference! And the conference was a lot more open and free of tension, too!"

Lloyd R. Leavitt, Jr., flew in combat in Korea and was a wing commander in Vietnam. He retired from the air force while a lieutenant general and vice commander of the Strategic Air Command. After retirement, he first became senior vice president of Cessna Aircraft Company, and then president of other corporations. He is currently president of Divaricate, Inc., in San Carlos, California. After thinking through some questions I had posed about combat leadership, he responded, "After watching many units perform in and out of combat, I have concluded that a leader must be himself. It is less important whether a leader is authoritarian or participative. Assuming what a leader is not is very dangerous because stress will usually cause a leader to revert to his 'natural' personality. When that happens, his followers become unsure of him and quickly lose confidence."[7]

Brig. Gen. William C. Louisell, who commanded infantry units in both Korea and Vietnam and was wounded in both wars and currently is president of the Foundation for Historic Christ Church in White Stone, Virginia, agrees. "The leader's style must be consistent with his character and personality, otherwise he will be marked as a phony by those he leads. Regardless of his personal style, he must have a highly contagious fire in his belly."[8]

TURN DISADVANTAGES INTO ADVANTAGES

If you really want to build your self-confidence, start turning disadvantages into advantages. When you know you can do that, you know you can do anything. Back in the early part of this century, the richest man of his day, steel magnate Andrew Carnegie, commissioned a young reporter by the name of Napoleon Hill to research success. Carnegie offered to provide introductions to some of the richest and most famous men in America if Hill would investigate and discover the reasons for their success. It took Hill twenty years, but he accomplished his mission. One of his discoveries was that hidden within every problem, drawback, disadvantage, or obstacle, there was an equally powerful opportunity or advantage. Hill found that successful people looked for these opportunities hidden within problems and used them. As a result, like the combat leaders I surveyed, they always seemed to expect positive results.

Let me give you some examples. The fellow who invented the ice-cream cone did so at the World's Fair in St. Louis in 1904. This man had several hundred gallons of ice cream the night before the fair opened. But he had a problem. A big problem. His vendor had run out of paper cups to hold the ice cream. The man had lots of ice cream, but no way for customers to eat it. His wife came up with the idea of using a waffle iron to cook waffle batter and roll the rectangle into a cone before it could cool. The ice-cream cone was such a hit at the fair that the man sold out. He made a fortune with his new invention as its popularity exploded all over the country.

In 1957 former combat leader Joe Cossman, whom we met in chapter 4, bought ten thousand pieces of costume jewelry in a closeout. Each piece was a bracelet with seven imitation gemstones. They looked very pretty, but he was stuck. He couldn't sell them.

About this time, Cossman heard of a young woman who underwent hypnosis and was regressed to an early age. Then the hypnotist did a strange thing. He asked the young woman to remember a previous lifetime. And she did! This American woman remembered a life in Ireland during the previous century as Bridey Murphy, a young Irish girl. Interest in hypnotism swept the country.

Always interested in new ideas, Cossman went to a course in hypnosis. He heard the instructor say, "To induce a subject to enter a hypnotic trance, you need a point of fixation. This can be anything on which the subject can focus all of his attention."

"How about an imitation gemstone?" asked Cossman. "Sure," answered the instructor. "Suddenly," Cossman said, "I realized I had seventy thousand points of fixation." Cossman made a deal with the hypnotist to record a hypnotic induction and other information on a record. They didn't have audiotapes in those days. Together with some printed instructions, and using a free "hypnotic gem" as inducement to buy, Cossman sold tens of thousands of units. He made more than a million dollars by turning a disadvantage into an advantage. As a young teenager, I was one of Joe Cossman's customers.[9]

Mary Kay Ash, who built her hugely successful company, Mary Kay Cosmetics, from a five-thousand-dollar investment, calls this turning "lemons into lemonade."

No matter how difficult the problem you face, one or more solutions, which can mean even greater benefit to you, are hidden right within it. Once you realize that, you can focus on finding those solutions. Moreover, the fact that you know they are there (and they always are) will greatly increase your self-confidence in any situation.

ONCE YOU DEVELOP YOUR SELF-CONFIDENCE, YOU CAN SET BIG GOALS

In combat, people don't put everything on the line for unimportant, insignificant goals — at least, not if they can help it. People in nonmilitary organizations are the same. They do not want to work hard and sacrifice for small things, only for big, important things. The sky is the limit on how big and how important. Successful leaders have visions and goals that are powerful and usually tough to reach.

The Royal Air Force has a motto that goes: "What man can conceive, man can achieve." Note that this motto doesn't say "up to a certain amount" or "to a certain point." If you can conceive of it, you can achieve it. Period.

George Washington is known as "the father of his country" because he had a big vision of that country's future. He conceived of an entirely new nation with freedom and liberty. He was not only general in chief and our first president, he was this country's number one visionary. He held his vision through the most trying times that this nation ever faced. In fact, although the Continental Congress appointed him commander in chief in June 1775, he was commander only of one soldier . . . himself. There was no Continental Army. If Congress changed its mood and decided to accommodate George III, King of England, Washington would be left "holding the bag," the most visible and conspicuous of traitors.[10] But Washington's vision was so large that it carried him and his army through six years of war against the major power of the day, to victory. Washington's big vision continues to inspire not only Americans, but also others in the world, today.

Remember Kenneth Lay from chapter 3, CEO of Enron who built that multibillion-dollar energy company? Mr. Lay has some very definite ideas about thinking big. "In addition to very ambitious visions, we have also set very ambitious one- and three-year goals. I have told our employees on a number of occasions that I am convinced that many organizations (and for that matter individuals) fail to realize their potential not because they do not set goals but because they set their goals too low. It's amazing what individuals and organizations can do if they set their goals high enough."[11] Yes, setting big goals will help you expect positive results.

BECOME A POSITIVE THINKER

It's a fact that what we think of we get, whether it's positive or negative. The successful leaders I surveyed and spoke with were not some kind of Pollyannas. Not at all. They were iron-hard and steely-eyed realists. But that didn't stop them from expecting to win.

What I noticed was this. These positive thinkers kept their eyes on the ball (what they wanted) and not on what they wanted to avoid by asking themselves, "What is the worst that can happen?" They would accept that worst as a possible result if all went wrong and then plunge ahead and do what needed to be done. Now do you think that someone who has already considered the worst that can happen, accepted it, even planned ahead as to what action to take if the "worst comes to worst" is less fearful and thinks more positively? You bet!

GEN. COLIN POWELL SUCCEEDED DESPITE ALL ODDS

One of the most positive-thinking military men I have ever met is Colin Powell, former Chairman of the Joint Chiefs of Staff (JCS). The position he held was the highest in our military. I met General Powell when he addressed the *Los Angeles Times* Management Conference in March 1993.

I had been invited to do a piece on combat leadership for the *Times's* internal newsletter for managers. As it happened, General Powell was slated to speak to the management conference shortly after my article was scheduled to appear. David Laventhol, then publisher and CEO of the *Times,* and Dickson Louie, a fellow graduate of the University of Chicago Business School who was conference president, asked whether I would like to attend the conference and meet General Powell. I was delighted and honored to accept.

I found General Powell to be positive and upbeat. I was surprised at his high energy. His executive officer told me that it was his third speech that day, in three different cities. The first was in Texas and the second in San Francisco. Here it was, three o'clock in the afternoon, his third speech in cities hundreds of miles apart, and Powell showed no sign of fatigue.

Everyone knew he was in for some tough questioning. One of President Bill Clinton's promises prior to his election was over the issue of gays in the military. The rumor was that it was the JCS that had convinced the president to adopt a compromise position. There were other issues. Why couldn't the military budget be cut more and faster? What was the future of the national guard? Many were unhappy with the way they thought the U.S. Army National Guard "round-out" brigades had been treated during the Gulf War. Powell was facing the media in the heart of "the enemy camp." He could be in for a rough time.

Well, it didn't happen like that. Powell was positive and in control right from the start. CEO Laventhol treated him to an elaborate introduction. During his accolades of Powell, Laventhol also revealed that before going into the newspaper business, he had once been a private in the signal corps. Powell came to the podium and thanked Laventhol for his introduction. Then with a twinkle in his eye he added, "And, private, that was done very well."

Powell gave a five-star speech. His positive thinking won over every one of the three hundred or so senior managers.

Powell came from the humblest beginnings. He was raised in the South Bronx in New York. Both of his parents were working-class immigrants, only one of whom had graduated from high school. Despite competition and prejudice, Powell entered and graduated from the City College of New York. There were no special admissions for minorities in those days. He competed for and got a regular commission in the army through the U.S. Reserve Officers Training Corps (ROTC). He was not an "affirmative-action success story" as some have suggested.

There was real, live bigotry and prejudice as Colin Powell rose through the ranks. There was no quota system to assist him. Powell made it to the very pinnacle of the U.S. armed forces on sheer guts, an incredibly positive attitude, and his own merit.

While still chairman, General Powell spoke to kids in the ghettos. And because he couldn't reach them all, he had ten thousand videotapes made, which went to high schools across the country.

Here's what General Powell told them. "There's nothing you can't accomplish if you're willing to put your mind to it, if you're willing to set aside the negative influences that are out there, if you believe in yourself, if you're committed to yourself, and if you believe in this country, and if you let nothing hold you back.

"Don't let the fact that you're Hispanic or black or any other attribute hold you back. Just go for it. I did it; you can do it. Don't look for a silver bullet. Don't look for 'a role model I'm going to follow.' Be your own role model. Believe in yourself."[12]

A POSITIVE THINKER REVITALIZES AN AILING OWENS CORNING

Companies are either growing or dying. There is no in-between. It's hard to think positively when a company is dying. Famed Owens Corning was dying. A recapitalization after fending off a hostile takeover left the company $1.65 billion in long-term debt. The company had retrenched to such a degree that investment in research development, sales — everything — virtually stopped. Sales plummeted by $74 million. Then the CEO the company brought in to try to turn things around was taken seriously ill. He retired after a little more than a year at the helm. Mighty Owens Corning was drifting in a downward spiral.

Enter Glen Hiner. Hiner had already proven himself by running the plastics division of General Electric. There he had grown a $750 million business to $5 billion during a thirteen-year tenure. A positive thinker doesn't think about additional opportunities for retrenching. A positive thinker like Hiner immediately thought about opportunities for expansion.

Here was a company worried about just keeping its head above water. Hiner shook things up by immediately setting the goal of reaching $5 billion by the year 2000. Owens Corning was at $2.8 billion in sales at the time. The year 2000 was only eight years away, but since Hiner had done it before at GE, no doubt he calculated that he could do it faster since he learned a lot the first time. Moreover, he set goals of almost doubling international sales and increasing productivity by 6 percent per year and increasing profitability twice as fast as sales. I imagine you would agree that Hiner expected positive results!

Now I don't want to suggest that being a positive thinker and expecting positive results is enough. You can't simply sit back and expect the results to roll in. Hiner got the company officers to rethink a lot of their former assumptions about the business. He made important acquisitions, and he moved capital around to concentrate resources where they were needed the most. He lent his personal prestige and was seen on the spot at important projects. He brought some talented people on board to help him, fired some who weren't getting the job done, and reassigned others. In other words, he orchestrated the execution of the company's new initiatives. Moreover, as Hiner says, "I'm a pretty good cheerleader, good at touching people and giving them a few kisses."[13] All of this together got the company moving toward the goals Hiner articulated. But consider this. Could Hiner have done any of this if he hadn't been 100 percent positive? Do you think Hiner could have shaken the company out of its "hold-on-to-what-we-have" mentality if he had been a leader with less positive feelings?

How is Owens Corning doing as a result of Glen Hiner's expecting positive results? Owens Corning has racked up twenty-one consecutive quarters of year-over-year improved profits. Long-term debt is down to less than $800 million. The company had record sales of $4.4 billion last year. Sales, service, marketing, and information systems have all been reworked. The company has completed fourteen acquisitions, building or acquiring facilities on every continent except Australia and Antarctica. In fact, things have been going so well that positive thinker Hiner has raised the bar. Now he has set the achievement of his original goals a year earlier![14]

Former Chairman of the Joint Chiefs of Staff Colin Powell says, "Perpetual optimism is a force multiplier."[15]

VISUALIZE THE RESULTS YOU WANT TO ACHIEVE

If you want to learn to expect positive results, you've got to see those results achieved in your own mind first. Psychologists call this mental visualization, and it is amazing what can be done with it. Mental visualization seems to work best in a very relaxed state, and I have witnessed as well as been involved in a number of experiments that illustrate just how powerful mental visualization is.

My wife is a clinical psychologist, and I studied psychology at the graduate level myself. As a consequence, I have attended a number of seminars on hypnosis. Under a hypnotic trance, a subject is extremely relaxed and open to suggestion. One common demonstration is to have the subject imagine himself in a lemon grove picking a lemon, slicing it in half, and squeezing a bit of juice into his mouth.

The amazing thing is that when people do this, their lips invariably pucker as they imagine the sweet-sour juice from the lemon in their mouth. One theory is that all hypnosis is really self-hypnosis, and to become entranced is quite easy. In fact, if you found yourself puckering your lips when you thought about the lemon juice, you did it to yourself!

But there is far more. When in a hypnotic trance, a subject can be told that a cube of ice applied to his bare skin is red hot. Believe it or not, it will actually raise a blister!

However one of the most amazing stories I ever heard about the power of mental visualization, especially regarding its use in expecting positive results, comes from a psychologist by the name of Charles Garfield. I first heard about Garfield from an article in the *Wall Street Journal* in January 1982. The article said that through visualizing a positive outcome, Garfield was able to significantly increase the speaking performance of top executives. Later, Garfield wrote a book, *Peak Performers*, in which he described the following incident.

In Milan, Italy, at a conference on peak performance, Garfield met some Russian scientists who began to discuss their current work. Learning that Garfield was an amateur weight lifter, they invited him to participate in an experiment. Garfield's maximum bench press was 280 pounds. When the scientists asked him what he thought was the most he could do, he told them three hundred pounds. After some encouragement, and working up to it, much to Garfield's amazement he did press three hundred pounds. However he said that he made the lift with great difficulty and it required every ounce of his strength and concentration.

Next, the Russians put Garfield into a relaxed state and took him through a series of visualization exercises that lasted more than an hour. During these exercises, he visualized himself lifting 365 pounds, which to Garfield seemed utterly impossible. However not only was he able to do this, but he felt it was easier to make this lift than the three hundred-pound lift an hour or so earlier![16]

Using visualization to expect positive results is really easy. Sit in your chair or someplace where you can relax and simply visualize your goal in every detail. If your goal is to make a speech, then imagine yourself on the stage waiting to be introduced. Hear the introduction given for you. Are there flowers on the dais? Smell their fragrance. Are some waiters still serving coffee? Listen to the sounds they make as they move about the room. Smell the aroma of the coffee. Imagine sipping some yourself, and savor its taste. Use all five senses to make the scene as real in your mind as you possibly can.

Listen to the applause as you are called forward to begin your presentation. Imagine looking out into the audience. Visualize the eager and expectant looks on the faces of those who are about to listen to you. Now give your speech and note the audience's rapt attention. See yourself connecting with audience, and see the audience responding to what you have to say, hanging on to every word. See yourself coming to a powerful conclusion, and see the audience leaping to its feet in enthusiasm.

After you have done this once, repeat it. If your project is several days ahead, I recommend repeating it several times a day. The night before your performance, you can repeat it a dozen times or more.

HE WAS BROKE, OWED $1 MILLION, AND BECAME ONE OF AMERICA'S RICHEST MEN

Bill Bartmann is the CEO of Commercial Financial Services, Inc. (CFS). CFS is the largest company of its type. It buys loans that have gone bad, those where the borrowers have defaulted and are not paying up. CFS is in the process of trying to collect on $7 billion in bad loans. Revenues have quadrupled, on average, every year since 1993. In 1996 CFS made $137 million in profits on revenues of $349 million. That's a 39 percent margin! According to *Inc.* magazine, Bartmann is worth $3.5 billion, one of the wealthiest people in America, just ahead of Rupert Murdoch and Ross Perot.[17]

Twelve years ago, Bartmann wasn't worth a plugged nickel. OPEC's oil cartel all but collapsed when Bill Bartmann owned a business manufacturing pipes for oil rigs. In one month, his sales dropped from $1 million a month to zero. The company closed its doors, and he found himself broke, owing the bank $1 million and trying to support a wife and two daughters with no income.

But Bartmann had seen tough times before. He dropped out of high school and left his impoverished home when he was fourteen. Yet he always expected positive results. This attracted others to help and follow him. Someone told him about a high school equivalency test. He took it, passed, and got into college. Successfully completing college, he went to law school and passed the bar. He hung out his shingle and made enough in five years as a lawyer to start his pipe company. It did just fine until the market dried up in less than thirty days.

Looking for a way to repay his debt, Bartmann saw an advertisement where the Federal Deposit Insurance Corporation (FDIC) was auctioning off delinquent loans. In other words, they were looking for some poor soul to buy loans that had already gone bad. Only a leader like Bartmann who expected positive results would even think of doing such a thing. Especially since he found his own portfolio among those being sold. But Bill

Bartmann went to his bank, to which he already owed money, and asked for another thirteen thousand dollars. Says Bartmann, "That was a tough sell." Bartmann, however, had a secret weapon. He knew how to visualize to turn his ideas into reality.

He made sixty-four thousand dollars from that initial thirteen thousand dollars. With increased confidence, he returned to the bank and asked for another one hundred thousand dollars to buy more bad loans. He promised to take out only twenty thousand dollars from the money he collected and to use the rest toward paying off his loan. Impressed with Bartmann's positive expectations, the bank president agreed. Several months later, Bartmann returned with more than two hundred thousand dollars and asked for more money. The bank was persuaded. Today, CFS has three thousand employees.

Bill Bartmann has never been in the military, but he believes in the military tradition. For example, all CFS employees attend a seven-week boot camp that is generalized training for everyone. "Admittedly, we brainwash them," he says. "We want them to be part of a cohesive unit. Afterward, they get specialized training for whatever they're going to do in the company." In an industry where turnover is 80 to 120 percent per year, turnover at CFS is about 20 percent during the first six months and then drops to 5 percent.

"My biggest thrill at CFS is watching people grow," he says. "I push people as hard as I can so they can achieve much more than they think. Then their self-esteem goes up, and they can achieve even more. I learned this in my own life. There was so much more I could do than I was doing after I dropped out of high school. What is true of me is true of other people. Once it is true in the mind, it becomes true in reality. I always expect to win, I expect our people to be successful, and I am rarely wrong."[18]

Brig. Gen. William C. Louisell notes that on the battlefield, a leader must "apply a realistic imagination to visualize the mission through to its successful conclusion."[19]

MAINTAIN YOUR ENTHUSIASM

If you aren't enthusiastic, no one else will be. That's a fact. You can't expect followers to enthusiastically accept a challenge that you haven't enthusiastically accepted yourself.

Some say that one reason for the failure of Gen. George Pickett's charge at Gettysburg during the Civil War was his superior, Gen. James Longstreet. Longstreet lacked enthusiasm for making the attack. Previously he tried to persuade Gen. Robert E. Lee not to order the charge, but he was unsuccessful. Having earlier warned General Pickett that Lee could order a charge, Longstreet was leaning dejectedly against a fence railing when Pickett came to him to receive the order to proceed.

"General, shall I advance?" asked Pickett, saluting. Longstreet returned the salute, but with his head bowed, said nothing.

Pickett repeated his request. Still not getting a response, he asked, "If it is your desire that I proceed, nod your head."

Longstreet, head still bowed, nodded in the affirmative. Pickett's charge, certain the most gallant in history, was also one of the most costly. Out of 10,500 men who made the advance, only 4,830 came back to Confederate lines unscathed.[20]

A MARINE SHOWS HOW TO MAINTAIN ENTHUSIASM WHEN CONDITIONS ARE BAD

In December 1950, the Chinese crossed the border into Korea in overwhelming numbers. United Nation forces under Gen. Douglas MacArthur withdrew to avoid capture. Col. "Chesty" Puller led a regiment of U.S. Marines in retreat from the Chinese border to the port of Hungnam in North Korea. It was during the bitter cold of winter, but the marines had only their summer uniforms. They had wounded men, carried limited food, and had gone for days with little sleep. Yet Puller was upbeat and positive. He told his troops: "You're the First Marine Division, and don't you forget it. We're the greatest military outfit that ever walked on this earth. Not all the communists in hell can stop you. We'll go down to the sea at our own pace and nothing is going to get in our way. If it does, we'll blow the hell out of it."

Puller got his regiment to the port of Hungnam successfully. Puller eventually retired from the marines with the three stars of a lieutenant general. He is also the only man in U.S. military history to win the Navy Cross, the decoration that is second only to the Congressional Medal of Honor, five times! Puller knew how to maintain his enthusiasm and expect positive results.

I've found that even if I'm not enthusiastic about a project initially, I can get worked up about it if it makes sense. Once I am excited and enthusiastic, I automatically expect positive results.

How do I get worked up? Well, my initial lack of enthusiasm may be for a variety of reasons. Maybe I've got another important project pending. Maybe I need more help. Maybe I haven't sorted everything out yet. What I do is think of all the good things that will happen when I complete this project or task. When I'm feeling a little better about it, I start pretending that I want to do this thing. Before long, I find that I really am enthusiastic. Then I expect positive results.

Four-star general Duane Cassidy, who commanded flying units in Vietnam and had senior responsibilities during the operation in Grenada, puts it this way: "The successful leader must know how to manage his own energy and transmit it to every man and woman in the unit."[21]

THE FOUR ACTIONS SUMMARIZED

If you want others to follow your lead and expect to win, then you must do so first. If you expect positive results, others will as well. To expect positive results as a leader:

1. Develop Your Self-Confidence
2. Become a Positive Thinker
3. Visualize the Results You Want To Achieve
4. Maintain Your Enthusiasm

It may be true that simply expecting positive results does not guarantee your success. However not expecting positive results will almost always guarantee your failure. So to increase your chances of success in any situation that you face:

EXPECT POSITIVE RESULTS

ENDNOTES

[1] Drucker, Peter F., *The Practice of Management*, (New York: Harper and Row, 1955), 194.

[2] Grant, Michael, *Classical Historians* (New York: Charles Scribner's Sons, 1992), 101.

[3] Xenophon, *The Persian Expedition*, trans. Rex Warner, (Baltimore: Penguin Books, 1949), 104.

[4] Vandenberg, Hoyt S., Jr., letter to the author, July 5, 1993.

[5] Stuberg, Robert, "An Interview with Bruce Jenner," *Insight* audio tape, no. 177 (1997).

[6] Williams, A. L., *All You Can Do Is All You Can Do* (Nashville: Oliver Nelson, 1988).

[7] Leavitt, Lloyd R., Jr., letter to the author, August 13, 1993.

[8] Louisell, William C., Ibid.

[9] Cossman, E. Joseph, telephone interview with the author, November 24, 1997.

[10] Flexner, James T., *Washington: The Indispensable Man* (Boston: Little Brown and Company, 1974), 61.

[11] Lay, Kenneth L., letter to the author, November 17, 1997.

[12] Powell, Colin L., address to *Los Angeles Times* Management Conference, March 19, 1993.

[13] Stewart, Thomas A., "Back from the Dead," *Fortune* (May 26, 1997), 126.

[14] Ibid., 118–126.

[15] Powell, Colin L., "Colin Powell's Rules," handout, *Los Angeles Times* Management Conference, March 19, 1993.

[16] Garfield, Charles, *Peak Performers* (New York: Avon, 1986), 71–75.

[17] Useem, Jerry, "The Richest Man You've Never Heard Of," *Inc.* (September 1997): 45.

[18] Bartmann, William, telephone interview with the author, October 28, 1997.

[19] Louisell, William C., letter to the author, July 26, 1993.

[20] Stewart, George R., *Pickett's Charge* (Greenwich, Conn.: Fawcett Publications, Inc., 1963), 232.

[21] Cassidy, Duane H., letter to the author, July 26, 1993.

TAKE CARE
OF YOUR PEOPLE

For people are only too glad to obey the man who they believe takes wiser thoughts for their interests than they themselves do.
— XENOPHON

Treat your subordinates right and they will literally die for you.
— MAJ. GEN. MELVIN ZAIS

Mark Peters was a star athlete and a fairly good student in high school, but he didn't know quite what he wanted to do with his life. He thought that maybe he wanted to go to college, only not right away. A friend was joining the army and persuaded him to join, too. The army gave him aptitude and other tests, and as a result, encouraged him to apply for advanced training in electronics or missile technology after he graduated from basic training. But Mark wanted to "experience life and see the world." He volunteered for Special Forces — the Green Berets. He qualified as a paratrooper, studied the Vietnamese language, and became a language specialist. In 1963 Mark was assigned to a Special Forces "A Team" in Vietnam.

Mark's unit worked with Montagnard tribesmen. He liked his job, both because of the mission and because of the Montagnards. His unit's mission was to find and attack enemy guerrillas. Unlike the regular army, the Special Forces operated just like the guerrillas they opposed. They taught the Montagnards the techniques of surprise, stealth, booby traps, and ambush. They attacked the guerrillas on what was considered the enemy's turf, and they were enormously effective. Much of their success was because of their students. The Montagnards were good fighters and were 100 percent trustworthy. Mark's team worked with several hundred men, and they not only led them in battle, but took responsibility for their feeding and the well-being of their families, who lived with the troops.

If a Montagnard said he would stay with you, he meant it . . . to the death. So the Americans trusted the Montagnards, and the Montagnards trusted the Americans. Where Peters saw much American military and other aid wasted because of the corruption of some Vietnamese officials, Uncle Sam got his money's worth with the Montagnards. The Viet Cong very much feared the Montagnards and their American "teachers."

One month American food and other aid promised for the Montagnards wasn't given to the Green Berets. Instead, it was diverted to a corrupt Vietnamese government official who promised to distribute it to them himself. Of course, he did not.

Peters's team leader, a warrant officer, complained through his command channels immediately. Without this food, the Montagnards and their families would starve. He was told that nothing could be done. The team leader was told to tell the Montagnards to feed themselves in the way they had before the Americans had come.

Instead Peters's team leader called his "A Team" together. There were ten men on this team. "We are responsible for the Montagnards," he told them. "They have fought with us faithfully and have always kept their word to us. However, I have been unsuccessful in getting the promised food for them. This has been given to 'X,' who, as you know, is corrupt. Several dozen of his troops who are considered part of Army of Vietnam are guarding the food. I propose to take the food tonight. Since this is an illegal operation, no one needs to come with me. I do not want casualties on either side, but it could happen. Who wants to come?"

Every man volunteered, Mark says. And the team leader kept his promise. That evening, they distributed booze to the corrupt official's troops. When they were drunk and asleep, the Americans escaped with enough sacks of rice and other foodstuffs to feed their several hundred charges.

Then they returned and began firing into the air. This awakened the drunken troops. They thought they had been attacked by Viet Cong troops and started firing wildly. The Americans faded into the jungle. There were no casualties on either side.

Later the official's troops examined the stores and found that a significant portion was missing. They suspected the Special Forces, but their commander was afraid to tell the corrupt official that he and his men had been duped. So they blamed the theft of the food on the enemy and took credit for driving the Viet Cong off. Mark Peters appreciated the extent to which his team leader had gone to take care of the people who looked to him for leadership. He did not forget this battlefield lesson.

MARK PETERS TAKES CARE OF HIS PEOPLE

Mark Peters left the army. He went to a small college in the Midwest and got a degree in engineering. He held a number of positions in different companies in industry. One day he was hired as director of operations by a Florida company that sold fire alarm systems to large corporations. Mark was responsible for the manufacturing and installing of the company's five product lines. Each product line was headed by a manager who reported to Mark. Four of his managers held degrees from universities. One engineer had come up from the ranks. His name was Irv. Mark found Irv to be extremely competent. If Mark wanted a difficult job done, he gave it to Irv. He considered him one of the best, if not the best, of his managers.

One day Mark sat down and reviewed the salaries of all his employees. He was amazed to discover that even though Irv had the same responsibilities as his other managers, he was paid considerably less.

Mark spoke with the vice president of finance. "Irv came up from the ranks of the workers," the vice president told him. "He has a couple years of college but no degree. Our salaries are based on a formula which weights a degree heavily."

"Irv is one of my best managers," said Mark. "We need to change the formula or make some kind of exception."

"Irv has never complained," answered the vice president. "I don't see any reason for doing this. However, if you insist, it can't be done all at once. Otherwise, the percentage increase would be too great. That's against company policy, too, and I won't budge on it."

Mark agreed that he would increase Irv's salary by giving him periodic raises until his salary was comparable with the others.

A few months later, it was the Christmas season. Mark received a memorandum from the president asking for recommendations for the coming Christmas bonuses. Mark called the president. "I don't know how this is done," he told the president. "I assume you assign each department a certain amount of money and then divide this pot up according to my input."

"That's correct, Mark," responded the president. "The vice president of finance and I get together and may make minor adjustments, but basically we will use the percentages you recommend."

Mark worked out percentages based on the contributions of each member of his department and sent them to the president. On the last day before the Christmas vacation, Mark received a large pile of sealed envelopes from the finance department with a note: "These are the bonuses for your department. Please distribute them."

Mark called the president right away. "These envelopes are sealed," he said. "Each recipient will assume that the bonus I hand him is what I intend. If anyone made an error, I won't know about it. I would like permission to open these envelopes to ensure they are correct before I give them out." The president told Mark to go ahead.

Mark called in his managers and told them to check the bonuses for their workers. He checked the bonus of each of his managers. All were as he intended. That is, all except for one. Irv, whom Mark wanted to get a larger bonus because of his greater contributions, got far less than any other manager.

Mark immediately called the president again and explained the problem. A few minutes later, the president called back. "We can't give Irv a larger percentage because the bonus percentages are limited by base salary. Until Irv's base salary is higher, the size of the bonus we can give him is limited."

"That is wrong," said Mark. "I am in the process of raising his salary to make it equitable with the others. But by company policy I can't do this all at once. However, to give him a bonus based on his salary, which is itself too low, and not based on performance is wrong. This is unfair. Moreover it sends the wrong message regarding this individual's performance."

"I'm sorry," answered the president. "These questions are up to the vice president of finance. It's his responsibility."

"Boss," said Mark, "if the company cannot give Irv more, I respect that, but I intend to give him an additional bonus out of my own pocket to make up the difference."

Mark knew he was taking a big chance. The vice president of finance had been with the company for many years. Mark was a new manager. The president could fire him. Mark's predecessor had been fired. However, Mark believed that taking care of his people was important. It was what he saw on the battlefield, and Mark knew it was the right thing to do. There were several seconds of silence. Mark waited and said nothing. Then the president spoke. "Bring Irv's bonus check to my office. It will be as you say."

And so it was. No wonder Irv, Mark's other managers and workers, and the rest of the employees and managers in the company respect and support Mark. When he asks his department to do "the impossible" in production, time, or budget, the workers never fail him. They don't fail him because he never fails them. Mark always takes care of his people. His future as a leader is assured.

Philip Bolte served in combat in armored vehicles in both Korea and Vietnam and retired as brigadier general. General Bolte puts it in a way shared by many combat leaders: "Take care of your men and they will take care of you."[1] Thomas Noel fought in Vietnam, then left the army to assume a senior executive post in the Department of Energy. He was in charge of the strategic petroleum reserves. He later became president of a succession of companies. Tom Noel credits what he knows about leadership to his general's inspirational leadership in Vietnam. "Believe in your people and take care of them," he says. "You are what your people are, no more, and no less."[2]

HOW FAR SHOULD YOU GO IN TAKING CARE OF YOUR PEOPLE?

Fortunately a civilian career does not normally require a leader to lay down his life for his people in order to take care of them. But make no mistake. You must be willing to go to enormous lengths in taking care of your people if you really expect them to follow you with the same devotion given to a successful battle leader.

They say that Thomas Watson, who founded IBM and later instituted extensive programs in education, health care, and recreation for IBM employees, was continually visiting his factories and spent hours talking to his employees. On one occasion, he told an employee, "If you have any problem at all, let me know."

Later the employee came to New York and asked to see Watson. On being ushered in to Watson's office, he told Watson that his younger brother had an incurable disease, and he had been told he would not live long. Remembering Watson's promise, he asked whether anything could be done that was beyond the medical resources of his small community. Watson immediately arranged for the brother to be put in a top hospital under the care of a famous specialist.

At this point, the employee began to feel a little guilty — perhaps he had overstepped Watson's invitation. He began to apologize. But Watson interrupted him. "When I said bring your problems to me, I meant exactly that."[3]

FIVE WAYS TO TAKE CARE OF YOUR PEOPLE

If you want to be a leader who follows the sixth universal law of leadership and who takes care of his people, here is what you must do:

1. Be the Leader When Things Go Wrong
2. Give Their Needs Priority
3. Really Care
4. Assume the Responsibility
5. Share the Gain

BE THE LEADER WHEN THINGS GO WRONG

When the chips are down and times are difficult — that's when those who follow watch to see what you do. Do you really take care of your people, or is it all for show?

One challenge of following the sixth universal law of leadership is that it can conflict with other laws, especially the first law, "maintain absolute integrity." The leader must always use his judgment to ensure he doesn't compromise his integrity when he is taking care of his people. We saw that in the case of General Lavelle in chapter 1. In attempting to take care of his people, General Lavelle compromised his own integrity and put many of his pilots in a position where they thought they had to lie.

So the leader is always walking the knife's edge, balancing a readiness to sacrifice himself for his people with doing what is right. Harry G. Summers, retired army colonel and syndicated columnist, states the commander has a responsibility "to shield his subordinate leaders from arbitrary and capricious attack."[4] He is 100 percent right.

Summers tells of a combat action in Vietnam in which he was involved to illustrate his point. Brig. Gen. James F. Hollingsworth, who was an assistant division commander, flew over Summer's battle position in a helicopter. He called Summer's battalion commander, Lt. Col. Dick Prillaman, on the radio and told him that one of his company commanders was all screwed up. "I want you to relieve him right now," he demanded. "Relieve" is the military way of saying "fire."

Prillaman responded instantly, "He's doing exactly what I want him to do. If you relieve anyone, it should be me."

General Hollingsworth could have done exactly that. Instead, he said, "Now dammit, Dick, don't get your back up. It just looked screwed up from up here. Go down and check it out." By the time he retired from the army, Prillaman was a lieutenant general.[5] Good leaders who take care of their people frequently get promoted. But, as we will see, not always.

WHEN THINGS WENT WRONG, THIS LEADER STUCK HIS NECK ALL THE WAY OUT

During the Vietnam War, the kinds of targets that could be attacked were controlled very closely. Many targets that would normally be attacked during a war were protected. This is why many claim that this war was fought "with both arms tied behind our back."

Those who violated the "Rules of Engagement (ROE)," even accidentally, were disciplined and sometimes court-martialed. They faced punishment that included grounding, discharge, and even the military prison at Ft. Levenworth, Kansas.

One June 2, 1967, two American F-105 pilots on a mission over Hanoi came under attack by guns protecting a ship unloading its military cargo in Haiphong Harbor. This was in an area that Secretary of Defense McNamara had declared a sanctuary for the enemy. The ship, and the area surrounding it, could not be attacked according to the ROE. However, to save themselves, the two pilots instinctively fired back. They didn't identify the ship. They simply opened fire to get away. The whole incident took less than five seconds. But the consequences could have been severe. It turned out later that the ship unloading munitions for North Vietnam was a Russian freighter.

The commander responsible for these pilots was a colonel by the name of Jack Broughton. Broughton was on the fast track to make general. He was a graduate of one of the most prestigious senior service schools in the armed forces, the National War College. He was smart, aggressive, and an outstanding leader. While many senior officers flew an occasional mission and spent most of their time behind a desk, Broughton scheduled himself to fly the tough ones. If there was a difficult combat mission over North Vietnam, you could bet Broughton was on it.

When the strike force the two pilots were a part of returned from its mission, the flight leader asked to see Broughton in private and told him what had happened. As Broughton commented, "That made it my problem."

Complicating the matter, the two pilots had landed first at another American base because of bad weather. Still somewhat punchy from combat and frightened by the potential consequences of the unauthorized attack they had made, one of the pilots signed a statement saying that he had not fired his guns. Both Broughton and his pilots knew that signing this report constituted a false official statement. Under military law, that in itself could lead to a dishonorable discharge, even if the statement were made under the pressures of the moment and without time to reflect.

The only evidence against the two pilots was their own gun camera film. Broughton took the film and exposed it to a truck's headlights. Then he burned it. Broughton said later, "This was not an easy decision nor was it made lightly."[6] He was not in favor of violating orders, and certainly not in favor of making false statements. However he believed that while what these pilots did was wrong, it was understandable and forgivable. Moreover, he knew that in this war, such mistakes were not forgiven. Pilots violating the ROE in the past had been punished severely for far lesser mistakes. Broughton was raised in an environment that required you to take care of your people. He made the personal decision that if anyone was going to be punished over this incident, it would be he and not the two pilots.

As a result of Broughton's actions, no one could prove which pilots were involved in this incident. Broughton was court-martialed. He freely admitted burning the film. He was found guilty, fined, and admonished. On appeal, a board of high-ranking civilians from the Office of the Secretary of the Air Force set these findings aside. But the mere fact that he was court-martialed effectively ended Broughton's career. He retired from the air force, and obviously he was never promoted to general. He did, however, write two best-selling books, *Thud Ridge* and *Going Downtown*. And on Broughton's last combat mission over North Vietnam, one of the pilots he protected saved his life. As Jack Broughton says today, "That's a type of poetic justice and in a real sense made it all worthwhile."[7]

Were his actions in destroying the gun camera film right or wrong? I don't know. You have to make your own call on this one. The point I want to make is just how far this leader was willing to go to take care of his people. He was willing to sacrifice his career, even go to jail, if necessary, to protect them from what he felt would be unduly harsh punishment for an instinctive act committed while under fire from a ship that was actually supplying the enemy.

How puny this makes other leaders look! Is it any wonder that many of their followers are unenthusiastic about working for them? Some of these so-called leaders go so far as to try to avoid responsibility when things go wrong by blaming subordinates. Others think nothing about inconveniencing those they lead, and are untroubled by employees' working conditions or whether their work schedules are causing family hardships or the decision to fire them to cut costs and bolster the bottom line a little. So far as they are concerned, their people are so much fodder for the system, and if a subordinate doesn't like it, he or she can go elsewhere! Is it any wonder that these corporate executives are not considered leaders by the people who work for them?

A SEVENTY-YEAR-OLD LEADER TAKES CARE OF HIS PEOPLE WHEN TIMES ARE TOUGH

Age or civilian clothes have little to do with this concept. You either take care of your people, no matter how bad the situation, or you do not. A man from Lawrence, Massachusetts, named Aaron Feuerstein did the former. On the night of December 11, 1995, while Feuerstein was celebrating his seventieth birthday, his factory, Malden Mills, burned down.

Malden Mills was a complex of nine buildings, and it

employed twenty-four hundred semiskilled workers. Most of them were immigrants. The manufacturer of upholstery and synthetic winter wear fabrics was a $400 million company and one of the largest employers in the region. Feuerstein's grandfather, a Jewish immigrant from Eastern Europe, founded it in 1906.

Feuerstein had laboriously worked the company out of Chapter 11 reorganization in the early 1980s. He had a reputation for taking care of his people and for paying what some termed "the best wages in the textile industry." Productivity had practically tripled prior to the fire.

His losses in the fire were significant. One of three boilers exploded in a building where nylon and velvet materials for chairs and other furnishings were made. This building and two others were leveled. Thirty-three workers were injured, thirteen of them severely. Almost half his workforce had no work to perform.

At a time when leaders of bigger, wealthier, stronger companies were firing employees simply to cut costs and improve their profit picture, Feuerstein pledged to continue paychecks and health benefits for as long as it took to rebuild. It cost him $1.5 million a week just to meet his payroll. He even paid the previously announced holiday bonus of $275 to each employee. Rather than take the insurance money and run, he vowed to rebuild on the same spot.

In a TV interview, he was asked to explain why he did this while other "smarter" and more prominent managers of large corporations smiled and said that he should cut his losses. Feuerstein quoted Hebrew and said his decision was in the Jewish tradition.

"Why am I doing it?" he asked aloud. "I consider the employees . . . the most valuable asset Malden Mills has. I don't consider them, like some companies do, as an expense that can be cut. I know in the long run that what I'm doing today will come back tenfold and will make Malden Mills the best company in the industry."

The response of Richard Lizotte, a Malden Mills machine operator prior to the fire, said Feuerstein's actions were typical. He said he wasn't surprised because Feuerstein's "a man of his word."[8]

Eventually it cost Feuerstein $15 million to keep his word. But last September, he rebuilt a $100 million factory on the site of the destruction. At the factory opening, U.S. Rep. Martin Meehan commented, "Feuerstein showed the difference when you have somebody who is passionately committed to his workers. It would have been easier for him to retire."[9]

Again, bean-counting managers at larger companies said he should have pocketed the insurance money, and if not, then rebuild farther south where labor costs were lower. That would be a good business decision, they said. I'm not so sure. I know it would have been a poor leadership decision. Feuerstein agrees. "Why would I go south to cut costs, when the advantage that I have is quality? And that comes from focusing on people, not cutting costs."

But Feuerstein is a businessman and nobody's patsy. Drawn into a discussion of Al Dunlap, who fired a third of the workforce at Scott Paper, Feuerstein said, "If one-third of the people of that company were wastefully employed, then Dunlap did the right thing. Legitimate downsizing as the result of technological advances or as a result of good engineering? Absolutely. I'm in favor of it. And we do it here all day long. . . . We try to do it in such a way as to minimize human suffering, but the downsizing must be done." However Feuerstein says that the trick is to do it "without crushing the spirit of the workforce." If all you are after is cutting costs, if you "just have a scheme to cut people — that sort of thing is resented by labor and never forgiven."[10]

Speaking at MIT, Feuerstein said, "Within four months, we had 85 percent of the people back. Were it not for the slow payments of the insurance company, we would have over 100 percent back today."

And how are Feuerstein's people performing today? As an example, Feuerstein told his audience, "The fourth plant, which prior to the fire had never produced more than 130,000 yards a week, is producing more than 200,000 yards."[11]

AN AIR FORCE CAPTAIN LEARNS TO GIVE HIS FOLLOWERS' NEEDS PRIORITY

If you are the leader, you've got to learn to give the needs of those you lead greater weight than your own personal needs. Again, you must balance your followers' needs with your mission. This entire balancing act sometimes makes for a difficult judgment call. Is it the mission you are primarily concerned with in ignoring or disregarding your people's needs, or is it your own needs?

If it's really your own needs, and taking care of your people just makes your job a little tougher, or a little riskier, then maybe you had better think again.

Capt. Dave Whitmore was the navigator of a "select crew" flying the giant nuclear B-52 bomber during the height of the cold war. The bomber crews of the Strategic Air Command (SAC) had an unusual motto for a group of warriors: "Peace is our profession." The reason for their motto was that these crews were our nuclear retaliatory force. The idea was that SAC crews were so well-trained and the weapons at their disposal so powerful that no enemy in his right mind would dare to start a nuclear war because of our retaliatory capabilities.

SAC select crews were considered the cream of the crop. Up to 10 percent of the bomber crews were designated as "select" based on their exceptional performance.

All SAC crews earned their pay. Having spent five and a half years in SAC myself, I can attest to the fact that the duty was no picnic. During two particularly rigorous years, the sum total of all holidays — Christian, Jewish, birthdays, and weekends — that I spent off-duty was less than ten days!

When the Vietnam War heated up, SAC crews did rotating duty flying combat missions with non-nuclear weapons from Guam. That heated things up for them even more. David Whitmore flew several rounds of these combat tours as well as training to go to a nuclear war.

Even though Whitmore spent so much time on his job, his real interest was in engineering, not flying. When he had first volunteered for flying duties, he anticipated a couple of years "in the cockpit" before being sent for an advanced degree in engineering and then applying this knowledge to aviation problems.

However shortly after Whitmore completed flying training, the air force more than doubled the amount of time a new flyer had to remain flying. Even so, he took tests and qualified for the air force's master's degree program in astronautics.

Unfortunately the air force put considerable pressure on unit commanders not to release SAC crewmen for other air force programs. Every trained SAC crewman replaced by one less experienced meant increased difficulties and problems for the commanders. Since competition for promotions for commanders was intense and their crews were constantly being tested, there was no question that the loss of Whitmore represented a significant career risk to his commander and other commanders at higher organizational levels. Would Whitmore's commander allow him to leave SAC to get his master's degree?

Says Whitmore, "My commander supported me 100 percent. He told me, 'Dave, if you wait around until the time is perfect for us you will never get your master's degree. That's important to the air force, too!'" So Whitmore left SAC and entered a master's program. Later Captain Whitmore discovered it hadn't been so simple. A higher leader had tried to block his transfer for graduate training. However his immediate commander had dug his heels in and stuck his neck out, literally guaranteeing no drop in crew performance despite Whitmore's leaving. Whitmore realized that his commander had taken risks for his sake. He had placed Whitmore's needs above his own, and Whitmore vowed to do the same as a leader himself.

WHITMORE GIVES HIS PEOPLE'S NEEDS PRIORITY AT IBM

With his air force service behind him, Whitmore joined IBM. Some years later, he was promoted to IBM marketing manager for a new region in New York that serviced utilities and telephone companies. Two of his most senior marketing team leaders serviced the two largest accounts in Dave's area. These accounts represented a considerable amount of money, and the pressure was incredible. The situation reminded Whitmore of SAC. If any of the computers went down, Whitmore could lose his job.

One day Whitmore became aware of a serious problem. Neither one of his senior team leaders had ever held a staff job. He was told that if they weren't assigned staff positions outside of his area within the next few months, chances were, they would never get them. If they never got a staff job, their future careers at IBM were limited. It was unlikely that they could ever get promoted to a more senior position. Yet these were talented, hard-working people. Their timing was just bad.

First Whitmore explained the situation to his two team leaders. What did they want to do? Both expressed a willingness to stay if they had to, but both understood the necessity of obtaining staff experience. Both wanted to go.

Whitmore was inexperienced in his new job. He had no other experienced team leaders, and none would be available if he let these two go. Yet it was Whitmore's decision, and it was his responsibility to take care of his people.

Whitmore's boss, a branch manager, counseled him. "Who cares whether they become managers or not? It's your fanny on the line. If you let them go, you're taking a chance on losing everything you've worked for. Screw up, and I can't guarantee whether you can ever become a branch manager. Your sending them to staff positions may help them, but it may limit your future in the company."

But Whitmore remembered SAC. He knew what he had to do. He saw that both team leaders were offered staff positions in IBM immediately. They both accepted and left.

What happened to Dave Whitmore? He made do without the two experienced team leaders. Later, because of his success at this job, he was offered what he calls "my dream job": international account manager in Brussels. Before retirement from IBM, he was promoted to branch manager and served in that capacity in Saudi Arabia.[12]

AMERICA'S LAST ACE LEARNS ABOUT LEADERS WHO REALLY CARE

If you want to be a leader, you've got to really care about the people you lead. If you really care about them, you will take care of them no matter what.

Steve Ritchie is a general in the U.S. Air Force Reserve. He is also the leading air force pilot ace of the Vietnam War and the last ace this country has produced. In his civilian job, he is president of a seminar company. Before that, he was the government's director of housing and welfare. He gives several hundred speeches every year on leadership.

Steve says that the greatest example of leadership he ever saw began with a defeat, not a victory. Maj. Bob Lodge and Capt. Roger Locher were shot down in their F-4 fighter while battling MIG-21s and MIG-19s over North Vietnam. No parachutes were seen. Though both men carried survival radios with extra batteries, radio contact could not be made with them. It seemed that both men had been lost.

Three weeks later, Ritchie suddenly heard a transmission on his radio while flying in the vicinity of Yen Bai Airfield, seventy miles northwest of Hanoi. "Any U.S. aircraft, this is Oyster — Zero — One — Bravo — Over." It was Captain Locher. Locher was five miles off the south end of one of North Vietnam's most important military airfields.

Ritchie passed the word, and they quickly planned and launched one of the deepest, most difficult, and most dangerous rescues ever attempted. But the ground fire was so intense that helicopters couldn't get to him. Here was Locher, still alive after successfully evading capture and living off the land for twenty-two days. They knew where he was, but so did the enemy. They couldn't get to him to get him out. Ritchie says everyone returned to Thailand discouraged and frustrated.

The next morning, Gen. John Vogt, the commander of all air forces in Vietnam, canceled the strike mission to Hanoi. He diverted hundreds of aircraft and assigned them to one mission — saving Locher — and they did. Later they learned that Lodge had been killed when the aircraft was shot down. But they got Locher out, despite everything the enemy did to try to stop them.[13]

Vogt was not publicly criticized for what he did. However there were those in the government at the time who were not pleased that all those resources had been diverted to save one flyer.

Ritchie never forgot the general who really cared — a leader who diverted the entire war effort to help one American return home. Neither did the thousands of other airmen under his command. They knew that if misfortune struck, their leader would stop at nothing to get them back.

REALLY CARING MEANS TAKING IT BACK

Remember Pat Patterson from chapter 4 who showed us what it meant to demonstrate uncommon commitment both in and out of combat? Patterson completed his combat mission in spite of terrible weather and no fuel. Then he filled the almost impossible fuel pump order as president of Ohio Precision Castings. The commander of Pat's squadron in Korea was a major by the name of Herb Mann.

Pat describes Herb Mann as "a leader because he cared for his troops and knew what he was there for. He did change his leadership style to fit the occasion. He could be very tough and demanding, yet always showed that he cared about his kids, whether pilots or ground crew.

"One day I had my third consecutive ground abort. They were all right according to the book, but I might have assumed a little more risk and gone anyway on the first two. However, this time it was due to fuel backing up in my pressurization system, which was a major hazard either in the air or on the ground. While I was climbing down the ladder, Herb came storming up in a jeep, with a cigar stub clenched in his teeth. His first words were, 'What's the matter, Pat, losing your nerve?'

"I replied, 'If that cigar is lit, keep away from me.' I unzipped my G-suit and poured out two gallons of highly inflammable JP-4 jet fuel.

"He didn't say a word. In a minute he had that plane swarming with specialists to fix the problem. He gave it first priority. I knew this was his way of showing that he was sorry for his question and that he really cared about me.

"And I never let him down by aborting unless I had a really major problem. In fact, I never aborted again for any reason."[14]

OTHER WAYS TO SHOW YOU CARE

Leaders in the corporate world, or those who lead other nonmilitary organizations, may not have the opportunity to save someone's life as many have in combat. But there are many other ways to prove to those you lead that you truly care about their welfare.

AN AGENCY SHOWS IT CARES BY GIVING
EMPLOYEES A WORK ENVIRONMENT THEY LIKE

Dahlin Smith White (DSW) is a $192 million advertising agency in Salt Lake City, Utah, started by John Dahlin, Darrell Smith, and Jon White. They show they care by giving their people incredible freedom in the work environment. Every office has a built-in, company-furnished boom box. Employees can play music as loud as they want as long as they don't disturb others.

If anyone wants to take a mid-day break to go skiing or to the movies, company policy permits it. Employees get an art budget to decorate their own offices. The company sponsors and pays for dinners, movies, mountain climbing, horseback riding, and snowmobiling and up to forty company-sponsored parties a year.

According to the three partners, showing they care pays off in that their people work harder and win more accounts.[15] In a little more than ten years, they have become the largest communications company in America focusing primarily on the technology customer. Last year *Marketing Computing* magazine named them "Agency of the Year," and *AdWeek* rated them one of the top interactive agencies.[16]

THIS RHINO LEADS PROEMPLOYEE CHARGES

Ted Castle founded Rhino Foods in Burlington, Vermont. They make specialty foods and gained some fame by coming up with the "cookie dough" in Ben & Jerry's ice cream of the same name.

The company has been called "A Workplace of the Future — Now."[17] Castle was determined that the business wouldn't run his life and that he would leave time for outside activities. And he wanted the same for Rhino's employees. To show he means what he says, he's started a number of highly innovative programs. One group called "Focus in Families" meets every Thursday on company time to oversee programs for employees and the community. Another, the "Nurturing Program," lasts fifteen weeks and works with parents and kids to develop better parenting skills. Rhino puts up the cash to fund it. Then there is Rhino's "Wants Program." Employees meet with a "wants" coordinator once every three months to work on goals they've chosen. The coordinator is especially trained to coach employees and help them reach their goals. Amazingly these goals are not necessarily work-related. We're talking about anything from buying a house to learning to skydive.

Mark Koenigsberg, the company's director of sales and marketing, says the company developed the programs to help promote a healthy life outside the workplace for its staff.[18] Marlene Dailey, director of human resources, explains, "We want people to be able to think for themselves, go after things on their own, and not become dependent on the company."[19]

Many Rhino Foods products are seasonal. Several years ago, President Castle came up with an innovative solution to show he cared and to avoid firing unneeded employees during the company's off-seasons. Castle found two noncompeting companies that also relied heavily on seasonal employees. He leased his unneeded employees to them. Rhino continued to pay all their employee benefits. In essence, he created an employee exchange program that benefited everyone. There were no unemployment costs, morale stayed high, and trained and experienced workers — ready, willing, and able — returned. Frequently they returned with ideas that further benefited Rhino Foods. Little wonder that in a small specialized market, Rhino Foods has doubled sales in five years and gets frequent attention from outsiders as a forward-looking company that really cares about its employees.[20]

GIANT 3M CARES FOR ITS PEOPLE BY SEEKING TO AVOID LAYOFFS

Minnesota Mining and Manufacturing Company in St. Paul, Minnesota, better known as 3M, is a $14 billion giant headed up by CEO L. D. De Simone. Back in the early 1980s, 3M had to address the possibility of layoffs for the first time in its history. To avoid or at least minimize them, company leaders came up with a system called the "Unassigned List."

The Unassigned List gives employees whose jobs have been eliminated through no fault of their own six months to find another position within 3M. Meanwhile workers continue to receive full salaries and benefits. Within the first four months, they have the option of taking a severance package. This includes a week and a half's pay for every year of service, plus six months of paid benefits. Those who are over age fifty but haven't yet reached retirement age can also receive a preretirement leave package that continues benefits until retirement age. Those over age fifty-five receive a special bridge to Social Security. For those who cannot find a position within the company, 3M also offers extensive help in finding new employment.

Says Dick Lidstad, senior vice president of human resources, "We're a company of long-service employees. That long service translates into less than a 3 percent turnover among the salaried staff. And pride."[21]

That pride translates into real results. Last year one of 3M's divisions won the National Malcomb Baldridge Award. Perhaps more important, CEO De Simone reported in 3M's annual report that income had increased by 11.7 percent and the company had record sales and earnings in its two business sectors and in U.S. and international operations.[22]

IF YOU REALLY CARE, YOU'LL TREAT THEM RIGHT

Erick Laine, CEO of ALCAS, Inc., manufactures and markets some of the highest quality kitchen knives in the world under the brand name Cutco. One division makes the K-bar knife, the official knife of the U.S. Marine Corps since World War II. Its sales today are more than $100 million worldwide. But when Laine took over as CEO in 1982, sales were only $5 million. That's a 2,000 percent increase in a field dominated by older, established brands from Europe.

When Erick became CEO of ALCAS, the manufacturing arm was in disarray. In a nine-year period prior to his becoming boss, there wasn't a single contract settled without a strike! No fewer than 270 outstanding grievances were on the books!

Erick is tough. He was born in Finland, and in addition to integrity, his parents taught him something that doesn't translate easily into English. The word in Finnish is "sisu." "Sisu" means a sort of stubborn persistence wrapped up with sheer guts. He knows what he is doing, and he is no pushover. But he truly cares about his people, and he insists on treating them fairly.

So Erick met with his union in a spirit of openness and listened. "When the union was right, I acknowledged it," he says. "And when I thought they were full of bologna, I told them that, too." But then, a strange thing happened. The two sides proceeded to work things through. Over a period of years they've developed great trust, and when they have a problem, they work together to solve it.

Every year at Christmas, a very unusual thing happens at Erick's plant. It's not mandated, and neither Erick nor any of his managers thought it up. It comes from his workers and their union. And though it has become a yearly tradition, there is no guarantee that it will happen. But it always does. The union leaders call Erick. They ask to meet with him and the other owners. At the meeting, they present cash to their management — money they have collected from the workers on a volunteer basis. Erick always accepts the money on behalf of management, but he always uses it to purchase something that will benefit the workers, like a TV or a clock for the cafeteria.[23]

Now why do you think the workers and their union do this? Obviously they could just collect the money, go out, and buy something themselves. I believe that this informal ceremony during which Laine is presented with money is a symbol of the trust between the ALCAS union and management, between the company leaders and their workers. It is rare and unprecedented. It happens only because Erick Laine really cares.

Kendall Young, who flew in combat in North Africa and Italy during World War II and flew in Vietnam, retired from the air force as a major general. He says, "Always look after the welfare of your subordinates — food, comfortable sleeping quarters, counseling on troubling situations (including family problems), etc. Let them know by your actions that you really care about them."[24]

THIS MAN IS FAMOUS FOR HIS COFFEE . . .
AND HIS CONCERN FOR HIS PEOPLE

If you want to embrace the sixth law, you don't need to run around saying what a wonderful "people person" you are. Actions speak louder than words. Howard Schultz grew up in Brooklyn and went to college on student loans and his salary as a salesman. In 1982 he joined Starbucks. Five years later, he bought the company and became CEO. The Seattle company then had six outlets and fewer than one hundred employees. Today Starbucks has more than thirteen hundred stores and twenty-five thousand employees. How did Schultz do it?

First, Schultz follows the sixth universal law of leadership as outlined in the previous chapter. In an excerpt from his book *Pour Your Heart Into It,* printed in *Fortune* magazine last September, he tells us, "Our first priority was to take care of our people, because they were the ones responsible for communicating our passion to our customers."[25]

Years earlier, he told a reporter, "Every dollar you invest in your employees shows up — and then some — on the bottom line." And he backed that up with a generous and comprehensive employee-benefits package that includes health care, stock options, training programs, career counseling, and product discounts for all workers. That includes both full and part time. "No one can afford not to provide these kinds of benefits," said Schultz.[26] So Schultz shares the gain. But he also shares the pain.

Not long ago he was asleep in his hotel room on a business trip to New York. The telephone rang. Three Starbucks employees had been murdered in a Washington coffee shop. Schultz immediately dressed, left the hotel, and went right to the airport. By the next morning he was on the spot comforting relatives and coworkers. Starbucks may have twenty-five thousand employees around the country, but Schultz knows he's the leader of all of them. "It's very important for me — or any CEO — to be visible," he says.[27]

Leroy Manor, who was a fighter pilot in the European Theater of Operations during World War II and a fighter wing commander in Vietnam, retired from the air force as a lieutenant general. General Manor says, "A leader must demonstrate sincere concern for the welfare of the people in his unit."[28]

TAKE PERSONAL RESPONSIBILITY

Every combat leader I surveyed spoke in some way about the importance of taking personal responsibility for his actions and for the actions of his organization. Whenever something went right, these leaders gave credit to their people. But when things didn't go right, they took personal responsibility. Most of the time, taking responsibility is as simple as General Lee's words after Pickett's charge failed at the Battle of Gettysburg. Lee told everyone, "It's all my fault." He took personal responsibility for the defeat. Sometimes, taking responsibility must be expressed in the physical sense. Other times, in the moral sense. The heroic leader does either, or both, in taking care of his people.

YOU CAN BANK ON THIS BANKER

Today Marshall Carter is chairman and chief executive officer of the State Street Corporation. The State Street Corporation is a bank, but not just any old bank. It is the largest processor of pension funds in the world. It has some $4 trillion under custodianship. Yes, that's trillion with a "t."

Capt. "Marsh" Carter spent twenty-six months in Vietnam where he served as a marine corps company commander. On January 14, 1967, the marines discovered secret orders for a conference of senior enemy officers to be held in a certain village behind enemy lines. Carter's company was given the job of a surprise attack on this conference. He and his company were transported by helicopter and landed right on top of the concentration of enemy officers. A terrific firefight broke out. Two of Carter's lieutenants and nine of his sergeants were hit in the first few minutes. But Carter's company got the job done and inflicted heavy casualties on the enemy.

However as Viet Cong in the area became aware of the attack and ran to provide support, Carter's withdrawing troops came under increasing fire from small arms, automatic fire, and mortars. The helicopters ready to depart, Carter heard that one of his platoons was pinned down.

Marshall Carter took personal responsibility and fought his way back to the platoon alone. He found that the platoon wouldn't leave because the men couldn't get to one of their number who was wounded. Under heavy fire, Carter crawled forward and got the wounded man to safety. Then he personally protected the platoon's evacuation by single-handedly hurling grenades at the enemy in close combat. Back at the landing zone, he supervised the loading of the entire company before he himself would leave.

Explains Carter, "I didn't think much about it then, or even later. We had been in tighter spots before. But an artillery officer assigned to me for the operation and an enlisted man from another unit went to higher headquarters with the story. I heard later that they wanted me to get the Congressional Medal of Honor, and I was very surprised. A leader must always take personal responsibility for the welfare of those he is responsible for."[29]

Said Frank Mason, who was one of Carter's lieutenants that day, "If it wasn't for Carter, we would have lost the entire company."[30]

Carter was awarded the Navy Cross. Like the Distinguished Service Cross for the Army and the Air Force Cross for the Air Force, it is second only to the Congressional Medal of Honor and is rarely awarded.

After leaving active duty, Carter continued to serve as a Marine Corps reservist, eventually rising to the rank of colonel. Meanwhile he began to build his career in banking. Starting first with Chase Manhattan Corporation, he rose to become head of its global securities services.

When Carter took over State Street Corporation, he faced severe challenges. There were talks of deep cost-cutting. There were talks of layoffs. But Carter didn't see things that way. He expected positive results. And he declared his expectations. He told people, "We're going to change, but not by losing people. Who cares about losing people? I'm interested in hiring." Others were concerned that Carter was being overly optimistic. But he took the responsibility. He did everything necessary to make sure his ideas of expansion worked. And when they did, he gave the credit to his subordinates who carried out his vision.

"I knew I was on the right track," he says. "If we were wrong, it would have been my fault, my responsibility. I didn't want to be wrong, but if I were, I would have taken responsibility. I would have done whatever was possible to take care of my people. A leader doesn't have that as a choice." In the six years since he's headed up the State Street Corporation, revenues have tripled while the number of employees has doubled.[31]

IF YOU WANT OTHERS TO FOLLOW, YOU'VE GOT TO SHARE THE GAIN

Rewards in both military and civilian life come in many forms. Monetary compensation is just one form, and it probably isn't the most important. Pay can be important in recognizing an employee's performance and sharing the success of the organization, but there are other rewards as well.

In the military, promotions and medals are ways for a leader to ensure that his subordinates "share in the gain." When Maj. Gen. William "Gus" Pagonis, General Schwarzkopf's top logistician, had completed the monumental job of improvising his own organization, setting up the infrastructure and supplies for half a million troops of various nationalities, and acting as commander for as many as ninety-four different reserve and national guard organizations mobilized from the States, Schwarzkopf took actions to have him promoted. Pagonis received the third star of lieutenant general before Desert Storm started. The difference in pay between a two-star and three-star general isn't all that much — a couple of thousand dollars a year. In fact, it wasn't too long ago that all generals, whether they wore one star or five, made the same pay. But visible promotion is still an important way of sharing the gain, and Schwarzkopf knew it. As noted in chapter 3, Gus Pagonis is now working his magic at Sears as executive vice president for logistics.

And Pagonis's boss at Sears, CEO Arthur Martinez, understands this concept very well. Martinez took over Sears Roebuck five years ago, and *Fortune* magazine has said of his performance that he brought Sears back "from its near-death experience." Former army lieutenant Martinez recognized that he'd have to take Sears's three hundred thousand employees and get them to work together. He didn't only want to make the situation better, he wanted a complete transformation. Noted Martinez, "It involves getting them used to risk-taking and innovation. And getting the very best out of our people."[32] To do this, he dropped Sears' longtime compensation program and substituted paying bonuses based on key measures such as customer satisfaction and employee morale. And he requires his senior managers to buy Sears stock equal to three times their annual salary. That way, they will share the gain . . . or the pain.[33]

Smart leaders in industry following the sixth universal law ensure that their people share in the gain as well. Bernard

Marcus and Arthur Blank founded Home Depot in 1978. Home Depot profits hit nearly $1 billion last year. What's the secret? Let's listen to what one of the two partners has to say.

Marcus believes Home Depot's success lies in their telling the employees they have hired over the years, "If we make it, you're going to get the rewards." The two partners elevated those who worked for Home Depot from simple employees to "mini-partners" by paying them in stock instead of inflated salaries, bonuses, or commissions. Today one secretary has stock worth more than $4 million. No wonder others also credit Home Depot's success to "famously loyal and knowledgeable store employees." Marcus says that Home Depot's policy of offering stock to all employees has resulted in as many as one thousand Home Depot millionaires.[34]

HE RUNS THE COMPANY THAT BUILT THE EJECTION SEAT HE RODE IN COMBAT

Ed Osborne flew 213 combat missions in the F-100 fighter aircraft in Vietnam. A little more than twenty years later, he became vice president, and later president, of the company that built the ejection seat he rode in the F-100 so many years earlier. AMI Aircraft Seating Systems was in an ownership battle in the courts and losing money rapidly. Osborne and two others took over the company and turned things around by changing the corporate culture. At the same time, AMI became a worldwide supplier of commercial aircraft crew seats with about 50 percent of sales outside the United States. AMI is now a division of Coltec Industries, Inc.

President Osborne says, "Integrity and the ability to focus on what's important make life much simpler and easier to handle. But for the grace of God, I was a goner on one of my last missions in Vietnam. Life has never been the same since. . . . The small worries of life seem inconsequential. . . . It is much easier to focus on what's important — both in the office and at home.

"To me this means taking care of your people. Just listening and respecting their input is one way of showing you care. But you have to do more than that. You've got to share in the rewards as well. That's been one of the secrets of our success, and I'm constantly looking for ways to do this. For example, at AMI we have a strong profit-sharing program for all employees. Our sales and profits rose by 50 percent this year.

Each employee has earned about six weeks extra pay as a result of this program. Our employees talk about 'their company and their money.' And they're right. So they think creatively about lowering costs and improving quality. I learned long ago in combat that once everyone begins to think creatively about things such as lowering costs and improving quality, it's contagious."[35]

THIS LEADER SHARES
THE GAIN THROUGH TRAINING

But sharing the gain doesn't need to be through ownership in the company. It's the concept of sharing the gain that I am talking about. In 1975 Donald Weiss became CEO of White Storage and Retrieval Systems in Kenilsworth, New Jersey. White Storage is a manufacturer of automated retrieval systems for the storage of small parts and documents. When Weiss took over, it was a profitable, small $4 million company. Through good leadership, the company grew.

In 1988 Weiss decided to share some of the gains by raising the quality of life in his company. He thought he would teach his employees advanced management and professional subjects. He quickly discovered that most of his employees didn't have basic English skills. Weiss saw it would be rather difficult to teach them if they didn't understand English. So Weiss began by paying a couple of teachers to come in and teach basic English. He started the teaching after hours but soon expanded to work hours as well. Before long, more than one hundred employees were involved, and he expanded the lessons to all sorts of topics, including math, blue-print reading, Japanese manufacturing techniques, and team building. He started preparing employees for high school equivalency diplomas. Then he began inviting customers in to train his employees. IBM instructors came to White to give "quality" workshops. At one point, White Storage offered seven thousand hours in training.

Weiss started the program because he wanted to raise his employees' quality of life. But it had dramatic and unexpected results. Said Weiss before he retired as CEO in 1996, "Turnover used to be 25 percent; now it's below 10 percent. . . . Workers' compensation claims filed has plummeted. We now pay one-tenth of what we paid four years ago. . . . In one year alone we saw the turnaround time on orders drop from seven days to one."[36] The company reported $50 million in annual revenues prior to Weiss's retirement.

Robert Gard is a Ph.D. and Harvard University graduate who is president of the Monterey Institute of International Studies. But lest the academic garb fool you, Robert Gard is also a retired army lieutenant general and combat leader from both Korea and Vietnam. Says Gard, "You must show your concern for your people and take care of them."[37] That's what Donald Weiss did at White Storage. And as it always happens when one follows the universal law of taking care of your people, his people responded and helped to boost him and his company to higher and higher levels.

Edward M. Straw is president of Ryder Integrated Logistics, Inc., a $1.7 billion global supply chain logistics service based in Miami, Florida and subsidiary of $5 billion Ryder Systems, Inc. However it was only a couple of years ago that Ed Straw wore the three stars of a vice admiral, spending four years running our armed forces Defense Logistic Agency before he retired in 1996. His service as a three-star admiral coming from the U.S. Navy's Supply Corps was extremely rare. He was one of only five to have attained this distinction in the last forty years.

Over the years, Admiral Straw has developed his own version of the "Stuff of Heroes." Not surprisingly, his "laws" closely parallel the ones I developed from my research. Regarding his extraordinary success he says, "I credit most of my success to the people who have worked for and with me . . . officer, enlisted, and civilian. The care and feeding, mentoring and training of those men and women in the trenches is the simple secret of successful leaders. Take care of your people, and they will take care of you. Never, never forget this."[38]

THE FIVE STEPS
TO FULFILLING THE SIXTH LAW

If you are a real leader, you must take care of the people who report to you. If you take care of your people, they will perform to the maximum extent of their capabilities. If you fail to care for them, you won't be their leader for very long. If you want to be a real leader, you must:

1. Be the Leader When Things Go Wrong
2. Give Their Needs Priority

3. Really Care
4. Take Responsibility
5. Share the Gain

Follow these guidelines, and others will follow you. Your people will take care of you because you:

TAKE CARE OF YOUR PEOPLE

ENDNOTES

[1] Bolte, Philip L., letter to the author, September 4, 1993.

[2] Noel, Thomas E., III, telephone interview with the author, January 6, 1998.

[3] Hay, Peter, *The Book of Business Anecdotes* (New York: Facts on File, 1988), 168.

[4] Summers, Harry G., "Take Care of the Troops," *Washington Times* (August 7, 1997): 14.

[5] Ibid.

[6] Broughton, Jack, *Going Downtown* (New York: Orion Books, 1988), 218.

[7] Broughton, Jack, telephone interviews with the author, December 4 and 8, 1997.

[8] No author listed, "After the Fire at Malden Mills," Workdoctor.com, May 5, 1996.

[9] Convey, Eric, "Malden Mills Celebrates a Special Day," Business Today.com., September 15, 1997.

[10] Teal, Thomas, "Not a Fool, Not a Saint," *Fortune* (November 11, 1996).

[11] Campbell, Kenneth D., "Malden Mills Owner Applies Religious Ethics to Business,"web.mit.edu:1962/tiserve.mit.edu/9000/43530.html (April 16, 1997).

[12] Whitmore, David C., interview with the author, November 8, 1997.

[13] Ritchie, Steve, "Leadership That Inspires Excellence," *AU-24 Concepts for Air Force Leadership* (Maxwell AFB, Ala.: Air University, 1987), 400–401.

[14] Patterson, G. K., letter to the author, July 28, 1993.

[15] Browkaw, Murphy, & Seglin, "What It Takes," *Inc.* magazine

archives, www.inc.com, ref no. 11921051 (November 1992).

[16] No author listed, *DSW Overview*, www.dsw.com/overview.html.

[17] No author listed, "Rhino Foods Is a Workplace of the Future — Now," www.workforceonline.com/ideas/hottopic/rhino.html.

[18] Op. Cit., Browkaw, Murphy, & Seglin, "What It Takes."

[19] Op. Cit., no author listed, "Rhino Foods Is a Workplace of the Future — Now."

[20] Carey, Patricia M., "Seven Ways to Keep Your Key Players," *Your Company*, www.pathfinder.com/moneyyourco/9608/960916 .cover.html.

[21] Anfuso, Dawn, "3M's Staffing Strategy Promotes Productivity and Pride," http://www.workforceonline.com/archive/2695.html.

[22] DeSimone, L. D., *3M Annual Report*, February 20, 1997.

[23] Laine, Erick, telephone interview with the author, December 22, 1997.

[24] Young, Kendall S., letter to the author, July 30, 1993.

[25] Schultz, Howard, and Dori Jones Yang, "Starbucks: Making Values Pay," *Fortune* (September 29, 1997): 262.

[26] Rothman, Matt, "Into the Black," *Inc.* (January 1993): 59.

[27] Zachary, G. Pascal, "CEO's Are Stars Now, But Why? And Would Alfred Sloan Approve?" *Wall Street Journal* (September 3, 1997): A-1, A-10.

[28] Manor, Leroy J., letter to the author, July 24, 1993.

[29] Carter, Marsh N., telephone interview with the author, December 16, 1997.

[30] Achstatter, Gerard, "State Street's Marshall Carter: Bringing His Battlefield Perspective to the Boardroom," *Investor's Business Daily* (October 6, 1997): 1.

[31] Op. Cit., Carter, Marsh N.

[32] Sellers, Patricia, "Sears: The Turnaround Is Ending; The Revolution Has Begun," *Fortune* (April 28, 1997): 110.

[33] Ibid., 118.

[34] Kaufman, Leslie, "There's No Place Like Home," *Newsweek* (August 4, 1997): 55.

[35] Osborne, Edward A., letter to the author, December 19, 1997, telephone interview with the author, January 27, 1998.

[36] Op. Cit., Browkaw, Murphy & Seglin, "What It Takes."

[37] Gard, Robert, letter to the author, July 29, 1993.

[38] Straw, Edward M., telephone interview with the author, December 22, 1997, and "Remarks by Vice Admiral Edward M. Straw to Supply Corps Officers," *Navy Supply Corps Newsletter* (November/December 1996), 8.

PUT DUTY
BEFORE SELF

You should do your duty in all things. You can never do more. You should never wish to do less.

— GEN. ROBERT E. LEE

And therefore the general who in advancing does not seek personal fame, and in withdrawing is not concerned with avoiding punishment, but whose only purpose is to protect the people and promote the best interests of his sovereign, is the precious jewel of the state.

— SUN TZU

When General Schwarzkopf was Major Schwarzkopf, he was an advisor to a South Vietnamese brigade. One of the senior Vietnamese officers was a colonel by the name of Ngo Quang Truong. Colonel Truong was short and skinny and didn't look like a military hero. Still, he was worshipped by his troops and feared by the enemy commanders who knew about him.

During a mission to find and destroy an enemy unit, Truong and Schwarzkopf were leading in an armored command vehicle. Suddenly a hidden machine gun fired and hit Schwarzkopf.

"I was in a little bit of shock as the medic bandaged me up," Schwarzkopf said. "Truong squatted beside me and said, 'My friend, if you would like, I will turn the personnel carrier around, and we will go back and get you a medevac. But I don't want to do that. We're in the position we need to be in, and I need your help.'"

Though wounded, Schwarzkopf agreed to keep going. They attacked using a plan Schwarzkopf helped develop. Truong's troops saw that Schwarzkopf put duty first. So they did the same. The result was a complete rout of enemy forces.[1]

Sixty years earlier, on June 3, 1905, a victorious Adm. Togo Heihachiro comforted his wounded prisoner after the Battle of Tsushshima during the Russo-Japanese War. The prisoner was Russian admiral Zinovy P. Rozhdestvenski, who had been badly beaten. "Defeat is a common fate of a soldier and there is nothing to be ashamed of in it," said Togo. "The great point is whether we have performed our duty. . . . For you, especially, who fearlessly performed your great task until you were seriously wounded, I beg to express my sincerest respect." Duty before self is a universal law of leadership that is as true in the boardroom as on the battlefield.

THIS AIRLINE'S CEO PUTS DUTY FIRST

Herb Kelleher is CEO of Southwest Airlines — the most profitable airline in the United States and first in quality according to customer surveys. Kelleher advises, "If there's going to be a downslide, you share it."

When Southwest Airlines ran into trouble a few years ago, he asked the board of directors to cut his salary. He cut his bonus by 20 percent and the bonus of all corporate officers by 10 percent. These cuts were made before firing a single employee.[2]

Leaders who practice duty before self help others to accomplish almost impossible tasks though they face major obstacles. Yet other leaders frequently fail, even when they face no major obstacles to their goals. Leaders don't need to be combat veterans. They just need to put duty before self.

WHAT IS DUTY?

If you look up duty in the dictionary, you will find several definitions. Two are essential:

1. The actions required by one's occupation or position
2. A moral or legal obligation

We will see that we need both definitions in our examination of what is required by this universal law.

THIS AVIATOR PUTS DUTY FIRST AS A SALESPERSON

Lt. Rosanne Ott flew as an army aviator in the Gulf War and led a platoon in the 227th Aviation Regiment. She earned both an Air Medal and Commendation Medal during Operation Desert Storm. In a 1995 interview, she told me that she only did her duty. Of course, her duty included flying in harm's way, taking care of her crew, staying up late at night to complete administrative tasks, and risking her life whenever necessary.

Out of the army and a sales manager for the Johnson and Johnson Corporation, she works in a hospital setting. Many sales managers sell their products and then disappear. They rely on product literature or company specialists to teach surgeons to use their medical devices properly.

Rosanne Ott considers it her duty to do a lot more. If surgery involving one of her products starts at 7:30 A.M., Rosanne shows up at 6:30 to make sure the surgeon knows exactly how to use the product. When not making sales calls, she hangs around the operating room, answering questions. As a result, when there is a question, physicians call on her. As you might imagine, others in her company look to her leadership as well. We will always turn to a leader who practices duty before self.[3]

WHAT MADE WASHINGTON A GREAT LEADER?

George Washington is known not only as "the Father of His Country," but as a great leader. Why? He was not perfect. He was not a great strategist. The highest rank he had held prior to the War of Independence was that of major in the British army. He made plenty of mistakes, including recommending Benedict Arnold for promotion and entrusting him with one of the most important commands. Later he made other errors. Why then is he considered such a great leader?

First, Washington had unquestionable integrity. The story about Washington as a boy cutting down a cherry tree and then admitting this act to his father rather than telling a lie may or may not be true. But the simple fact that such a story is told helps to confirm what his countrymen thought about him both during his life and after his death. Because of his integrity, others followed him in situations when they would not follow others. However, rivaling Washington's integrity was the fact that he always put his duty before his own self-interest.

WASHINGTON SAVES THE UNITED STATES FROM A MILITARY DICTATORSHIP

After the Revolutionary War, the Continental Congress failed to provide proper subsistence to the army. Soldiers and officers alike went begging for food and clothing. Again and again Congress made promises that it was unable to keep. Washington himself was frequently blamed. Finally many senior officers, men such as colonels Alexander Hamilton and Henry Knox, who became our first secretary of the treasury, could take no more. They wanted to march against the Continental Congress and take charge of the country. They felt that a military dictatorship was the only solution to get the resources they needed. Washington was at the height of his popularity. These men wanted Washington to become military dictator of the United States.

Washington had every reason to be frustrated, and a lesser man might have succumbed to their offer. It would have been easy to march on Congress and see them get what many thought they deserved.

However Washington would not agree to do this. His duty to his country came first. It came before his own need to gratify his frustrations after so many months and years of broken promises. It came even before the needs of his soldiers who suffered from Congress's inability to do anything. He tried to dissuade his officers from their plans. They refused to listen.

With so many involved, he could not order a general arrest. There was apparently nothing he could do. He could at least, however, stay out of the controversy. This would have preserved his popularity. But one day an opportunity appeared. Those in potential rebellion against Congress asked Washington to speak at a general meeting of their membership. They were again trying to persuade Washington to agree to lead them.

Although he had nothing to gain by his interference, and much of his personal popularity to lose, Washington repeated his attempts to convince them to abandon their scheme. He could see by the looks on their faces that they were not persuaded.

Suddenly he thought of one last idea. Washington had never before revealed the fact that he was near-sighted. He had never worn spectacles in public. Today poor eyesight means little or nothing. However in Washington's day, the image of a senior commander without disabilities was very important. A commander did everything possible to maintain that image. In some instances, one's image seems important in modern times. It may be a sad commentary on the way some think, but remember that when Franklin Roosevelt ran for president, he took great pains to conceal the fact that he was an invalid.

But not hesitating, Washington reached inside his uniform cloak and took out his glasses. He donned them for the first time before all his officers. There was a gasp from the audience. Slowly he spoke these words: "I have grown old in your service . . . and now I am growing blind." Having given everything he had left to give, he turned and left the meeting.

At first there was dead silence. Then someone spoke. His voice cracked slightly: "Maybe General Washington is right. Perhaps we should give Congress another chance." And this is what they agreed to do. It was not Washington's physical disability or the way he presented it that saved the country from a military dictatorship. It was Washington's integrity and his willingness to put duty before self.

THIS LEADER SAYS DUTY BEFORE SELF IS ESSENTIAL

Harry Walters is one of those unusual leaders whose experience spans the army, the civilian world, and government service. After graduating from West Point and serving three years in the army, he went into industry. He worked himself up to marketing manager of a company, then vice president, and finally president. At that point, President Reagan asked Walters to enter government service as assistant secretary of the army, and two years later, Veterans Administration administrator. Leaving government, Walters became CEO of Great Lakes Carbon Corporation, CEO of DHC Holding, and is today general partner of Lafayette Equity Fund.

Reflecting on his intercollegiate background in sports including football, basketball, and baseball, he says, "I always felt I was playing in a team environment whether in government or industry. If that environment didn't exist, I always felt it was my job to create it. That's the only way to win. If you don't put duty before self, you can't create a team environment.

"Unfortunately, that was the situation at the Veterans Administration at first. A team environment just didn't exist.

No one put duty first. There was a $30 billion budget to take care of eleven million veterans, and it seemed that too many were looking out for themselves and protecting their own turf. Lincoln had started the Veterans Administration 'to care for him that has born the battle.' By the early 80s, it seemed that Lincoln's philosophy had gotten lost somewhere and the purpose of the VA was to restrict the benefits to which veterans were supposedly entitled, and to make things as tough as possible for them. The VA had taken on an adversarial role to veterans when it should have had an advocacy role. Moreover, there was no mission statement, no planning, no nothing.

"To me, duty before self means inclusion with no secrets. Why should there be any secrets when the leader puts his own interests last? So I brought everybody into the party. That meant the veterans organizations like the American Legion, the Veterans of Foreign Wars and the Jewish War Veterans, Congress (which both represented the veterans and was our banker), and even the press. I held a press conference every Monday morning. When things went wrong, the press didn't need to call me, I called them. I think I was one of the few people in government whom the press never harassed.

"I gave the VA employees a mission: to help vets, with no politics and no secrets from anyone. Duty before self meant that the well-being of the veteran came before any individual in the VA. We measured progress and held everyone accountable. We developed a motto, 'America is number one thanks to our veterans.' When people realized this was for real, we got cooperation from everyone, from both parties in the U.S. Congress to the media. The VA employees were superb.

"Industry is no different. I spent a lot of time with unions. But not fighting with them. I wanted them to understand my perception, and I began to understand theirs. We spent far more time on how we could master the environment than we did with complaints. And in my opinion, that's the way it should be. We were both on the same side. If there was 'an enemy,' it was the competition, not me, and not them. When a leader puts duty before self, he helps to create that team environment, whether it's in government or private industry, that is absolutely essential for success."[4]

Sometimes a Rarity in Industry

Is the attitude displayed by these military and corporate heroes common in industry? Unfortunately not. In many companies, the automatic solution to any slip in profits or in the stock market is downsizing. A few years ago, a *Newsweek* article stated, "After causing the problems through poor decisions, many CEOs offer up their employees as human sacrifices, hoping to get their stock prices up. If they do go up, they get a raise even while their employees suffer."[5]

The *Newsweek* article may have overstated the case. For example, when workers are doing jobs that are no longer needed, or corporate survival is at stake, it is the leader's duty to take action, which may include layoffs. Otherwise the company will ultimately fail and no one will have work. However *Newsweek* correctly made points that no leader should ignore:

1. A leader does not use his people as corporate fodder simply to look better on the bottom line.
2. A leader does everything possible to assist and prepare people who must be released for their future.
3. A leader takes personal cuts himself before laying off anyone, and shares the pain by taking more personal cuts if layoffs are unavoidable.
4. A leader never benefits from the misfortunes of those he leads.

As Akio Morita, former chairman of the Sony Corp., commented, "American management treats workers as just a tool to make money. You know, when the economy is booming they hire more workers, and when the recession comes, they lay off the workers. But you know, recession is not caused by the workers."[6]

Maybe all American managers do not treat workers as "a tool to make money." But many do. They transpose the correct order of priorities and put their own welfare before the needs of those they lead. They accepted salary increases and bonuses while firing loyal, productive workers. That's not duty before self, and it's certainly not the stuff of heroes.

The Combat Model of Leadership

For many years I have been working on the concepts contained in this book. I call them the "combat model of leadership."

Researchers are fond of creating models . . . and for good reason. If you can develop a model that represents the real world and works successfully, then you can substitute new variables and repeat your successes again and again. Your model is somewhat like a cookie cutter. Once you've constructed it correctly, you can use your cookie cutter to create another great looking cookie every time.

The Stuff of Heroes is such a model. Some parts of this model are more difficult than other parts. In the previous chapter, I pointed out instances when two laws are in conflict, and the leader must use his or her judgment to decide which takes precedence.

The development of the part of the model making up the seventh law has also been more of a struggle than developing some of the other laws. Computer programmers would describe this as a difficulty with one of the subroutines.

Here is the problem. Duty before self encompasses three priorities of a leader: your mission, your people, and yourself. I quickly found that there was never a question in placing your own welfare after that of your mission and your people. Combat leaders easily showed what must be done in setting that priority.

THIS COMMANDER ORDERED
HIS SUBMARINE TO DIVE WITHOUT HIM

In early 1943, Howard Gilmore was the commander of the USS *Growler*, an American submarine on its fourth war patrol in the Southwest Pacific. Evading continuous air and antisubmarine patrols, the *Growler* penetrated an enemy convoy's protective screen of destroyers and attacked and sank an enemy freighter. The *Growler* managed to escape a severe depth charge attack. Some time later, the *Growler* found and attacked another enemy ship. This time, *Growler's* torpedoes only damaged its target. Again the *Growler* survived the depth charge attack and escaped.

Forced to surface to recharge the submarine's batteries on the dark night of February 7, 1943, Gilmore and his crew didn't see a Japanese gunboat until it was too late. The gunboat closed range to ram the surfaced submarine. By skillful maneuvering, Gilmore was able to move the *Growler* aside to avoid the gunboat's attack. He immediately pivoted the sub and rammed the gunboat. The gunboat stopped dead in the water. Still, its crew fired on the *Growler* with its all of its ammunition. If it could damage the *Growler* and delay its escape for only a few minutes, other enemy ships not far away could finish her off.

Gilmore had already ordered those on deck to clear the bridge. He intended to follow his men into the submarine for an immediate dive to safety below the waves. Before he could do this, he was hit by enemy fire. He was alive, but he could barely move. He knew his crew and submarine were in danger from the gunboat and other approaching enemy ships. He could not get to the hatch to enter the submarine by himself. For his men to climb out of the submarine to drag him into the submarine would result in further delay. That delay could be fatal. The submarine had to crashdive immediately. So he gave his last order from the submarine's deck even though he knew it meant his own death: "Take her down."

The crew of the *Growler* reluctantly obeyed their captain's order as they had been trained to do, and the submarine dived. The USS *Growler* was seriously damaged but under control. Gilmore's crew brought her safely to port. No doubt they were inspired by the courageous fighting spirit of their captain, who had sacrificed his life, truly putting duty before self. Commander Gilmore was awarded the Congressional Medal of Honor posthumously, this country's highest decoration for bravery.[7]

John Gutherie served in combat in Vietnam and retired as a general officer from the U.S. Army Reserve. As a civilian, he also served in the government's Senior Executive Service (SES). General Gutherie states quite emphatically, "What is really important is for your soldiers to believe that you put them first, before yourself."[8]

George Miller, who flew combat missions in an A-1 in the 22nd Special Operation Squadron during the Vietnam War and retired as a lieutenant general puts it this way: "Your crews must know that you'll go all out for their well-being, that you'll 'go to the mat' for them."[9]

Fortunately business endeavors do not require us to sacrifice our lives for our mission or our people. However even if we sacrifice ourselves in other ways to put mission and our people before our own welfare, which I believe leaders should, where does that leave the order of the other two priorities?

IS IT MISSION FIRST, THEN PEOPLE?

In combat, if you always put mission before people, you soon run into some major challenges. The implication of a simple "mission first" doctrine is that you sacrifice yourself or your people for any goal. History is replete with disasters of great magnitude, with tremendous loss of life, which have occurred when military commanders have attempted to do this on an ongoing basis. For example, on July 1, 1916, the British Fourth and French Sixth armies attacked the German Second Army astride the Somme River during World War I. This was one of the strongest sections of the German line. The battle raged almost five months until November 25. The losses on both sides were enormous. The British lost four hundred thousand. The French, two hundred thousand. The Germans lost five hundred thousand. The British and French captured a small strip of land, no deeper than seven miles at best. At the end of the battle, the lines on the Western Front were practically the same as when the battle started.

With the continual sacrifice of people for mission, pretty soon, you've got no people to accomplish the mission. As we will see, this is as true in civilian organizations as it is in battle.

On the other hand, you would run into difficulties if you always put people first. There are examples in combat of that, too: leaders who were so solicitous of their soldiers that they lost the battle, with the result that more men were lost than would have been if the leader had placed a greater emphasis on the mission. General McClellan was unwilling to attack Lee's army although he had greatly superior numbers. And General Meade failed to attack Lee's Army of Northern Virginia after he had defeated it at the Battle of Gettysburg. Both decisions, in being overly solicitous of followers, cost thousands of casualties. These losses might never have occurred had these commanders been more concerned with completing the mission than with the welfare of those they led.

In business, if you always put employees over mission, you are also likely to run into difficulties. There will be times when you and your employees must work late and work over holidays or weekends in order to satisfy your customer. There are other times when the personal wishes of individuals must be sacrificed for mission. For example, Joe or Josephine Smith may want to be a sales manager, but he or she may be far better placed as a salesperson.

In fact, contrary to everything you may have heard, studies done as long as thirty years ago concluded that there is no necessary relationship between job satisfaction and performance, except that turnover and absenteeism rates are generally more favorable for satisfied than for dissatisfied workers.[10] Those times when work must come before an employee's wishes are critical. Ignore them at your peril!

Many combat leaders point out that concern for mission and people are so closely intertwined — since without people, you cannot accomplish the mission —that they cannot be considered separately or prioritized in a fixed order. If you adopt the priorities of mission or people in any fixed order, it will eventually be wrong for a particular situation.

HIGH CONCERN FOR BOTH MISSION AND PEOPLE IS NOT A NEW CONCEPT FOR BUSINESS

The notion that you must have high concern for both mission and people may have originated centuries ago with combat leadership, but it was documented for the corporate world by researchers Drs. Robert Blake and Jane Mouton since the early 1960s. Their books, *The Managerial Grid* and *The New Managerial Grid*, describe a matrix of managerial effectiveness showing concern for production on one axis and concern for people on the other. Management books were only then gaining in popularity, but their original book sold almost one million copies. Their conclusions sound almost self-evident today. Essentially, they said that a leader's high concern for both production and for people ("head and heart" they called it) lead to a number of beneficial and synergistic consequences.[11]

So if you follow the universal laws of leadership or "the combat model," both people and mission must be considered before self but not in a fixed and unchanging priority. There are times when the very top priority must be given to mission (work). At other times your people must be given top priority. As a leader, you must ensure that both priorities are at the top of your list, and judge which gets the primary call in a specific situation.

DUTY BEFORE SELF, REGARDLESS OF SACRIFICE

Gen. Ronald Fogleman, former Chief of Staff of the air force, pointed out that duty before self, or "service before self" as one of the air force core values describes it, must be accomplished regardless of difficulty, and sometimes at tremendous sacrifice. Because of prejudice against African-Americans, Lt. Gen. Benjamin O. Davis, Jr., suffered terribly while at West Point for his entire four years. But he persevered. On graduation with the class of 1936, he was commissioned a second lieutenant, the same as his classmates. However he was denied the opportunity to take flying training. The West Point superintendent was sympathetic but could only get him assigned to the infantry.

Despite confronting additional forms of bigotry, "He would not be denied the chance to serve his country," General Fogleman observed. "He aggressively pursued the opportunity to fly and led the initial cadre of Tuskegee airmen through flight training in 1941. Next, he commanded the first all-black U.S. fighter squadron in combat during World War II, helping disprove myths about blacks' inability to fly and fight.

"Subsequently, General Davis led the first all-black group to great distinction in Europe. His 332 Fighter Group never lost a single bomber on 200 escort missions. Moreover, it earned a Distinguished Unit Citation for a 1,600-mile escort mission to Berlin that resulted in the downing of three ME-262 jets in March 1945. Ultimately, General Davis enjoyed a long and distinguished military career in which he played a pivotal role in the successful integration of African-Americans into our Air Force. We can learn much from his extraordinary perseverance and willingness to subordinate personal concerns to serving his country — even under the toughest of circumstances."[12]

FIVE WAYS YOU CAN PRACTICE DUTY BEFORE SELF

1. Focus on the Mission
2. Rejoice in the Success of Others
3. Consider Yourself Last
4. Share the Pain
5. Demonstrate High Moral Courage

FOCUS ON THE MISSION

Recently I watched a rerun of the second of Herman Wouk's epic novels, *War and Remembrance*, on television. I had both read the book and seen the series on television previously. It is a tale worth rereading or re-viewing and has some major lessons regarding duty before self.

Wouk's story is that of a navy family during World War II. A prior book, *Winds of War*, chronicled the family's experiences just prior to the war. Robert Mitchum played the lead as Victor "Pug" Henry, a career naval officer, in the miniseries based on both books.

Prior to the war Henry is a naval attaché in Berlin. Because of his unique abilities in judgment and dealing with others, he performs top-level confidential services for President Roosevelt all over Europe. In doing so, he defers his own personal ambitions to attain command of a battleship. Not only was command of a ship the sinecure of a successful navy career but a requirement for further promotion in the navy. However in performing his diplomatic duties, he concentrates on the mission he is given and puts duty before self. In late 1941, he is finally released from other obligations. They finally give Henry command of the battleship Virginia, which is assigned to the Pacific fleet.

Henry arrives in Hawaii to take command only hours after the Japanese attack at Pearl Harbor. The battleship USS *Virginia* had been sunk. Henry was to be assigned as chief of staff to the commanding admiral in the Pacific. Chief of staff is another route to quick promotion to admiral, even without having had a major ship command. However Henry has two sons. One is a naval aviator, the other an officer on a submarine. After Pearl Harbor, the one son's submarine is missing and is presumed lost. Henry asks the chief of personnel for the Pacific fleet, an Annapolis classmate, to change his orders so that he be given command of any fighting ship.

Henry's grief over the apparent loss of his son and his request for a change of assignment is Henry's only lapse of duty in Wouk's story. Henry is given command of a cruiser, which is still a major ship, but smaller than a battleship. In battle, Henry fights well. His ship is sunk despite his skillful handling. Henry is given leave to Washington, D.C., prior to reassignment.

Now Henry's abilities as a naval commander are as sought after as his diplomatic talents. Admiral Nimitz requests Henry for a major naval command. It means promotion to admiral. However before the assignment can be made, he is called to see the president. President Roosevelt explains that there is much concern that Stalin will make a separate peace with Hitler. Roosevelt's senior military representative in Moscow feels that

Henry can make a difference because of the previous contacts he established in the Soviet Union. Henry instantly agrees to request new orders and go to Moscow, although it means deferring any chance for promotion to admiral.

After successfully completing this assignment, the president again needs Henry for a stateside job having to do with the war effort. He knows that accepting this assignment will once again have a negative impact on Henry's career. Henry learns of the president's wishes through the president's assistant, Harry Hopkins. Although disappointed, again Henry concentrates on the overall mission. He volunteers for what the president wants him to do immediately.

Eventually Henry gets his major combat command. At the end of the book, he not only is an admiral but wears the three stars of a vice admiral.

What is so important about this account of a fictional naval officer? The importance is that except for the single incident where Henry is overcome by emotion at the apparent death of his son, he is 100 percent focused on the overall mission. That mission is that of the diplomatic interests of the United States, and once the war has begun, to win the war. Henry knows that his mission is not his career, and he knows that his becoming an admiral is not of primary importance.

In this fictionalized account, Henry eventually becomes an admiral. In real life, I have known many like Henry who gave up numerous opportunities for advancement for the good of the mission and were eventually promoted to the top ranks in their profession.

Eisenhower volunteered repeatedly for combat duties in France during World War I. However, superiors felt that his services were most needed in training soldiers in the States. In *At Ease: Stories I Tell My Friends*, former president and general of the army Eisenhower noted: "I had missed the boat in the war we had been told would end all wars. A soldier's place was where the fighting went on. I hadn't fully learned the basic lesson of the military — that the proper place for a soldier is where he is ordered by his superiors."

Of course, not all leaders who focus on mission reach the top. However, when leaders haven't gone as far as they might have in their careers, it is not because they focused on the mission and put duty before self that they have not realized their ambitions.

Rather, it is for some other reason, either personal or situational. In all cases, those who have focused on the mission — who have put duty before self — have had the total respect of those they lead and have been far better leaders because of their choice.

REJOICE IN THE SUCCESS OF OTHERS

As a leader, you are responsible for everything your organization does or fails to do. Since your organization is made up of people, you are responsible for everything your people do or fail to do. Thus, if your people are successful, that makes you successful. Conversely, if they fail, that makes you a failure.

Amazingly some leaders have the idea that they must be seen as the one who brings all success to the organization. Such "leaders" seem to take the attitude that they would like to see their organization succeed, but their people fail. They take credit for all successes, and blame their people for all failures. What a stupid, short-sighted philosophy. No wonder good employees look elsewhere for employment, and these so-called leaders get stuck with followers who have difficulty in finding a position elsewhere. Such leaders are invariably doomed to eventual failure.

A leader who puts duty first rejoices in the successes of those who report to him and does everything possible to help subordinates achieve those successes. As noted in an earlier chapter, such a leader takes full responsibility for failure. As for the successes, that the leader gives as much credit as he can to his followers.

THIS MAN DID THE NEAR IMPOSSIBLE TWICE
AND THE IMPOSSIBLE ONCE

You probably haven't heard the name of Professor Richard Roberto. I didn't hear much about him, and I am on his home turf of California State University Los Angeles (CSULA). Roberto is an engineering professor. He is also the chief faculty advisor to students who participate in a special competition. In 1990, with no prior experience in solar vehicle technology his students designed and built the university's first solar-powered electric car and entered the sixteen-hundred-mile race from Orlando, Florida, to Warren, Michigan. Amazingly his students came in fourth place, competing against some of the top universities in the country. CSULA is not known as an engineering school. Moreover, it has one of the highest percentages of students who are the first in their families to go to college, and the students' families are the lowest in overall income. But not only was CSULA's solar car fourth in the nation, it accomplished the near impossible. It was number one in California, besting such well-known schools as the University of California at Berkeley and Stanford.

A fluke? Maybe. Except that in 1993, in the second national solar race that CSULA had ever competed in, the school did the same thing all over again with a new car, Solar Eagle II. This time, the CSULA team came in third nationally racing from Dallas, Texas, to Minneapolis, Minnesota. Again, CSULA beat out much better funded, much better researched cars to finish number one among California universities in the race.

In 1997, Roberto's students built Solar Eagle III. This time CSULA raced from Indianapolis, Indiana, to Colorado Springs, Colorado. It was 1,250 miles, and it took nine days. Impossible to win against thirty-six top-flight entries, such as MIT, Yale, a combined team from Stanford University and the University of California at Berkeley, and even my own alma mater, West Point? Guess again. The Stanford/UC Berkeley team came in third. MIT came in second. CSULA came in first nationwide. Roberto had done the impossible.

The *Los Angeles Times* quoted CSULA spokeswoman Carol Selkin. "In the past, the winners were big-name schools with four-year research institutions and big money. We're a state university with no research arm. These other schools had people clamoring to support their team — doctors and lawyers. We just didn't have that."[13]

What CSULA had was a leader by the name of Dick Roberto. In interviewing Professor Roberto, I discovered something that didn't come out in much of the press coverage, besides his rarely mentioned name. Ninety percent of Roberto's students on the solar team are undergraduates. Their competitors at MIT, Stanford, and Berkeley are mostly graduate students. The students received no academic credit for their work. Most had to work part-time jobs, too. "About 50 percent of the students have family incomes of less than $20,000," Roberto told me. And only about 5 percent of CSULA students want careers in engineering compared with a national average of better than 7 percent.

"How did you do it?" I wanted to know. Roberto told me that the secret was reliability. "Our car just didn't break down, not once," he said.

But I knew there was more. At first, he was evasive. Finally, he told me his secret. "I'm like an unknown basketball coach," he said. "And that suits me fine. It is how it should be for the good of the team. The press wants to talk to our winning players, our drivers, those who had their hands on building the car. I stay in the background. Outsiders don't need to know me or know my name. The less I am in the forefront, the better for the team. This way, our team members get the publicity, and they get the job offers. They work hard for it, and they deserve it. I always refer questions to the students or to public relations. I'm proud to be coach."[14] Professor Roberto is a leader who rejoices in the successes of those he leads.

NORDSTROM REJOICES IN THE SUCCESSES OF THOSE WHO FOLLOW

Everyone is familiar with Nordstrom, the $4.5 billion, Seattle-based specialty retail chain, because of the world-famous service these stores give to their customers. But Nordstrom's famed service isn't all that centralized. *Forbes* once described it as "building the stores, then getting out of the way."[15]

Giving great service may be more difficult than it seems. What is good service to one group may be considered poor service to others. For example, some customers like it when waiters or waitresses in restaurant come to their tables every few minutes to ask how they are doing. Other customers don't like having their meals interrupted.

When you are striving to give the absolute best in customer service, implementing the Golden Rule of treating others as you yourself would like to be treated might not work. As James MacGregor Burns noted in his Pulitzer Prize–winning book, *Leadership*, "But even the Golden Rule is inadequate, for it measures wants and needs of others simply by our own."[16]

James Nordstrom told his managers, "This is your own business. Do your own thing. Don't listen to us in Seattle. Listen to your customer. We give you permission to take care of your customer."[17]

Nordstrom encourages his store managers around the country to take care of their customers in the way their customers want to be taken care of. And when they are successful, he rejoices in their success and rewards them for doing it. In this way, he puts the mission and his people ahead of his own ego.

CONSIDER YOURSELF LAST

Sure, you have to consider yourself. You owe something to yourself, and you have responsibilities to your family as well. If you never consider such things as personal health, don't get proper sleep, fail to spend the time you need with your family, you are heading for massive trouble, which can negatively impact your entire life, not to mention your ability to lead.

The difficulty arises when those who claim to be leaders almost always consider themselves first. As a leader, others will do as you do. If you always consider your own well-being first, before others and before your mission, so will those you expect to follow you. In all likelihood, they won't willingly follow you at all. They will be too busy looking out for themselves, too!

THE WORLD CONQUEROR WHO TOOK CARE OF OTHERS BEFORE HIMSELF

By the time of his death in June 323 B.C., except for Genghis Khan who maintained his empire for but a short period, Alexander the Great controlled the largest area of the earth's surface ever to be conquered by a single individual. It is said that Alexander mourned the fact that there were no further worlds to conquer. I do not know whether this was actually true or not. However what is most certainly true is that a good deal of Alexander's success is due to his being an exceptional leader who looked out for those he led before he looked after himself. He made certain his soldiers were well fed before every battle. After the Battle of Granicus in 334 B.C., Alexander took the time to visit all his wounded. He personally examined their wounds and even encouraged them to boast of their exploits. As noted by military historian John Keegan, "excellent psychotherapy, however wearisome for the listener."[18] Only afterward did Alexander look to his own needs and get some rest.

At the Battle of Issus in Mesopotamia in 333 B.C., Alexander received a sword wound in the thigh. It was not life-threatening, but Alexander was in considerable pain. The doctors advised him to stay put for a couple of days. Alexander ignored their advice. Though uncomfortable, he again personally made the rounds to visit his wounded soldiers before calling it a day.[19]

Hap Arnold Risks Death as a Four-Star General During World War II

Not looking after your own well-being first could be at some risk. Henry H. "Hap" Arnold commanded the U.S. Army Air Forces during World War II. Fighting to build an air force that was second to none in the world, he drove himself unmercifully. He worked seven days a week, every week.

In the middle of the war, Arnold had a heart attack. Some doctors told him that he must retire and give up the job commanding the army air forces. Others told him that he must at least slow down significantly and delegate many of his responsibilities. His condition, they told him, was life-threatening. Arnold would not follow their advice. He fought to stay on active duty and succeeded. He restricted his activities only long enough to avoid forced retirement. Then he pressed on with his busy schedule. He had another heart attack. Now his doctors were really insistent on curtailing his mind-numbing schedule.

But Arnold told them, "I cannot ask my air crews to do something which I am unwilling to do myself. I know that in not slowing down, as you advise, I am risking my life. But we are at war. My airmen risk their lives every day. Until the war is over, I can do no less." All told, he had four heart attacks before the war ended.[20]

Arnold finally succumbed to a fatal attack. However, it was not until 1950, four and a half years after the war was over. Like Alexander the Great, Hap Arnold disregarded his personal well-being. Like Alexander the Great, he put his self-interest last and practiced duty before self.

Arnold's legacy continues in the U.S. Air Force to this day. Even the buttons worn on the current air force uniform are called "Hap Arnold buttons" because the insignia on them is reminiscent of the insignia worn by the army air force under Arnold's command. Arnold's major contributions were recognized with his promotion to the five-star rank of general of the air force toward the end of the war, the only five-star general the air force has ever had.

Emmitt Smith's Agent Puts Others First

Today Michael L. Ferguson is an attorney with McDonald, Fleming, Moorhead, and Ferguson in his hometown of Pensacola, Florida. While he primarily practices business law, he is also an NFL players' agent and sports attorney, handling such sports greats as world-class athlete Emmitt Smith. "I believe that Emmitt knows in his heart that I'm going to choose the harder right instead of the easier wrong for him, and take care of him and his family regardless of the consequences to me," he says.[21]

A few years ago, Mike Ferguson was an army general, and a few years before that, a young major who was an advisor to a regiment of the Army of Vietnam (ARVN) in the ancient city of Hue in Vietnam. During the religious holiday of Tet in 1968, the North Vietnamese and other Communist forces launched a surprise attack throughout Vietnam. Hue was especially hard hit.

"We were attacked with devastating surprise and overwhelming numbers," Ferguson remembers. "All of our units were cut off from one another. The weather was miserable. There was no visibility whatsoever. We were low on ammunition, low on food, and without significant fire support. Most devastating, our intelligence was the pits and very few, if any of us, had any real idea of what was going on. . . . In spite of our high casualties, due to the almost continuous mortar, rocket, and periodic small-arms attacks, we held out in our area and, along with our RF/PF units,[22] protected all the roads from the north leading into Hue."

After about a week, the civilians and friendly militia forces in Hue began to run out of food. American and Vietnamese army officers got together and decided that the priority effort would be directed to moving rice and other food stuffs into the area even before additional ammunition and other supplies they needed to fight the enemy. They were responsible for these civilians and militia. They justified this decision by saying that starving civilians might have forced them to surrender. But still, it was mission and people before self.

"The American and Vietnamese leaders involved deserved considerable credit for recognizing that sometimes the small things mean the difference between victory and defeat on the battlefield," says Ferguson. "In this case, getting the food to the civilians was a correct decision that saved the day for them and for us. All of the leaders involved had been confronted with something totally unexpected in warfare and reacted in the middle of a violent combat situation with a sense of humanity and integrity that left me indelibly imprinted with a story of selfless multinational civilian and military leadership that has probably never been told before."[23]

Duty before self and choosing the harder right rather than the easier wrong was a key factor in the battle for Hue.

SHARE THE PAIN

Sharing the pain means that when things go wrong, you are there to show your concern. However showing concern shouldn't be just a display. You must really share your subordinates' pain whether or not it is inconvenient, difficult, or it costs you time, money, or other resources.

THIS HIGH-TECH BOSS
HAS THE SMALLEST OFFICE

Sharing the pain can be shown by simple things, such as the size of your office or your lack of a private secretary. Ann Price is CEO of Motek Information Systems, Inc., a multimillion-dollar company that designs inventory-control software for warehouse/distribution centers. Not only is Price's company profitable and growing, but in 1994, Motek won the prestigious Computerworld Smithsonian Award for Information Technology in the Workplace.

Motek's facilities are limited in space, so no one has a spacious office. But the smallest private office belongs to Ann Price. It is just large enough to comfortably seat one visitor. No one has a private secretary. Motek has more than twenty employees and the employee turnover rate is almost zero. Incidentally, Ann Price is not without her military experience. She served two years in the Israeli army.[24]

A BILLION DOLLARS IN SALES
AND NO PRIVATE OFFICE

Michael Bloomberg owns a billion-dollar company that publishes financial news electronically. It's called *Bloomberg News*. The subscribers are seventy-eight thousand financial professionals in one hundred countries who pay roughly $1,150 a month for the service.

Bloomberg has four thousand employees. Bloomberg doesn't have the smallest office of any of his employees. Neither Bloomberg, nor any of his employees, has a private office or a secretary.[25] Moreover, Bloomberg believes and insists that as his employees rise up the ladder, they shouldn't expect to work less and take more vacations. Explains Bloomberg, "You're more valuable, you get paid more, and your co-workers should get more out of you."[26] Like Motek, the employee turnover rate is very low — single digit.

Now before you fire your private secretary, or lease out most of your office, you should know that the employees of these two companies are taken care of in other ways. At Motek, although wages aren't necessarily high, permanent employees own a piece of the company. And they are not permanent until they have proven themselves. Bloomberg's employees are also all on a revenue-sharing plan. The point isn't that these executives don't have large offices or other symbols of power. Other successful leaders do. These leaders do feel that it is important to limit office space and not employ private secretaries, but they feel that it is equally important to share whatever problems may be associated with this approach.

Maj. Gen. Thomas Greer, an infantry officer who commanded troops in combat in Vietnam, says, "A leader must share all dangers and hardships with his men."[27]

THIS LEADER SAVED HIS COMPANY BY TANGIBLY SHARING THE PAIN

Ken Iverson is the CEO of the $4.2 billion Nucor Corporation. Nucor has consistently high profits in what can only be termed a declining industry — steel manufacturing. Nucor's seven thousand employees are the best-paid workers in the steel business, but Nucor has the industry's lowest labor cost per ton of steel produced. Nucor is a Fortune 500 company, but there are only twenty-four people assigned to corporate headquarters and four layers of management from the CEO to the front-line worker. Nucor has no R & D department or corporate engineering group. Yet the company was the first major operator of "minimills" and the first to demonstrate that minimills could make flat-rolled steel, the first to apply thin-stab casing, which "Big Steel" had determined couldn't be done, and the first to produce iron carbide commercially.

In simple terms, Ken Iverson took over a failing business and built it into a highly successful giant. How did he do it? What happened a few years ago might give us some insight.

When times were really bad for the steel industry back in 1982, the total number of steelworkers dropped like a stone from four hundred thousand to two hundred thousand. At

Nucor, they had to cut production in half. Iverson did not, however, "downsize" anyone. How did he avoid doing what every other steel company did? Department heads took pay cuts of up to 40 percent. Iverson and other company officers cut their salaries up to 60 percent and more.

It wasn't enough. So Iverson cut back work weeks from five to four days, and then three days. This meant that on average his workers suffered a 25 percent cut in pay. "You know that had to hurt," said Iverson. "Still, as I walked through our mills and plants, I never heard one employee complain about it. Not one."[28] That's not too surprising when those workers fully understood that their leaders were taking significant cuts also.

Iverson, who was once a naval officer, says, "I was in the navy for three years and ended up as a lieutenant, junior grade. But I probably did not get my philosophies from the navy. I was much too young (in at 17, out at 20)."[29] Nevertheless, Ken Iverson clearly follows the universal law of leadership recommended by combat leaders and puts duty before self: "I took a 75 percent pay cut from $450,000 to $110,000," he said. "It was the only right thing to do. Of course, nothing is written in stone. If we have to lay people off someday to save Nucor, we'll do it. But not before we try everything else first. We call that pain sharing. When times are good, we share the benefits, and when times are bad, leaders have to share that as well. For all of us, but leaders especially, there is a duty that comes before personal interest, and certainly before my personal interest."[30]

DEMONSTRATE HIGH MORAL COURAGE

Combat leaders must frequently demonstrate high physical courage. Leaders of other organizations rarely need to do that. However, both military and civilian leaders must demonstrate high moral courage. High moral courage manifests itself in a variety of ways. It may mean making decisions that damage the careers of longtime friends, or one's own career. It may mean taking a high risk. And it may mean doing what is right, however unpopular.

MACARTHUR OFFERS TO RESIGN
AS CHIEF OF STAFF OF THE ARMY

Gen. Douglas MacArthur was chief of staff of the army in the early 1930s during the Great Depression. In seeking major budgetary cuts, President Roosevelt decided to make significant cuts in the national guard and the army reserve. MacArthur felt the cuts were excessive. He tells what happened in his book, *Reminiscences:*

"I felt it my duty to take up the cudgels. The country's safety was at stake, and I said so bluntly. The President turned the full vials of his sarcasm upon me. He was a scorcher when aroused. The tension began to boil over. For the third and last time in my life that paralyzing nausea began to creep over me. In my emotional exhaustion I spoke recklessly and said something to the general effect that when we lost the next war, and an American boy, lying in the mud and with an enemy bayonet through his belly and an enemy foot on his dying throat, spat out his last curse, I wanted the name not to be MacArthur, but Roosevelt. The President grew livid. 'You must not talk that way to the President!' he roared. He was, of course, right, and I knew it almost before the words had left my mouth. I said that I was sorry and apologized. But I felt my Army career was at an end. I told him he had my resignation as Chief of Staff. As I reached the door his voice came with that cool detachment which so reflected his extraordinary self-control. 'Don't be foolish, Douglas; you and the budget must get together on this.'

"Dern (Secretary of War) had shortly reached my side and I could hear his gleeful tones, 'You've saved the Army.' But I just vomited on the steps of the White House."[31]

MORAL COURAGE PAYS OFF AT NBC

Robert C. Wright, the General Electric (GE)–trained lawyer who has led NBC since 1986, would agree that moral courage pays off. GE acquired NBC when it bought the Radio Corporation of America (RCA). RCA had been NBC's sole owner since 1932. When GE CEO Jack Welch sent Wright to run NBC, the creative folks at NBC were not overly thrilled. Recalls news anchor Tom Brokaw: "My heart sank. GE people were engineers and accountants. They came from a different gene pool."

Not to worry, Tom. Wright transformed NBC from a traditional broadcaster into a global media powerhouse, expanding the company through domestic and international cable ventures and significant investments in new media opportunities. Under Wright's leadership, "must-see TV" entered the popular lexicon. Moreover, the network has dominated the prime-time ratings battles in recent years with such successes as the drama *ER* and the sitcoms *Seinfeld, Friends, Frasier,* and *3rd Rock from the Sun,* to name a few. Meanwhile NBC is in its fifth consecutive year of double-digit earnings growth, with more than $5 billion in revenues and $1 billion in profits in 1997, even with declining network-television viewership.

According to an article in *Fortune* magazine, Wright was considered a stiff, colorless outsider when he arrived at NBC. But brainpower, integrity, and decency are considered his best qualities. Moreover, Bob Wright had more than his legal background to draw on. At one time he left GE to run Cox Cable Communications as president. He grew Cox from five hundred to five thousand employees. Then he came back to run GE Capital. When GE acquired NBC, he was the only key executive with a background in the consumer communications business.

Says Bob Wright, who spent five years as an officer in the army reserve: "It's a lot easier to demonstrate integrity when the environment demands it, and that was true at GE. Moreover, my upbringing included a very religious mother who made certain I had a very disciplined education in the home. But I needed it all when I came to NBC."[32]

When he came on board, the situation was challenging. The relationship between NBC and RCA was not good. Moreover, NBC employees wanted to be applauded. "They had a seven- to eight-year stretch when ratings had been poor. Finally, they had a hit year. They felt they deserved a break, or at least a breather from new goals," explained Wright.

Why not do it? After all, ratings weren't so bad. Why not just give them a pat on the back? Why not be popular with old NBC executives and all these creative people? Unfortunately there were some challenges on the horizon that many couldn't see. Wright could. As Peter Drucker has said, "A company which continues to do what has made it successful in the past will eventually fail." It was no time to rest on the laurels of the past year.

Wright risked everything and put duty before self. He told NBC executives and professionals what they needed to hear rather than what they wanted to hear. He didn't waste time with accolades. He gave them a stiff dose of reality about the need for change. Sure, the ratings were high. But so were costs, and viewers were abandoning network television for cable. Says Wright, "They certainly weren't interested in hearing about diminishing shares."[33] But Wright knew that high moral courage meant telling the truth and doing what has to be done, not winning popularity contests. Wright is a leader, not a caretaker.

Wright cut costs. He brought in strong people. He got into the cable business by launching CNBC and MSNBC and acquiring interests in other cable networks. It was not an easy time for him. His subordinates did not instantly fall into line. Many gave him a hard time. Some had to be replaced. But Wright stuck to his guns. "If you don't pay attention and do what you have to, you'll get yourself whittled down to nothing," he says.[34]

His sacrifice of popularity paid off when NBC and Bob Wright faced the even greater challenge of the 1992 recession. "Many saw that the recession didn't hurt us nearly as much as it could have because of the changes we instituted," he observes.

Today, broadcasting viewership is still in decline. The network news business is in turmoil. But MSNBC is creating the first true television-Internet service hybrid and offering NBC the cost advantage it needs in the TV news business. Network rival and president of CBS News Andrew Heyward says, "MSNBC has added to the perception that NBC is on all the time and that NBC is a significant player."[35] Thanks to Wright, NBC is strong and well positioned to meet the challenges of the future.

"Our new challenge is finding the right role in major program relevance, and that's not easy. Still, if you don't see great challenge as a leader, you're going to fail because you drop back to becoming just a manager. If you are clear and consistent with your ideas, you can set an honest and straightforward agenda to get everyone committed."[36]

LOGICALLY, THEY SHOULD HAVE QUIT

Homer Laughlin China Co. manufactures china. The company managed to survive and even prosper during the Great Depression because theaters were giving away dishes as door prizes to try to attract customers. However in the late 1970s, cheap imports almost did in the company. At that point, CEO Joseph Wells II and President Marcus Aaron headed Homer Laughlin. Their grandfathers had bought the company from its founders in 1897.

By the 1970s, Homer Laughlin China was producing cheap dinnerware for the restaurant trade. The imports wiped out their price advantage, and sales plunged. Neither owner needed the money. They were tempted to call it quits. However, both knew that liquidating the company would decimate the community. Said CEO Wells, "These plant employees are the fourth and fifth generation at Homer Laughlin. I went to school with some of them."[37] So the two owners made a moral decision to stick it out, not for their own good but for the welfare of their employees. Just to survive meant spending an additional half million dollars on a new kiln and reconfiguring their entire manufacturing process. The reconfiguration eliminated dozens of steps, reduced costs by 15 percent and cut production time from one week to one day. This in turn enabled them to reduce inventories by 75 percent.

To do more than survive, they brought out old molds for a once popular design called Fiesta. Bloomingdale's launched the revived brand, and Homer Laughlin was back in business. Using cash flow from their Fiesta line, they moved into the custom china business with additional lines.[38] Naturally Homer Laughlin workers responded to the high moral courage displayed by their leaders. Today Homer Laughlin China is the largest domestic pottery company, employing more than 700 skilled workers on a 37-acre lot, with sales of more than $100 million a year.

Dan McKinnon is the president and founder of North American Airlines, a worldwide large-jet charter airline located at JFK International Airport in New York. Previously he served as chairman of the Civil Aeronautics Board for President Reagan. It was McKinnon who oversaw implementation of airline deregulation in the United States. Before that, he owned and operated several country music radio stations in San Diego. Dan McKinnon is also the author of *Bullseye One Reactor*, the story of the Israeli air force's successful raid on the Iraqi nuclear bomb factory outside of Baghdad in 1980. Before all this, McKinnon was a navy helicopter pilot.[39] Says McKinnon in one of his books, *Words of Honor*, "Leadership has its penalties — you don't always get to enjoy the same things other people do, but you do get the enjoyment of accomplishing your duty, and that more than compensates for all the pleasures of life you miss. Yet, by doing your duty, you'll find exciting and challenging opportunities that the people who relish the small pleasures of life never dream about."[40]

IT ISN'T ALWAYS EASY

Leaders who want to succeed know that they cannot get others to follow them by putting their own interests ahead of the mission or those they lead. They know that they must put their personal interests last. This isn't always easy, but you can accomplish this goal if you will:

1. Focus on the Mission
2. Rejoice in the Success of Others
3. Consider Yourself Last
4. Share the Pain
5. Demonstrate High Moral Courage

Do these things and others will follow because you:

PUT DUTY BEFORE SELF

ENDNOTES

1 Schwarzkopf, H. Norman, *It Doesn't Take a Hero* (New York: Bantam, 1992), 148.
2 Waxler, Robert P., and Thomas J. Higginson, *Industrial Management* (July–August 1990): 26.
3 Ott, Rosanne, telephone interview with the author, June 6, 1995.
4 Walters, Harry N., telephone interview with the author, January 12, 1998.
5 Sloan, Allan, "The Hit Men," *Newsweek* (February 26, 1996): 44–48.
6 Op. Cit. Waxler, Robert P., and Thomas J. Higginson, 24.
7 Citation awarding the Congressional Medal of Honor to Howard Walter Gilmore, The American War Library, http://www.familyville.com/wirlibrary/moh/w2b.shtm#28.
8 Gutherie, John S., Jr., letter to the author, July 26, 1993.
9 Miller, George D., letter to the author, July 20, 1993.
10 Lawler, E. E., "Job Satisfaction and Employee Motivation: Theory, Research, and Practice," *Personnel Psychology* (1970): 223–237.
11 Blake, Robert R., and Jane S. Mouton, *The New Managerial Grid* (Houston: Gulf Publishing Co., 1964), 95.
12 Fogleman, Ron, "The Profession of Arms," *Policy Letter Digest* (August 1995): 3.
13 Glionna, John M., "A Solar-Powered Surprise," *Los Angeles Times*

(June 29, 1997): 1.

[14] Roberto, Richard, interview with the author, November 4, 1997.

[15] Lubove, Seth, "Don't Listen to the Boss, Listen to the Customer," *Forbes* (December 4, 1995): 45.

[16] Burns, James MacGregor, *Leadership* (Harper & Row: New York, 1978), 4.

[17] Op. Cit. Lubove, Seth, 45.

[18] Keegan, John, *The Mask of Command* (New York: Penguin Books, 1988), 46.

[19] Ibid.

[20] Coffey, Thomas M., *Hap* (New York: Viking Press, 1982), 296–299, 300–301, 304–305, 334–336, 348–354.

[21] Ferguson, Michael L., letter to the author, November 13, 1997.

[22] RF/PF were friendly local forces and militias.

[23] Op. Cit. Ferguson, Michael L.

[24] Price, Ann S., interview with the author, October 16, 1997.

[25] Turner, Richard, "The Information Mogul of the 1990s," *Newsweek* (August 4, 1997): 52–53.

[26] Whitford, David, "Fire in His Belly, Ambition in His Eyes," *Fortune* (May 12, 1997): 158.

[27] Greer, Thomas U., letter to the author, August 2, 1993.

[28] Iverson, Ken, *Plain Talk* (John Wiley & Sons, Inc.: New York, 1998), 13.

[29] Iverson, Ken, letter to the author, October 21, 1997.

[30] Iverson, Ken, telephone interview with the author, October 30, 1997.

[31] MacArthur, Douglas, *Reminiscences* (New York: McGraw-Hill Book Company, 1964), 101.

[32] Wright, Robert C., telephone interview with the author, January 20, 1998.

[33] Gunther, Marc, "How GE Made NBC No. 1," *Fortune* (February 3, 1997): 92–98, 100.

[34] Op. Cit. Wright, Robert C.

[35] Pope, Kyle, "As the Focus Shifts, the Picture Brightens at MSNBC," *Wall Street Journal* (October 28, 1997): B1.

[36] Op. Cit. Wright, Robert C.

[37] Oliver, Suzanne, "Keep It Trendy," *Forbes* (July 18, 1994): 88.

[38] Ibid., 89, 94.

[39] McKinnon, Dan, telephone interview with the author, January 6, 1998.

[40] McKinnon, Dan, *Words of Honor* (Jamaica, N.Y.: House of Hits Publishing, 1996), 76.

CHAPTER 8
The Eighth Universal Law of Leadership

GET OUT IN FRONT

If you want an army to fight and risk death, you've got to get up there and lead it. An army is like spaghetti. You can't push a piece of spaghetti, you've got to pull it.

— Gen. George S. Patton, Jr.

If it weren't for one leader pulling from out in front instead of pushing in the Gulf War, the casualties might have been ten times what they were. Yet it was not the actions of a senior leader like General Schwarzkopf or Colin Powell that made the difference, but rather a young naval officer.

Lt. Cdr. Steve Senk was on board the USS *Tripoli* when it struck an Iraqi mine. Seawater rushed in and mixed with volatile helicopter fuel from ruptured tanks stored below decks. The air was thick with highly flammable and toxic paint thinner fumes. The flame from a single match would have ignited this mixture and caused instant detonation. It probably would have incinerated all aboard. This included 1,375 marines who were being transported into action.

The greatest danger was below decks where dangerous gases, both toxic and explosive, congregated. They had to be cleared, but no one was eager to enter that hellhole. Lieutenant Commander Senk did not order anyone into the increased danger. Instead he got out in front and rushed below decks where he could immediately begin the hazardous work himself. Because he went, others followed.

For four hours Senk personally led the efforts to decontaminate the space below decks. Though fatigued, he refused relief.

Several times, he almost collapsed due to the fumes. In the end, he and his men succeeded in cleansing the area. The engines were restarted, and the crippled ship reached port safely.

Norman Boyter was a combat infantry captain during the Vietnam War. Today he is vice president and general manager of the Westinghouse Electric Company. General Manager Boyter says that under the desperate circumstances of combat leadership "the competence, determination, and leadership by example of the leader and the cohesiveness, trust, and spirit of the team together can prevail against fears and even bad odds to successfully achieve the goal(s) and objective."[1]

If business leaders could motivate their employees to perform at only a small fraction of the dedication of Lieutenant Commander Senk and his sailors, what couldn't their organizations accomplish? I believe they can, if they get out in front. Employees don't follow leaders who spend all their time behind a desk. They follow leaders who get out in front where they can see and be seen. These are leaders who set the example. These are take-charge leaders who aren't afraid to mix with the people actually doing the work.

SUCCESSFUL COMBAT COMMANDERS GET OUT IN FRONT

Gen. Robert E. Lee exposed himself so frequently in the front lines of battle that his soldiers were terrified he might be killed. They promised him victory if he would just go to a more protected area. They would take up the cry, "General Lee to the rear! General Lee to the rear!"

Grant also was in the company of his private soldiers as much as his generals were. One soldier wrote home that Grant, as their general in chief, was so much exposed to enemy fire that soldiers were ashamed to do less or be thought a coward.

Generals in modern times get out in front as well. In the Philippines in World War II, Douglas MacArthur was frequently up front with his troops in combat. As reported by one veteran newsman, he shocked one private, who exclaimed, "General MacArthur, we killed a sniper not ten minutes ago, right over there." "Good," responded MacArthur, "that's what to do with them."

In the first B-52 raid in Vietnam, two generals were killed when the airplane in which they were flying collided with another. In Desert Storm, in Panama, in all wars, successful commanders try not to take what they consider to be unnecessary risks. However, at times these risks are necessary. When they are, these senior leaders get right up front where the action is.

When on active duty, Brig. Gen. Harry "Heinie" Aderholt was the dean of air force air commando leaders. He led in combat in World War II and Korea and had nine years combat experience during the Vietnam War. Says General Aderholt: "There's no secret about leadership. You've got to know your people, live with them, and be seen always out front."[2]

JULIUS CAESAR'S LEADERSHIP SECRET

Perhaps because of Shakespeare's immortal play, we tend to focus on the final hours in the life of Julius Caesar. We think primarily of his role as a politician and of his assassination. Yet he was first and foremost a great military leader. That's what brought him to the front rank in politics.

Julius Caesar had one trait that set him apart from other successful Roman generals and emperors. He spent an inordinate amount of time in the company of his soldiers. It was said that he committed not only the names of his officers, but also the names of thousands of his legionnaires to memory. He greeted all of them by name.

Because of this, Caesar's troops knew they were not just numbers to him. They were important! Wherever the action was, and whatever happened, they knew he would be there to share in it with them.

There is no way of leading from the rear in combat, and there is no way of leading from the rear in corporate life. You have to be "up front" where the action is. That way you can see what's going right and what's going wrong. You can make critical decisions fast without those decisions having to work their way up and down the chain of command for approval. You can see your employees, and they can see you. There is no question in anyone's mind as to what you want done, and the fact that you are there on the spot lets people know just how committed you are to getting things done. It lets your people know you think what they are doing is important. It lets all who would follow you know that you are ready, willing, and able to share in their hardships, problems, successes, and failures in working toward every goal and completing every task. Moreover, going where the action is gives you an opportunity to set the example. Remember, to be a leader, you have to lead. To lead means to be out in front.

YOU DON'T NEED TO BE THE COMMANDER OR MANAGER TO GET OUT IN FRONT

A couple of years ago, the town of Montgomery, Alabama, offered to purchase and donate an aircraft for a memorial at Air University. Air University is located at Maxwell Air Force Base near Montgomery. It offers advanced professional military education for air force officers, senior noncommissioned officers, and officer trainees. Among its schools are the Senior NCO Academy, Squadron Officers School, Air Command and Staff School, and Air War College.

Lt. Gen. Charles G. Boyd was then commander of Air University and made a counterproposal to Montgomery's offer. "Why not a statue of an air force leader who had a major impact on the air force?" he suggested. The town enthusiastically agreed to raise the money for such an award. They left it to General Boyd to suggest the leader to be portrayed.

Who would General Boyd select to inspire future generations? The list of potential honorees was long. Perhaps Brig. Gen. Billy Mitchell, who fought hard for an independent air force after World War I? Or General of the air force Hap Arnold. He held the highest rank any air force officer ever held — five stars — when he led the army air force during World War II. Or maybe he would chose Gen. Curtis LeMay. He built Strategic Air Command and through strong deterrence, did much to prevent World War III. He also served longer wearing the four stars of a full general than anyone else. And there were many other candidates.

General Boyd chose none of these distinguished leaders. Instead he chose a lieutenant by the name of Karl Richter who lost his life in the Vietnam War. How could a mere lieutenant inspire others more senior? Why would a young lieutenant even be considered over these distinguished senior officers each of whom served the air force and the country in positions of high responsibility?

Karl Richter graduated from the U.S. Air Force Academy in 1964, went to pilot training, and completed operational training in the F-105 "Thud" fighter-bomber. First Lt. Karl Richter had leave coming. "Leave," short for leave of absence, is the military term for vacation. However he turned it down to fly his fighter-bomber directly to Korat Royal Thai Air Force Base in Thailand and join the 388th Tactical Fighter Wing. He arrived in April 1966.

The 388th attacked targets in "Downtown" Hanoi in North Vietnam. These were considered the most heavily defended targets in the history of air warfare. Five months after arriving, he became one of the first F-105 pilots, and the youngest, to shoot down an enemy MiG-17. He was able to accomplish this even though the F-105 was used to attack ground targets and was not considered to have the necessary maneuverability for air-to-air combat.

These were tough days for our air force. Losses were high. Pilots needed to complete one hundred missions to go home. This was far from easy. Forty-three percent were either killed or declared missing in action before reaching one hundred missions. Richter completed his missions successfully. He promptly volunteered to fly another one hundred. He felt that his extensive combat experience could be used to further the war effort and help others to complete their missions. His superiors agreed to let him fly the additional missions. He personally led many raids. He taught many more senior officers, including some of his commanders, how to survive while flying and fighting in this intensely hostile environment. Along the way, Richter won numerous decorations for his heroism and leadership. On one occasion, he was awarded the Air Force Cross, the second highest decoration, just below the Congressional Medal of Honor, for leading a flight that successfully suppressed enemy antiaircraft artillery and surface-air-missile crews despite bad weather and intense fire. This enabled the strike force to destroy an important railroad target.

Karl Richter completed his second one hundred missions. He had already volunteered for a third tour of combat duty, this time to fly F-100s in missions supporting our soldiers on the ground in South Vietnam. Before his transfer, he was once again out in front, checking out a newly assigned pilot. Their target was a bridge. The defenses could be heavy. The enemy knew that bridges were primary targets because they were logistical lines of supply for military material heading down the Ho Chi Minh Trail into South Vietnam. Richter told the new wingman to stay high and observe while he attacked the bridge by himself.

But Richter's luck had run out. His aircraft was hit and disabled on his first pass. His wingman saw him eject successfully and his parachute open. Air Rescue Service aircraft were on the scene as rapidly as they could get there. They heard the beeper from his emergency radio. With other armed aircraft suppressing the flak, a helicopter landed and pararescue personnel, nicknamed "P.J.s," rushed to his aid. When they got to him, they saw he was near death. Richter had sustained multiple injuries, probably caused by being dragged into rocky karst formations by his parachute. He died aboard the rescue helicopter.

The statue of First Lt. Karl Richter bears an inscription from the Bible. It quotes the prophet Isaiah, who says: "Whom shall I send, and who will go for us? Here am I. Send me."[3] Lieutenant Richter wasn't a squadron commander or the wing commander of the units he flew with. Still he got out in front and led, and leaders more senior than he followed him gladly. He will continue to lead and inspire other air force leaders into the future.

We don't expect business leaders to sacrifice themselves to this extent. However there are occasions when they, too, take risks when they get out in front. When they do, others follow for the same reasons as they followed Karl Richter.

A Texas CEO Gets out in Front with the Headhunters and Piranhas

As president of Inland Laboratories in Austin, Texas, Dr. Mark Chandler heads up a $100 million company with a different kind of product. Inland sells toxins, viruses, and other biochemical products to medical researchers.

A few years ago, Inland needed two rare plants to refine into a cancer medicine. Unfortunately these plants grew only in a Brazilian rainforest hundreds of miles from civilization. Chandler couldn't buy them anywhere. Someone had to go into the jungle and harvest the plants on-site. Perhaps he could have sent employees to find this rare foliage. However, their job descriptions did not include facing piranhas, deadly snakes, and headhunters. He knew this was one trip that no one else should lead. So Dr. Chandler got out in front.

Mark Chandler personally organized and led an eight-day expedition up the Amazon. This wasn't easy. Several days into the journey, he thought he was going to die. Burning up with fever and wracked by diarrhea, he plunged into the river to cool off, forgetting about piranhas and poisonous snakes. He was so sick he just didn't care. Two days later, the fever broke. A little after that, with the help of native guides, he got his plants. David Nance, president of Intron Therapeutics and a customer for more than ten years, says, "Mark is equally comfortable in a loincloth, lab coat, or a three-piece suit." Do you think employees want to work for a leader like Dr. Chandler? Do you think customers want to do business with him? They know that Chandler can be counted on to be out in front where the action is. No wonder *Forbes* gave Inland Laboratories a price/earning multiple of forty.[4]

Gen. Wallace "Wally" Nutting retired from the army as a four-star general, and the commander in chief of Southern Command, a major regional command. General Nutting says that successful combat leaders set the example. They should be willing to do everything they ask their followers but more. "Once I entered a defensive minefield at night with a French sergeant to remove an injured Korean woman — a necessary act at the time, but not one I felt I should ask one of my platoon to accomplish," he explains.[5] Like Lieutenant Richter or Mark Chandler, General Nutting believes you've got to get out in front to lead properly.

WHY YOU MUST GET OUT IN FRONT TO LEAD

There are leaders who feel they must maintain total detachment. They believe they must coolly and carefully analyze the facts and make a decision without being influenced by outside complications. From their viewpoint, this decision making must be done away from the action because the action's noise, pressures of time, and other problems distract from their ability to think calmly and clearly.

There is a place for contemplative thinking and measured analysis in leadership. But many leaders have their priorities all wrong. The first priority is to get out where the action is, where those who are doing the actual work are making things happen. You cannot lead from behind a desk in an air-conditioned office. John Keegan is a military historian. He has written many professional books on command and strategy. In his classic treatise on the essence of military leadership, *The Mask of Command*, he concludes, "The first and greatest imperative of command is to be present in person."[6]

WOMEN ALSO LEAD FROM THE FRONT

You hear a lot of talk nowadays that women must lead differently from men to be successful. In fact, some say that women lead differently from men, anyway. Maybe, but I doubt it. Everything I've seen demonstrates that women who follow the eight universal laws of leadership get the same results as men. Successful leaders of both sexes lead from the front.

As a young lieutenant, Carol Barkalow, one of the first female graduates of West Point, led a Nike Hercules platoon in Germany. Her platoon was part of Air Defense Artillery and had the capability of firing both conventionally armed and nuclear-tipped missiles at invading aircraft. However an Air Defense unit also had to be able to defend itself. On one occasion, Lieutenant Barkalow was assigned to head up the Aggressor Unit to test the battalion's defenses.

Barkalow was ordered to attempt to take control of an air defense artillery site manned by 150 soldiers. She divided her group of marauders into teams of two soldiers each. She didn't exclude herself. She got out in front and assigned herself to the main assault team.

The soldiers at the site to be tested knew her Aggressor Unit was coming, and, within certain time parameters, they knew when. This made real surprise somewhat difficult. Since the site expected an attack, she decided on a strategy of waiting. She wouldn't attack immediately after dark, but would wait all night and attack at daybreak. That way, the 150 soldiers at the site would wait all night with increasing nervousness and weariness. At 4 A.M., four of her teams would start firing sequentially to create a division. Then she and another soldier would cut through a barbed-wire fence, infiltrate the site, head for the command post, and capture it.

She and the other soldier, one of her noncommissioned officers (NCOs), crawled on their hands and knees across an open field for a hundred yards to reach a road at the perimeter of the site. They made it without being discovered despite bright moonlight. Then they waited. It was cold, and it was uncomfortable. They were too close to "the enemy," to talk. They waited quietly without speaking for hours. Every few minutes, Lieutenant Barkalow checked her watch. The time passed very slowly. She wondered whether she or the soldiers at the site would become more weary of the waiting. At 3:30 A.M., thirty minutes before her planned assault, the area suddenly exploded with dozens of star clusters. It illuminated the area like daylight.

Someone started firing. "We'll go now," she ordered. Taking advantage of the defense's own actions as a diversion, she ordered her team forward. In the confusion, she and her NCO breached the defense and rushed to the site command post. Her Aggressor Team took possession of the site. Said Barkalow, who is now an army major, "Each member of the team received a certificate of achievement commending us for our professionalism and discipline while infiltrating and destroying the enemy."[7]

Notice, Lieutenant Barkalow didn't sit behind a desk, make decisions and plans, and send her team forward. She went forward herself, right in front of everyone.

Hoyt S. Vandenberg, Jr., who was an F-4C "Phantom" fighter squadron commander in Vietnam in 1966 and 1967 and retired as a major general, also graduated from West Point. He fully agrees with Major Barkalow: "You've got to stay visible and lead from the front," he says.[8]

WOMEN OUT IN FRONT LEAD
IN BATTLE AND IN BOARDROOMS

According to the Bible, Deborah was a judge of Israel. Among her duties was military advisement. Called to advise the Hebrew general Barak in the Israelite's war against the Canaanites of Jabon, Deborah suggested that Barak recruit ten thousand troops to invade Jabon. Barak was not entirely convinced. "If thou will go with me, then I will go; but if thou will not go with me, then I will not go."

Deborah did go, and her presence up front inspired the Israelites to victory. She received full credit: "The people were oppressed in Israel, until you arose, Deborah, as the mother of Israel," Judges states.

Almost two thousand years later, a young French girl was despondent because of the English invasion of her country during the Hundred Years War. We know her as Joan of Arc.

When she was thirteen, Joan began to hear voices that she identified as those of three saints. They gave her a mission: liberate France from English domination. For five years she was uncertain and did nothing. Then she went to her monarch, Charles VII, and boldly asked for command of the French army.

"Not likely," you may think. Not only was Joan a young woman, but she had no military experience at all. St. Cyr, the famous French military academy, did not exist in Joan's age. But it would have made no difference. St. Cyr still doesn't admit women as cadets. Joan's king gave her the command she desired anyway. He was that desperate. He had tried everything else. The situation was so bad that even the king's counselors agreed Joan might be their only chance.

Prior to Joan's appointment as French commander, the English siege of Orleans had lasted eight months despite the best efforts of the French army to relieve it. Joan lifted the siege in just eight days. Her orders to her soldiers before attacking were simple: "Go boldly in among the English." But she didn't just give orders. She got out in front. "I go boldly in myself," she told the chroniclers of her time.

Joan personally hated fighting and killing. Though she commanded the French army and gave the orders, she did not struggle in hand-to-hand combat. Mounted on a horse, she carried a huge banner. She rode with these colors and her staff to the place on the battlefield where the situation was most critical, where most of the action was, and where the danger was the greatest. The French soldiers saw that their commander was out in front, so that's where they went, too.

Being out in front is not just for show. In Joan's case, it led to her capture while attempting to relieve Compiegne a year later. Eventually her captors executed her as a witch. They thought that for any leader to be so successful, particularly a young girl with no military training, she had to have demonic power. She had special power all right. It was the power of the universal laws with emphasis on the one that tells the leader to get out in front.

There are modern Joans in the boardroom as well as on the battlefield who get out in front today. Beth Pritchard is the chief executive of the nation's leading bath-shop chain, Bath & Body Works. Pritchard gets out in front and demonstrates a special power, too. In addition to her corporate duties and responsibilities, she spends two days a month working "in the trenches" in a Bath & Body Works boutique. At the boutiques, she doesn't sit around observing or handing out advice to employees. She sees and is seen; she teaches and she learns. She helps set up displays, stocks shelves, and arranges gift baskets. "Though I'm not really good on the cash register," claims Beth Pritchard.

Whether she is good on the cash register or not doesn't matter. The power of getting out in front has paid off. Her cash registers are full. When she took over Bath & Body Works in 1991, it had ninety-five stores and sales of $20 million. Five years later, the number of stores had increased to a whopping 750, and sales hit $753 million.[9]

HOW TO GET OUT IN FRONT

If you want to be a leader, obey this natural law. Here's how to do it:

1. Go Where the Action Is
2. Set the Example
3. Be Willing To Do Anything You Ask Your People To Do
4. Take Charge
5. Be an Up-Front Leader

MARCH TOWARD THE SOUND OF THE GUNS

Napoleon Bonaparte advised commanders always to march toward the sounds of the guns. It was his way of saying, "Go where the action is." This is good advice for commanders in uniform or executives in mufti. Well-known management author Tom Peters, who himself served as an officer in the navy recommends going where the action is, too. He calls it "management by wandering about."

HOW GENERAL SHERIDAN WON A VICTORY BY SIMPLY BEING WHERE THE ACTION WAS

In the summer of 1864, Confederate general Jubal Early, commanding the Second Corps of the Army of Northern Virginia, invaded the North. In response, General in Chief Grant formed the Army of the Shenandoah and put thirty-three-year-old Maj. Gen. Philip Sheridan, who had formerly commanded his cavalry, at its head. By mid-October, Sheridan had beaten Early's corps and forced it to retreat. Sheridan was recalled to Washington for a conference to decide what to do next.

The Union leaders moved too fast. Unknown to their intelligence, Lee had scraped together enough men to significantly reinforce Early's defeated corps. While Sheridan was in Washington, Lee moved these troops into position. Early launched a surprise attack against the Union forces at a point

THE STUFF OF HEROES

on their left flank called Cedar Creek. The attack was highly successful. One Union Corps stampeded and wasn't re-formed until two days later. What was left of Sheridan's army fought successive delaying actions. It was clear that Early had won a great victory. The Union Army was not only defeated, but in a sudden turnabout, the capital of the United States was in danger of falling to Early's victorious forces.

It was at this point that General Sheridan, returning as fast as he could from Washington, galloped up the Pike from the city of Winchester, Virginia. His mere presence up front rallied his army. He regrouped on the battlefield and drove Early from the field. His victory was so decisive that this was the last great battle fought in the Shenandoah Valley.

The poet Thomas Buchanan Read immortalized this military turnaround in a poem entitled "Sheridan's Ride." The poem was not entirely accurate. At every stanza, Buchanan threw in another mile. Read had Sheridan galloping for twenty stanzas. The distance was actually a little less. But close enough. Even Herman Melville, the author of *Moby Dick*, wrote a poem entitled "Sheridan at Cedar Creek." They knew that the difference between victory and defeat was the leader being out in front on the field of battle where the action was.

HOW A YOUNG BUSINESSMAN BECAME *TIME* MAGAZINE'S MAN OF THE YEAR

Does being where the action is help in the civilian world? Peter Ueberroth was still in his forties when *Time* magazine named him Man of the Year. President Reagan invited him to the White House, and he was routinely introduced to audiences as "the man who brought honor to America."

Ueberroth didn't win these accolades in uniform. He wasn't a military leader. Ueberroth is a self-made businessman who made a great deal of money in the travel business. A head-hunting firm suggested Ueberroth's name to a Los Angeles committee searching for someone to run the 1984 Olympic Games. Ueberroth took the job at a 70 percent cut in pay. Later he changed his status to volunteer worker. He refused to take any money at all for his work on the Olympics.

Some said Ueberroth declined to take a salary because there was no way the games could turn a profit. Many experts said it was unlikely that the L.A. games could break even. The media agreed.

The Soviets and their satellites were likely to boycott the games in retaliation for the American boycott of the Soviet games. Other countries in the Soviet sphere of influence would follow. Cities had had financial problems hosting the Olympics even without the Soviet problem. How could Los Angeles do any better?

His first week on the job, Ueberroth couldn't even get into his own new office. He and members of his staff could hear the phones ringing inside. But the landlord was so certain that the Olympics would lose money and not pay the bills that he wanted his money up front.

But as Harry Usher, who functioned as Ueberroth's chief of staff said, "Leadership and inspiration are his managerial gifts."[10] Ueberroth plunged right in. He managed by getting out in front and going where the action was. Taking over an old helicopter hangar as headquarters, he encouraged everyone to eat lunch in the hangar's cafeteria to save time. Ueberroth ate lunch there with everyone else.

Frequently he would stroll through the hangar talking to his employees and asking questions. "Peter is demanding and self-demanding. That makes you try as hard as you can," noted Agnes Mura, one top staffer.[11]

Ueberroth personally negotiated contracts totaling millions of dollars. As the cash flow started in the right direction, he cultivated the ministers of sport from each country. Once the Soviets announced they wouldn't be coming, Ueberroth kept the pressure on and did everything he could to stop other countries from joining the Soviet boycott. He flew to Cuba and met face to face with Fidel Castro. While Castro said he had to follow the Soviet lead, he did agree not to pressure other Latin American countries into boycotting.

Once the Soviets made their boycott official, the experts again announced there was no way Los Angeles could do anything to avoid losing money. Big money. Ueberroth ignored the naysayers. He claimed that even without the Soviets, they would make $15 million profit. The naysayers laughed. Make $15 million profit? Impossible!

As the games opened, Ueberroth continued to go where the action was. He was constantly on the move, racing to the scene of action and even riding a helicopter over Los Angeles freeways to check the traffic. Every day, he wore the uniform of a different Olympic worker as he made the rounds. One day it was a bus driver's uniform, the next an usher's blue and gold, the day after perhaps a cook's whites with apron. And every time he spotted a security worker, he ran over to shake his or her hand.

When the smoke cleared, Ueberroth was proven wrong. The Los Angeles Olympics didn't make $15 million. But the experts were wrong, too. Under Peter Ueberroth, the Los Angeles Olympics made $215 million profit, $200 million more than he had predicted.

And so Ueberroth got to dine with President Reagan and his photograph graced the cover of *Time*. Many Americans thought he should run for president. But others said he was just very lucky. Ueberroth didn't say much. He accepted an appointment as baseball commissioner and continued to be lucky because he knew his real luck was that he went where the action was.

Brig. Gen. Dick Dunwoody flew 130 combat missions as an A-1 "Sandy" lead pilot. Sandys flew old navy single-engine prop planes. A little old by Vietnam standards, the planes were, however, terrific for their mission — providing close-in support for air rescues in enemy-held territory. Like Ueberroth, General Dunwoody found "when it's time to produce, be right there. Talk to your people and personally brief the troops. Don't delegate leadership that demands a leader. If you want to succeed, be everywhere!"[12]

TWO GENERALS SET THE EXAMPLE BY JUMPING OUT OF AN AIRPLANE

Another way to get out in front is to set the example. Two generals showed us how this is done. When the C-17 air transport aircraft was accepted by the air force, Gen. Ronald Fogleman enthusiastically received it. General Fogleman, who afterward became air force chief of staff from 1995 until 1997, then wore two hats. He was commander of Air Mobility Command (AMC) at Scott Air Force Base, near Belleville, Illinois. AMC would operate the C-17. In addition, he was commander in chief of U.S. Transportation Command, responsible for strategic logistical support by all means — land, sea, and air — around the world.

The C-17 represented a giant leap forward in air transport. It could fly farther and faster and carry more weight than other air force strategic transports. Moreover, it could get into unimproved fields where other military jet transports like the C-141 or C-5 could not. Like the C-141, it was capable of carrying and dropping a full load of army paratroops.

However some army officers involved in airborne operations — operations involving parachutes — were not happy. There was a rumor that the spoiler extended to help reduce airspeed of the C-17 during airdrops would pose a hazard to paratroopers as they exited the aircraft. Sure, the spoiler had been tested previously, and it had worked. "But," said these officers, "that doesn't mean there still isn't a potential problem." There was talk that some troops might even refuse to jump from a C-17 because of the risk of striking the spoiler.

Shortly thereafter, an unannounced airplane landed at Edwards Air Force Base in California where the C-17 was undergoing its final tests. Two generals got out of the plane. One was Lt. Gen. Henry H. Shelton, a master parachutist with hundreds of jumps. He probably had more jumps than any other general in the armed services. In 1997, President Clinton appointed him Chairman of the Joint Chiefs of Staff, after commanding the U.S. Special Operations Command. In those days, he was commander of the army's Eighteenth Airborne Corps at Fort Bragg, North Carolina. His organization included the Eighty-second Airborne Division, which would be the prime user of the C-17 as a jump vehicle. The other general was Ron Fogleman. He normally flew airplanes rather than jumped out of them, but he was a rated parachutist. He had graduated from the army's parachute school at Fort Benning, Georgia, thirty years previously and made his required five jumps to earn his parachute wings. He had gone back to parachute school to get requalified.

Both generals suited up and received instruction about the peculiarities of jumping out of a C-17. Then they took off and jumped. They termed the C-17 acceptable as an air-drop vehicle. That squelched rumors about the C-17 being unsafe for jumpers. How can business leaders set the example like these generals did?

He Sets the Example
by Going through Garbage

Remember Phil Rooney? We met him back in chapter 3. When Phillip Rooney was CEO of WMX Technologies, Inc., of Chicago, Illinois, he found a way to set the example. WMX founder Dean Buntrock hired him shortly after he completed his second tour in Vietnam as a marine corps officer. WMX

Technologies manages waste, and every founder's day at the corporation, Rooney and other managers go through garbage. They take off their suits and ties and donn the appropriate clothing to sort through the garbage with the troops.

Rooney's first international work with WMX was back in 1976. He was sent to Riyadh, Saudi Arabia, to pull together a $250 million garbage-hauling contract. He set the example then, too. To get the work done, he had to create a town for two thousand workers. Rooney helped put in the electricity and sewage systems himself. Not bad for a former relatively junior marine corps officer.

Some years later, Buntrock sent Rooney to Chicago to take over the main WMX operation in the United States. He was out in the field five days a week working with front-line managers and salespeople. He pushed sales managers to get out and talk to clients more. Or rather, he pulled rather than pushed, because he dropped in on customers himself.

Because Rooney set the example, others followed. WMX's head of sales and marketing said about Rooney: "He moves as easily among low-level [employees] as among CEOs."[13] And Rooney knew what he was doing. He acknowledges getting out in front as one of the keys to his success in both his professional career and his home life.[14]

Army major general Joseph Fant, with combat in Korea and Vietnam, became president of the Marion Military Institute in Alabama after his retirement. "If you're going to be a leader, you've got to set the example and be seen by your troops," he says.[15]

THIS COMPANY PRESIDENT LEARNED YOUR PEOPLE WANT TO SEE YOU DO IT FIRST

Today Jodie Glore is president and chief operating officer of Rockwell Automation, a $4.5 billion company located in Milwaukee, Wisconsin. During the Vietnam War, he was a front-line infantry company commander in the U.S. Army's 101st Airborne Division. Early in his tour of duty, his unit got in a fierce firefight with the enemy. One of his men who was out toward the front stood up and was instantly shot in the shoulder. Captain Glore ordered another man to crawl forward and bring the wounded soldier back to cover. No one moved. Glore looked around and realized that his men were waiting to see what he would do. Without hesitation, he handed his M-16 to a noncommissioned officer crouching nearby and crawled out to retrieve the wounded man himself.

"From then on," states Glore, "they knew I was for real. When I gave an order, they obeyed it instantly because they knew that I was ready to do it myself. This is a lesson that has served me as well in my civilian career as it has in combat."[16]

THIS "TUNNEL RAT" DID ANYTHING
HE ASKED HIS SOLDIERS TO DO

A successful leader has to be willing to do anything he or she would ask of others. Capt. Fred Meurer served as battalion intelligence officer and commander of an elite unit called "tunnel rats" in the First Infantry Division north of Saigon in the "Iron Triangle" during the Vietnam War.

What were "tunnel rats"? They were a special volunteer unit of only six men. Their extremely hazardous mission was to explore and then destroy the tunnels constructed and used as operational headquarters and supply depots by enemy forces throughout South Vietnam.

Whenever American troops discovered one of these tunnels, they would contact Fred. He and his boys would either rotate the lead or draw straws to see who would lift the trap door and go down first. Almost anything could happen. The tunnel could be long abandoned with nothing left behind. Then, if possible, they just blew it up.

Or the enemy might have been scared off when the tunnel was discovered. That was ideal. They frequently discovered maps, war plans, guns, ammunition, and other equipment. That was very satisfying. It meant that their actions had a direct effect on future actions and saved American and allied lives. After removing this valuable material, they would blow up the tunnel, or if they couldn't do this, they would contaminate the tunnel with a gas similar to what is found in a pepper spray.

But sometimes, the enemy was either still there or had time to set booby traps before leaving. These were the worse cases because the first one going down the tunnel had trouble or a fight on his hands, usually against superior odds. That is why they drew lots. And Captain Meurer drew lots with everyone else. He says he soon learned that if you are going to lead in combat, you've got to be there, out in front where the action is.

You've got to be ready, willing, and able to do anything you demand your subordinates to do.[17]

CITY MANAGER FRED MEURER SAVED THE TOUGHEST JOBS FOR HIMSELF

Twenty-five years later, retired colonel Fred Meurer was the city manager of Monterey, California. With the end of the Cold War, many military bases around the country had to be closed. There was no alternative. When you have a much smaller military, you don't need as many bases, and every base cost the Department of Defense a lot of money to maintain.

But every base also represented considerable business for the local civilian community. No community wanted to give up the military base, which helped to support its citizens. Closure of some bases would destroy the community. The Department of Defense didn't want this to happen. It formed Base Closure Commissions to study each situation and make recommendations based on the potential impact of closure on the local communities.

To the little town of Monterey, closure would be devastating. Despite this, the base was initially on the "hit list" and slated to be closed. So, Fred went to work in the same way he once led the tunnel rats. He got out in front. He wrote letters, made presentations, and helped gather data. He formed a special team. When his team worked nights and weekends, so did Fred. Those on his team knew he was with them in meeting every challenge and enduring every hardship.

They say that victory has many fathers, while defeat is an orphan, but Fred is widely credited with taking on the toughest job and being the sole "father" of this victory. The Base Closure Commission took Monterey off the closure list, saving thirty thousand jobs and a half-a-billion-dollar payroll.[18]

FIELD MARSHALL MONTGOMERY TAKES CHARGE AND HELPS WIN AFRICA

Getting out in front means to take the initiative, to be proactive, to take charge. Early in World War II, Lt. Gen. Bernard L. Montgomery was a relatively unknown general who had performed well during the allied defeat at the Battle of France in 1940. On August 13, 1942, Prime Minister Churchill gave Montgomery command over the British Eighth Army in

North Africa.

Earlier the British Middle East Command and the Eighth Army had gone through several commanders while unsuccessfully fighting the German general Erwin Rommel and his Afrika Korps. General Sir Claude Auchinleck, Montgomery's immediate predecessor, had won a victory over Rommel but had been persuaded to attack again prematurely. Rommel then defeated the Eighth Army decisively.

The situation for the British was now very bad. It was possible that the allies would be entirely driven out of Africa. Moreover, the Eighth Army itself was not in good shape. After its latest defeat, it had made withdrawal after withdrawal. Withdrawal is simply another word for retreat. The enemy retreats. You withdraw. Morale in the Eighth Army was at an all-time low. Then Lt. Gen. Montgomery arrived. Here are the steps he took right away:

1. He canceled all previous orders about withdrawal.
2. He issued orders that in the event of enemy attack, there would be no withdrawal. The Eighth Army would fight on the ground it held. Or in Montgomery's words, "If we couldn't stay there alive, we would stay there dead."
3. He appointed a new chief of staff.
4. He formed a new armored corps from "various bits and pieces."
5. He changed the basic fighting units from brigade groups and ad hoc columns to full divisions, a major change in the organization's structure.
6. He initiated plans for an offensive saying, "Our mandate is to destroy Rommel and his army, and it will be done as soon as we are ready."

Later he wrote of the actions he took on his first day in charge: "By the time I went to bed that night, I was tired. But I knew that we were on the way to success."[19]

Only a few months later, Montgomery's Eighth Army attacked at El Alamein and won a major victory. It was the turning point of the war in the North African theater of operations. Eventually it forced the Germans to withdraw from Africa completely. Montgomery was promoted to field marshal. That's the British equivalent of full general in the United States. The victory also won for him knighthood and a special title — Montgomery of Alamein.

Successful combat leaders not only get out in front of a situation physically, they also get out in front of a situation psychologically. They do not sit and wait for things to happen. They take charge and make things happen.

TAKING CHARGE IS IMPORTANT AT ALL LEVELS OF AN ORGANIZATION

Joe Anderson is chairman and chief executive officer of Chivas Products Ltd. This former White House Fellow built this company, which he owns, to $47 million in annual sales and about four hundred workers. Chivas makes automotive parts for Detroit. Before striking out on his own, Anderson learned the automobile business by heading up a billion-dollar division of General Motors with seven thousand people reporting to him. But he learned the leadership business in two tours of duty as an infantry officer in the First Cavalry Division in Vietnam.

"The eight fundamental principles are baseline values, which you must interpret," he says. "Those who become successful on the battlefield learn those rules real fast.

"For me, the most critical factor was getting out in front and taking charge. I had never worked with flare ships, used artillery support, or anything of that kind previously. I'd had it all in school, of course, but I'd never done it. But, there was no one else to do it, and I was the leader. Both my men and my superiors expected me to get the job done and keep them alive as best I could, so I did.

"I remember one time early on when we had to rescue another platoon that had been ambushed and taken casualties. Suddenly I was doing all kinds of things that I had never done before. And it was my responsibility. Doing that successfully really sealed my relationship with my men.

"When you realize what you did and apply the same principles as a civilian leader, it works. And I think that's especially true as an entrepreneur. If I don't take charge, no one else is going to do it, and I'm playing with my own money."[20]

THE ASTRONAUT AT EASTERN AIR LINES TAKES CHARGE

Two of my West Point professors who convinced me to enter

the air force were "Pat" Patterson, who instructed me in ordnance engineering my first-class (senior) year and astronaut Frank Borman. I told you about Pat and how his showing uncommon commitment helped him to be an extraordinary leader in chapter four. Frank Borman, in those days, was Captain Borman, an air force fighter pilot. He was one of my instructors in thermodynamics my second-class (junior) year.

On retiring from the air force as a colonel, Eastern Air Lines recruited Borman as a vice president. Five years later Borman took over as president and CEO of a very troubled airline.

Eastern was a billion dollars in debt. Their airplanes were fuel inefficient and mostly obsolete. Their best plane, the L-1011, was too big for most of their routes, and they had too many of them. Corporate headquarters was split between two locations — New York and Miami. This separation led to continual infighting between senior executives at the two locations.

The entire company was top-heavy with useless managers. Dozens of executives clogged the lines of communication between the people at the top and the people on the firing line. One department had sixty people assigned to do a job that a larger competitor was doing with twenty.

In one typical situation, computer experts were hired to establish information control systems. They did. However, after the systems were set up, the experts were never given new work. They sat around doing virtually nothing. Bonuses were given to company officers based largely on subjective appraisals by fellow officers. Losing money, the company furloughed or fired hundreds of employees. However at the same time, Eastern supported executive cars and a private executive jet. Earlier, customer service had been so bad that a group of former customers had formed the WHEAL (We Hate Eastern Air Lines) Club.[21]

When Frank Borman became CEO, like Montgomery, he took charge. Here's what he did right away:

1. He fired, forced into early retirement, or demanded the resignation of twenty-four vice presidents.
2. He sold the executives' JetStar and informed executives that in the future they would travel on regular Eastern flights.
3. He reduced the limousine fleet and its drivers to a single car and driver in each of three major cities.

4. He canceled the leased company automobiles for executives and eliminated the private club membership dues the company was paying.
5. He transferred all major executive functions to Miami, making this the single headquarters location.
6. He sent a large number of people who had contact with the customer to a "charm school." The school was based on the customer service training syllabus from a company that had a first-class reputation for dealing with customers — Disney World.
7. He abolished the subjective executive bonus and established a new profit and deficit-sharing plan that applied to everyone, rank and file as well as senior executives. The plan was directly tied in to how the company did and what the individual accomplished.
8. He visited Eastern Air Lines employees in almost every city in the system. In his own words, "I cajoled, pleaded, argued, and demanded. I courted not merely the rank and file but their union leaders on both the local and national levels."[22]

For the next four years, Eastern had the most profitable period in its history. Customer service went from dead last in the Civil Aeronautics Board's passenger complaint ratings to number two in the industry. As Borman said, "You could actually see and even feel the new pride developing, growing, and taking hold in the way our people looked and worked.[23]

When Borman was still serving as vice president of operations, Eastern Flight 401, a Lockheed L-1011 Tristar, crashed into the Everglades at night while on final approach to Miami International. Borman heard the news and headed for the systems control center. No one knew exactly where the plane had gone down. Borman ordered the systems control director to charter a helicopter for him.

The darkness was pitch black; the swampy waters prevented the aircraft from burning. They located the crash site when they spotted a couple of U.S. Coast Guard helicopters in the area.

With difficulty, they located a surface hard enough to land the helicopter. It was 150 yards from the downed airplane. When Borman ran up, the scene was one of confusion and horror. Borman helped the dead and the dying and assisted survivors into helicopters. "When I was satisfied that there were enough rescue personnel on the scene, I finally left on one of the last choppers," he said. With two of the surviving flight attendants, he flew straight to the hospital with a woman who had lost her baby.[24] With this history, it was no surprise that Borman obeyed the universal laws and took charge when he became Eastern's president and CEO.

Later a new union president succeeded in destroying the incentive compensation system Borman set up. Then the company was bought, Borman was fired, and many of his changes were dropped. Within months, Eastern Air Lines no longer existed.

OFF DUTY, THE COMMANDER IN CHIEF COACHES A GAME

Somehow some leaders have got the idea that they are supposed to keep their distance from employees and subordinates. Nothing could be further from the truth. You should see and be seen every chance you get. And if you can get to know them after normal duty hours, so much the better.

When I was promoted to the rank of brigadier general in the air force reserve, I was sent to a special course along with about forty other new general officers from the active duty air force, the air force reserve, and the air national guard. Other services have similar courses. Officially the course is entitled "Brigadier General Officers Orientation Course." Unofficially it is known as charm school, the joke being that the orientation course is somehow supposed to teach all general officers how to be charming.

The real intent is to widely instruct officers who up to now may have been specialized in one area of military work. As a general officer, your responsibilities are broader, and "charm school" helps to orient you toward these responsibilities and teach you what other organizations do. Each of the four-star commanders of the major air force commands briefed us in closed sessions at his headquarters. In Washington, the chief of staff of the air force, the chairman of the joint chiefs of staff, the secretary of defense, and others talked to us. They told us what they did, and they helped us to understand what it meant to be a general officer and what would be expected of us.

When we got to Air Mobility Command at Scott Air Force Base near Belleville, Illinois, the youngest four-star general in the air force greeted us. His command was responsible for air transportation of people and material all over the world. He was "dual-hatted." He was also commander of U.S. Transportation Command and so was responsible for military transportation of all services worldwide.

This young "four-star" had been commander less than a week. However he was already clearly in charge. His accomplishments during this week were impressive. But most impressive was how he related to those who were in his command. Earning their respect didn't stop him from mixing with them easily at both work and play. "You know," he told the colonel who introduced him to us, "your hair is getting as gray as mine. Or did you put something on it?" "No sir," the officer answered smilingly. "It's naturally gray."

There was a dinner at the Officer's Club the night we were with him. After dinner, he led all forty of us to the basement of the club. In one of the rooms a pool table had been converted to a "Crud" table. The game of Crud is unique. It is said to have originated in the Royal Air Force and then been learned by U.S. fighter pilots. It is a much more physical game than pool, with players smacking into one another and more than one participant ending up on the floor. Pool sticks and balls are still used in the play, however.

We took off our ties and jackets, and the four-star, with his sleeves rolled up on his formal white shirt, taught us how to play Crud while he acted as referee. As required by the rules, he assigned penalty points when a young brigadier, engrossed in the game, ran into him and knocked him down!

It was no surprise when three years later this officer, Gen. Ronald Fogleman, became chief of staff of the air force, establishing core values and primary competencies for the first time in its history and getting it on track to become this nation's space force in the next century. As chief of staff, he stayed an up-front leader, visiting his "employees" at their bases around the world and getting to know them on and off the job.

AN "UP-FRONT" LEADER AT COCA-COLA

When Julie Culwell became manager of editorial services at the Coca-Cola Company, she first tried distancing herself from her subordinates. "I'd read a lot of management books that warned me not to get personally involved with my team," she says. But things weren't working out, so she threw these books away and became an up-front leader.

"We helped pull each other through professional and personal crises. We spent time together after hours. And what happened was, the more I nurtured them, the more they produced. In fact, they became passionate about their work — putting in long hours at the office and taking projects home with them. Nobody ever missed a deadline, and the feedback we got from our clients was consistently outstanding."[25]

What we're talking about here is not being a good guy and clapping people on the back. We are talking about being unafraid to be with your people, look them in the eye, help them when you can, and listen to what they say. It is not important that they like you and think of you as a "good guy." It is important that they respect you and think of you as a human being willing to share their victories and defeats.

THIS DISK-DRIVE KING
IS AN UP-FRONT LEADER

Alan F. Shugart is CEO of Seagate Technology, the number one disk-drive maker. You could probably call him the disk-drive king. Seagate Technology in Scotts Valley, California, owns 33 percent of a $25 billion industry. Al Shugart is known to be gruff and hard driving. Yet those who work with him and for him credit his success to his leadership ability, a surprising attribute because of his considerable technical ability. This is the man who developed the first disk drive for a computer at IBM way back in 1961.

When he left IBM for the Memorex Corporation in 1969, he took two hundred IBM engineers with him. This is especially noteworthy because these were the golden days of IBM, when "Big Blue" was the place to be for prestige, security, and monetary rewards. James N. Porter, a market analyst who worked at Memorex then recalled, "All he had to do was raise the flag to get people to work with him."[26]

Shugart demands hard work, and he's not a leader who avoids difficult decisions. He demoted former Vice President Robert Martell who is now president of Avatar System Corporation. He offered him a lower-ranking job and convinced him to take it. Martell went to Europe to take charge of Seagate's new European subsidiary. Within a year, he tripled sales and was back in a better position. Today Martell says, "I'd do almost anything Al asked me to do."

What's Shugart's secret? One of his current vice presidents, Stephen J. Luczo, says, "He's the most up-front guy I've ever worked with."[27] After hours, Shugart holds impromptu staff meetings at local bars. Since he shows up everywhere wearing short sleeves and never wears a tie, he is always ready for these informal meetings. The most popular location currently is a place called Malone's. Employees call it "Building 13," a reference to Seagate's twelve-building complex. Shugart is successful because he has mastered the art of getting out in front and leading twenty-four hours a day.

AN UP-FRONT LEADER
HEADS SOUTHWEST AIRLINES

Successful leaders take every opportunity they can to get to know their employees — at work or at play. You've got to admire the leader of Southwest Airlines. When every other airline in the industry was losing money, somehow Southwest Airlines kept making it.

Successful people are successful because they do the things that unsuccessful people won't do. I don't know about the presidents of other airlines. I do, however, know about Southwest Airlines president Herb Kelleher. He is an up-front leader. In addition to doing other things right, he is enthusiastically at the center of Southwest's frequent off-duty festivities, whether it is an employee dinner at a Dallas restaurant, someone's retirement, or just an end-of-the-week socializer. But Kelleher isn't doing this for the purpose of being some kind of a social butterfly. Steve Lewins, an analyst at Gruntal & Co. who has been following Southwest since the early 1970s, says: "He is the sort of manager who will stay out with a mechanic in some bar until four o'clock in the morning to find out what is going on. And then he will fix whatever is wrong."[28]

THE FIVE MOVES UP FRONT

Commander Senk didn't sit at his desk and ponder the decontamination job below decks on the USS *Tripoli* when it struck a mine. He got down there with his men and took the same risks and suffered the same hardships. So did Fred Meurer in leading the tunnel rats. So did Karl Richter. So do other good combat leaders. The same was true of Fred Meurer, the civilian leader, and of Al Shugart, Beth Pritchard, Mark Chandler, and Frank Borman. It's all part of getting out in front.

All these people know if you want people to follow you, you must lead from the front. To do this:

1. Go Where the Action Is
2. Set the Example
3. Be Willing To Do Anything You Ask Your People To Do
4. Take Charge
5. Be an Up-Front Leader

If you really want to be a highly successful leader:

```
GET OUT IN FRONT
```

ENDNOTES

1 Boyter, Norman C., letter to the author, May 28, 1996.
2 Aderholt, Harry C., letter to the author, September 7, 1993.
3 Frisbee, John L., "Here Am I. Send Me," *Air Force Magazine* (December 1992): 71.
4 Mack, Toni, "Indiana Jones, Meet Mark Chandler," *Forbes* (May 23, 1994): 100–104.
5 Nutting, Wallace H., letter to the author, September 13, 1996.
6 Keegan, John, *The Mask of Command* (New York: Penquin Books, 1988), 329.
7 Barkalow, Carol, *In the Men's House* (New York: Poseidon Press, 1990), 189–191.
8 Vandenberg, Hoyt, S., Jr., letter to the author, July 26, 1993.
9 Bongiorno, Lor, "The McDonald's of Toiletries," *Business Week* (August 4, 1997): 79-80.
10 Ajemian, Robert, "Peter Ueberroth: Master of the Games," *Time* (January 7, 1985) in *Time 1995 Almanac* CD-ROM (Cambridge: Compact Publishing Co., 1995).
11 Ibid.
12 Dunwoody, Dick, letter to the author, July 28, 1993.
13 Melcher, Richard A., "How Phillip Rooney Reached the Top of the

Heap," *Business Week* (June 17, 1996): 80.

[14] Rooney, Phillip B., letter to the author, January 30, 1998.

[15] Fant, Joseph L., letter to the author, July 26, 1993.

[16] Glore, Jodie K., telephone interview with the author, January 9, 1998.

[17] Meurer, Frederick E., letter to the author, May 3, 1996.

[18] Ibid.

[19] Montgomery of Alamein, *The Memoirs of Field-Marshall Montgomery* (World Publishing Company: New York, 1958), 94.

[20] Anderson, Joseph B., Jr., telephone interview with the author, December 9, 1997.

[21] Borman, Frank, with Robert J. Serling, *Countdown* (New York: William Morrow, 1988), 329–330, 326.

[22] Ibid., 323, 328, 335.

[23] Ibid., 341, 334.

[24] Ibid., 285–286.

[25] Glasner, Connie, and Barbara Steinberg Smalley, *Swim with the Dolphins* (New York: Warner Books, 1995), 50.

[26] Burrows, Peter, "The Man in the Disk Driver's Seat," *Business Week*, (March 18, 1996): 71.

[27] Ibid., 72.

[28] Labich, Kennet, "Is Herb Kelleher America's Best CEO?" *Fortune* (May 2, 1994): 46.

WITHOUT ACTION THE UNIVERSAL LAWS ARE WORTHLESS

Strong determination and perseverance in carrying through a simple idea are the surest routes to one's objective.
— FIELD MARSHAL HELMUTH GRAF VON MOLTKE

From the past to as far as we can see into the future, the universal laws of leadership are immutable. Over the millennia, they have not changed. They are as true today as they were in the times of the ancients, and they will be as true thousands of years from now for those who come after us. But unless leaders take action on their knowledge, the laws are without value.

FAILING TO APPLY THE UNIVERSAL LAWS EXACTS A GREAT COST

War is a terrible thing. To date, man seems to have learned little regarding how to avoid it and its terrible consequences of misery and destruction. But as in all things good or bad, man at least can learn something from what he does, no matter how undesirable. That is how I see the universal laws. They have been bought at a terrible price. They cannot by any means be considered worth the price, for it was far too high. Still, the universal laws of leadership are something of substance, something of worth. The prophet Isaiah foresaw that the day would come when man would beat his swords into plowshares. The lessons of leadership, the universal laws, are such swords. They are long overdue in their transformation.

Yet knowledge of the eight universal laws alone cannot complete this transformation. Mere knowledge is not power. But the laws of leadership do constitute potential or stored power. If knowledge of the universal laws is acted upon, the resulting plowshares are exceedingly powerful. If not, they are worthless.

Leaders who apply the eight universal laws to their actions will lead more effectively. The organizations they lead will be more productive. There will be fewer failures and more and greater successes. Those who lead and those who follow will be happier, wealthier, and more content in the work they produce and in the tasks in which they are engaged. My research of combat leaders now serving as leaders in all types of organizations proves this. Seven thousand years of recorded history confirm it. There is no possibility of error. But to repeat, to reap the power in the universal laws, they must be acted upon.

WHY CAN'T LEADERS LEAD?

The eight universal laws of leadership are immutable. Following them results in almost perfectly predictable results. Failing to do so also results in almost perfectly predictable results. In some form, the universal laws of leadership are listed, talked about, explained, and analyzed in every serious book on leadership. They are on almost everyone's "must do" list in one way or another. Leaders from all fields and of all backgrounds agree. Yet, though they are universally praised in government, in business and industry, and even in the military that uncovered them, they are obeyed far too infrequently. Why is this so?

THE UNIVERSAL LAWS
OF LEADERSHIP AREN'T COMMON SENSE

The universal laws may be pervasive and unchanging over the millennia, but they are not always easy to apply. We are not born with knowledge of them. They may appear to be "common sense" or "obvious" if we think about them after the action is over and the results are in, or observe them as stand-alone commandments without thinking through their application to what we are doing. But though the laws are simple conceptually, implementing them can rarely be accomplished without thought.

The operation of complex machinery, such as an automobile, makes a good metaphor. After we learn the basics of driving and gain a little experience, we can drive an automobile, turn the wheel, and push the right levers at the right times. In doing so, we obey the laws of physics automatically, without thinking about it. Still, as driving safety experts tell us, there is danger in instinctive driving. When situations that are out of the ordinary occur, we are unprepared to meet them and react too slowly, regardless of our driving proficiency and our experience on the road. Safety experts exhort us to "drive defensively." Defensive driving requires us to think. We cannot drive "on automatic" but must assume an active role in our driving activities. When we do this, we drive more safely and we have fewer accidents.

Similarly, with experience, we gain proficiency in leading and we can do it almost instinctively. But beware — leadership situations that are "out of the ordinary" occur every day. The work of leaders must be grounded in the universal laws of leadership just as the practice of driving is grounded in the universal laws of physics. Once we understand the laws of physics, they may seem obvious. We take them for granted. We must be thinking leaders. Unfortunately many are not.

How else can we explain leaders who ignore the universal laws in practice? It may be obvious that a leader who cannot be trusted to tell the truth or to do the right thing will not have followers who will follow without reservation and under all circumstances. Consciously or unconsciously, followers will analyze every situation and obey only when they perceive it to be in their best interests to do so. They will take nothing on faith from such a leader. Yet leaders of low integrity are not rare.

There is no question that those who follow expect their leaders to know their stuff. Yet the shelves are filled with self-help books explaining how to acquire power over others through trickery or manipulation rather than through merit. I recall seeing a book that recommended locating a desk so as to ensure the light shined in the eyes of visitors. This was defined as a "power position." Nowhere did the author recommend that you know what you were talking about over that desk, no matter where it was located.

Maybe it is obvious that leaders must declare their expectations. Yet many leaders keep their real intentions secret, as if even revealing what they want done will put some sort of curse on their goals, or as if they think they will look bad in the eyes of others if they fail to attain their vision.

How can any leader believe that his followers can be made to be more committed than the leader himself? Yet some leaders pride themselves on their coolness and detachment in the pursuit of required organizational tasks, as if their attainment mattered not at all.

How can anyone succeed when he or she expects to fail? On rare occasions, I suppose this happens. But it is not the norm. All the research shows that you tend to get what you expect in life. If you expect positive results, that's what you'll generally get. And if you expect the opposite? Well, you'll generally get that, too. Yet some leaders actually begin their declarations with "I don't think we can do this but . . ." or "I doubt you'll be able to accomplish this, but . . ." Such leaders disregard the fifth universal law and set things up for failure.

It would seem obvious that you must take care of your people. You want their minds free of problems so that they can follow you without distraction, don't you? Still, some leaders seem to care less. They let those who follow fend for themselves. Worse, they sometimes make a point of caring for themselves and ignoring their followers. It is as if they think this demonstration of their power somehow enhances their ability to lead. Perhaps, like abused children, that's how they were treated as followers, and so somehow having found themselves in a position of authority over others, that's how they behave.

A leader's duty is derived from his purpose or mission in life. Isn't it obvious that his duty must then be primary? If not, the leader strays from his personal mission, his or her very reason for existing. Yet some leaders do subvert their duty, simultaneously destroying, or at least injuring, their own life missions. Is it any wonder that followers can fail to work up much enthusiasm for following, or even obeying, such incongruent behavior?

When we were children, many of us played a game called "follow the leader." We lined up behind the leader we elected. The leader then led us in a variety of feats of strength, agility, bravado, or just plain silliness. But there is an important lesson in this childhood activity. The leader led from the front. Always. If the leader was not in front, he or she was no longer the leader and was not followed. Several years ago Robert Fulghum wrote a best-selling book. Its title was *All I Really Need to Know I Learned in Kindergarten.* Clearly there is much truth in Fulghum's words. Can anyone doubt that a child or an adult can lead in any other way than by getting out in front?

APPLYING THE UNIVERSAL LAWS IS THE STUFF OF HEROES

Applying the eight universal laws of leadership is far from easy. It takes courage to maintain absolute integrity. It takes courage to put one's career on hold while taking the time and actions necessary to know your stuff. It takes courage to risk looking silly or being wrong by declaring your expectations. It takes courage to risk all by showing absolute commitment. It takes courage to expect positive results, when others tell you that you are certain to fail. It takes courage to take care of your people and protect them from others, sometimes from your own boss. It takes courage to put your duty toward your mission and your people first. It takes courage to get out in front despite multiple demands on your time, and risk exposure to what others think, say, and can do to you. But those leaders who take these actions have earned the right to lead their organizations into the future.

That's why the universal laws are the stuff of heroes. As Mike Armstrong, the new CEO of AT&T, advises, "If you want to lead, you've got to put yourself in the shoes of those that are going to help you build the future. Do what you know is right and that will earn the respect and trust of those you lead. If a leader honors respect and trust, so will the organization. And it is the organization that honors respect and trust that sets it off from other organizations now and in the future."[1]

As a result, heroic leaders with the stuff of heroes will help us build a better, more productive future in all aspects of our lives. Who are these heroes who will lead us to a superior destiny? Who are these leaders of tomorrow? Some are already known. Most are not. Some of them will reach great fame. Others will never be well known outside of the world of those they lead. They will quietly perform their duty as leaders in such a way that others will say, "Well done." They will be equally great. Who are these heroic leaders of the future? I cannot say today. But I hope and pray that one of them is you.

ENDNOTE

[1] Armstrong, C. Michael, telephone interview with the author, March 1, 1998.

INDEX

ACKNOWLEDGMENTS

This project was an eight-year labor of love, and I owe much to many people who helped or participated in the research, read and assisted with drafts, made suggestions, participated in interviews, provided quotes or stories that helped to illustrate the eight universal laws, and gave insight and encouragement. During the years I have been working on this project, several of them have gone on ahead. In soldiers' myth, they now enjoy that special place set aside for them known as Fiddler's Green. The good they accomplished lives on after them, and I greatly appreciate their contributions to this project.

To all, thank you for what you have done. This book could not have been written without you. Among those to whom I would like to give special thanks are the following. They are truly of the stuff of heroes.

General Harry C. Aderholt, USAF, Ret.
Maj. Gen. Albert B. Akers, USA, Ret., CEO, The Gallatin Group Brigadier
Joseph B. Anderson, Jr., Chairman and CEO, Chivas Products, Ltd.
C. Michael Armstrong, CEO, AT&T
Mary Kay Ash, Chairman Emeritus, Mary Kay Cosmetics
Major General Edward B. Atkeson, USA, Ret.
Brigadier General Walter J. Bacon, USAF, Ret., Superintendent, Castle Heights
   Military Academy
Lt. General Edward P. Barry, Jr., USAF, Ret., ICBM Systems Div.,
   The Boeing Co.
Dr. William Bartlett, Senior Manager of Editorial Services, NBC
William Bartmann, President, Commercial Financial Services Inc.
Major General Walter H. Baxter, III, USAF, Ret., President, Baxter Seed Co.
David C. Beard, Director, Manager of Ethics, Northrop Grumman Corp.
Captain William F. Bina III, MD, USN, Ret., Residency Director, Medical Center of
   Central Georgia
Colonel Robert E. Blake, USAF, Ret., Deputy Director Autonetics and Missile
   Division Rockwell International
Major General Lucien E. Bolduc, Jr., USA, Ret.
Brigadier General Philip L. Bolte, USA, Ret.
Norman C. Boyter, Jr., Vice President and General Manager, Westinghouse Electric
   Corp.
Simon Burrow, CEO, Brandon International
Colonel Jacksel M. Broughton, USAF, Ret., Author
Brigadier General Edward N. Brya, USAF, Ret.
Colonel Marshall N. Carter, USMCR, Ret., Chairman and CEO, State Street Corp.
General Duane H. Cassidy, USAF, Ret.
Major General Robert W. Clement, USAF, Ret., President, Haines City Citrus Assoc.

Commander John W. Conrad, MS, DC, USN, Ret., Owner, Chiropractic Wellness Center

Captain Jan W. Cook, USN, Ret., Deputy Associate Director, Plant Engineering, Lawrence Livermore National Laboratory

E. Joseph Cossman, CEO and President, Cossman International

Major General Hugh L. Cox III, Adjutant General, Alaska National Guard

Major General Albert B. Crawford, Jr., USA, Ret., Exec. Vice President, AMEXTRS Co.

Brigadier General Theodore P. Crichton, USAF, Ret., President, American Nucleonics

Ralph Crosby, Corporate Vice President and General Manager, Northrop Grumman, Commercial Aircraft Division

John B. Curcio, Chairman and CEO, Mack Trucks, Inc.

General James E. Dalton, USAF, Ret., General Manager, Defense Technology Group, Logicon

Colonel Alfred H. Davidson, III, Director, Network Operations, Voice of America

General Bennie L. Davis, USAF, Ret.

Nicole Dionne, President, Primal Scream

Dr. Peter F. Drucker, Marie Rankin Professor of Management, Peter Drucker Management Center, Claremont Graduate University

Brigadier General Richard T. Drury, USAF, Ret.

Brigadier General Dick Dunwoody, USAF, Ret.

Major General B. J. Ellis, USAF, Ret.

Brigadier General Uzal W. Ent, Pennsylvania Air National Guard, Ret., Supervisor, Pennsylvania Dept. of Public Welfare

Major General Joseph L. Fant, USA, Ret., President, Marion Military Institute

Brigadier General Michael L. Ferguson, USA, Ret., Attorney

General Ronald R. Fogleman, USAF, Ret.

Rear Admiral G. M. Furlong, Jr., USN, Ret., Exec. Vice President, Naval Aviation Museum Foundation

Lt. Colonel Anthony J. Garcia, USMC, Ret., Director, Litton Data Systems

Lt. General Robert G. Gard, Jr., USA, Ret., President, Monterey Institute of International Studies

Jodie K. Glore, President and Chief Operating Officer, Rockwell Automation

Colonel Sherwood D. Goldberg, USA, Ret., Director, Worldwide Associates, Inc.

Senator Barry Goldwater, Major General, USAFR, Ret.

General Andrew J. Goodpaster, USA, Ret., Chairman, The Atlantic Council of the United States

Major General Thomas U. Greer, USA, Ret.

Lucius Gregg, Vice President of Corporate Communications, Hughes Electronics Corp.

Major General John S. Grinalds, USMC, Ret., President, The Citadel

Dr. Richard N. Groves, Chairman and CEO, NAVCO

Major General John S. Guthrie, Jr., AUS, Ret., Chief of Staff, Military Order of the World Wars

Colonel John J. Haas, USAF, Ret., Director, Operations Research, BDM Federal, Inc.

General Alexander M. Haig, Jr., USA, Ret., Former U. S. Secretary of State

Major General Richard L. Harris, USA, Ret., Vice President, Radian Corp.

Lt. Colonel Edward N. Hathaway, USA, Ret., Senior Associate, Booz Allen & Hamilton, Inc.

Thomas C. Hayes, Executive Director, Communications, Tenneco Corporation

Major General John A. Hemphill, USA, Ret., President, 6th Region, Association of the United States Army

Lt. Colonel David G. Hofstetter, USA, Ret., Property Manager, Koger Equity

Captain John Jay Hummer, USN, Ret., Director, Corp. Environmental Health and Safety, Lockheed Martin Corp.

Captain Paul Ibsen, USCG, Ret., CFO, Pace Academy

F. Kenneth Iverson, Chairman, Nucor Corp.

Jeff J. Jarvis, COO, Touchscreen Solutions, Inc.

Maj. Gen. (Chaplain) Kermit D. Johnson, USA, Ret.

Lt. General W. D. Johnson, USAF, Ret., Corporate Vice President, Baxter, International

Lt. General Jay Kelley, USAF, Ret.

Lt. Colonel Charles A. Kennedy, USAF, Ret., Manager, Systems Safety and Human Factors, B-2 Division, Northrop Grumman

Brigadier General Benjamin King, USAF, Ret.

General Frederick J. Kroesen, USA, Ret.

Erick J. Laine, CEO, ALCAS Corp.

Dr. Kenneth L. Lay, Chairman and CEO, Enron Corp.

Lt. General Lloyd R. Leavitt, Jr., USAF, Ret., President, Divaricate, Inc.

Dr. Ronald B. Lee, CEO, Vantage Marketing International

Richard B. Lieb, President, SEI Investment Systems and Services

Brigadier General William C. Louisell, USA, Ret., President, Foundation for Historic Christ Church

Robert A. Lutz, Vice Chairman, Chrysler Corp.

Colonel Micharl J. Lynch, USAF, Ret., Quality Engineer, Motorola

Lt. General Jack V. Mackmull, USA, Ret.

Colonel Michael G. Major, USAF, Ret., Program Manager T-38, Northrop Grumman Corp.

Frederic V. Malek, Chairman, Thayer Capital Partners

Lt. General Leroy J. Manor, USAF, Ret.

Brigadier General Edward M. Markham III, USA, Ret., Director, Management Information Systems

Brigadier General James R. McCarthy, USAF, Ret.

Colonel Clay McCutchan, USAFR, Historian, U.S. Air Force Special Operations Command

Dan McKinnon, President, North American Airlines

Lt. General Thomas H. McMullen, USAF, Ret.

Captain James E. McNulla III, USN, Ret., Vice President and General Manager, Sparton Electronics

Colonel Dana G. Mead, USA, Ret., CEO, Tenneco

Major General Charles F. Means, USA, Ret.

Colonel Frederick E. Meurer, USA, Ret., City Manager, Monterey, California

General Edward C. Meyer, USA, Ret., Chairman, Association of Graduates, United States Military Academy

Lt. General George D. Miller, USAF, Ret.

Colonel Jacques C. Naviaux, USMC, Ret., Director of Business Planning, Hughes Aircraft Co.

Lt. Colonel Thomas E. Noel III, USA, Ret., President, Commodore Advanced Science, Inc.

Captain Douglas M. Norton, USN, Ret., Principal, Korn/Ferry International

General Wallace H. Nutting, USA, Ret., Senior Fellow, National Defense University

John D. Ong, Chairman, The BF Goodrich Company

Dr. Edward A. Osborne, Lt. Colonel, USAF, Ret., President, AMI Aircraft Seating Systems, Coltec Industries, Inc.

Rosanne F. Ott, Sales Representative, Johnson & Johnson

Lt. General Edward A. Partain, USA, Ret.

Brigadier General George K. Patterson, USAF, Ret.

Major General Don H. Payne, USAF, Ret.

Lt. General Ernest D. Peixotto, USA, Ret.

Colonel Thomas E. Pence, USA, Ret., Vice President of Operations, Summit Plastic Solutions, Inc.

Major General Elmer D. Pendleton, USA, Ret.

Charles W. Petruska, President, Human Resource Services

Colonel John Phillips, USAF, Ret., Contracts Manager, Standard Missile Company

Frank Popoff, President and CEO, The Dow Chemical Company

Ann S. Price, President, Motek, Inc.

Major General Walter B. Putnam, USAF, Ret., Director Emeritus, Tech-Sym

General William R. Richardson, USA, Ret., Defense Consultant

Professor Richard Roberto, Professor of Engineering, California State University, Los Angeles

Leonard Roberts, CEO Tandy Corp.

Phillip B. Rooney, Vice Chairman, The ServiceMaster Company

Dr. Stan Rosen, Lt. Colonel, USAF, Ret., Director of Strategic Planning, Hughes Space and Communications Company

Michael J. C. Roth, Vice President and General Manager, United Service Automobile Association Investment Corp.

Brigadier General Roswell E. Round, Jr., USA, Ret.

Brigadier General Maurice D. Roush, USA, Ret., Dean, College of Engineering, St. Martins College

Lt. Colonel William L. Schwartz, USA, Ret., Director, International Marketing, Litton Applied Technology

Lt. General Winfield W. Scott, Jr., USAF, Ret., Superintendent, New Mexico Military Institute

Major General Richard V. Secord, USAF, Ret., President, CTI

Major General Stan R. Sheridan, USA, Ret., Special Assistant to the President, Teledyne Vehicle Systems

Major General John K. Singlaub, USA, Ret.

Major General Clyde W. Spence, Jr., USA, Ret.

Lt. Colonel C. West Stewart, USA, Ret., Practice Manager, McIntosh Trail Family Practice

Colonel Rice St. John, USA, Ret., Vice President, Total Systems Services, Inc.

Vice Admiral Edward M. Straw, USN, Ret., President, Ryder System, Inc.

G. Craig Sullivan, Chairman and CEO, The Clorox Co.

Colonel Clarence S. Summers, Jr., USAF, Ret., Project Engineer, The Aerospace Corp.

Colonel Harry G. Summers, Jr., USA, Ret., Syndicated Columnist and Partner, On Strategy, Summers and Cunningham

Major General W. H. Tankersley, USAR, Ret., Vice Chairman of the Board, Sterne, Agee & Leach, Inc.

Donald D. Thompson, President and CEO, Farmers and Merchants Bank

Lt. Gen James M. Thompson, USA, Ret.

Lt. General Richard G. Trefry, USA, Ret., Executive Vice President, MPRI

Lt. General Stanley M. Umstead, USAF, Ret.

Major General Hoyt S. Vandenberg, Jr., USAF, Ret.

General Henry "Butch" Viccellio, USAF, Ret.

Harry N. Walters, general partner, LaFayette Equity Fund

Major General William F. Ward, Jr., USA, Ret., Chairman, REALICAM

Brigadier General Daniel H. Wardrop, USA, Ret.

General Volney F. Warner, USA, Ret., President, VW Warner Associates

Lt. General Alexander M. Weyand, USA, Ret.

Major General Albin G. Wheeler, USA, Ret.

David C. Whitmore, Marketing Consultant

General John A. Wickham, Jr., USA, Ret., Former Chief of Staff, USA, President and CEO, Armed Forces Communications & Electronics Association

Edward B. Wild, Indigence Examiner, Seventh Judicial Circuit, Florida

James Wood, Chairman and CEO, The Great Atlantic and Pacific Tea Co., Inc.

Colonel Royce G. W. Woodell, USAF, Ret., F-16 Instructor, McDonnell Douglas Aircraft Systems Co.

Robert C. Wright, President and CEO, NBC

M. Monique Yellin, Managing Director of Events, *Chief Executive* magazine

Major General Kendall S. Young, USAF, Ret.

Admiral R. J. "Zap" Zlatoper, USN, Ret., CEO, Sanchez Computer Associates, Inc.

Admiral Elmo Zumwalt, USN, Ret.

William F. Zuna, Program Administrator, Florida Department of Revenue

Special thanks to my agent, Stedman Mays, my editors, Suzanne De Galan and Sherry Wade, and Scott Bard, who once commanded a company in the ROTC. Without these individuals, you would not be reading this book.